ROAD TO FREEDOM

ROAD TO FREEDOM

A Sociological Study on the Abolition of Scavenging in India

BINDESHWAR PATHAK

MOTILAL BANARSIDASS PUBLISHERS
PRIVATE LIMITED. DELHI

First Edition: 1991

Also available at
MOTILAL BANARSIDASS
Chowk, Varanasi 221 001
Ashok Rajpath, Patna 800 004
16 St. Mark's Road, Bangalore 560 001
120 Royapettah High Road, Mylapore, Madras 600 004
41 U.A. Bungalow Road, Jawahar Nagar, Delhi-110 007

ISBN: 81-208-0704-9

PRINTED IN INDIA
BY JAINENDRA PRAKASH JAIN AT SHRI JAINENDRA PRESS, A-45 NARAINA INDUSTRIAL AREA, PHASE I, NEW DELHI 110028 AND PUBLISHED BY NARENDRA PRAKASH JAIN FOR MOTILAL BANARSIDASS PUBLISHERS PVT. LTD., BUNGALOW ROAD, JAWAHAR NAGAR, DELHI 110007

To

Mahatma Gandhi

whose centenary celebrations
marked a turning point
in my life

Foreword

To write a foreword to a book is generally a routine exercise. However, at times it is a privilege of which one is proud. To me, this is one such occasion.

The present work is an updated and revised version of the doctoral thesis, 'Liberation of Scavengers through Low-Cost Sanitation in Bihar', submitted to Patna University in 1985 by Dr Bindeshwar Pathak. As a teacher and guide, I have been associated with the dissertation for long; hence the added pleasure in seeing that it is being presented in the form of a book.

The research that this book is based on is a radical departure from the general trend of doctoral dissertations. Generally, a Ph.D. scholar adopts one of two methods of doing research: (i) he chooses a topic, reads books, articles in journals by eminent scholars, synthesizes and analyzes the information he has collected, and writes his thesis; (ii) he does field work, collects data using different tools and techniques of research, tabulates and interprets the data, and then writes his thesis. The present work goes beyond both these two categories of research work. It is a pace-setter in that it lays down a new approach for action research in the social sciences.

Dr Pathak has collected data (facts), but not merely as objects of the historical processes in India's socio-cultural life. The writer develops a concept, works it out as an action sociologist, tries to bring about a directed change, and evaluates the results of his own action programme. In sum, this book is a critical appraisal made by a person who has tried, in his own way, to bring about social change.

Dr Pathak, true to the style of an action sociologist, takes up a very old social problem of Indian society: the inhuman practice of scavengers cleaning latrines and carrying night-soil on the head. He ponders over the problem, develops a strategy, prepares an action plan, and initiates action to eradicate it. The plan involves providing low-cost flush latrines to replace the traditional dry latrines which require the services of scavengers to manually clean them. Further, Dr Pathak has developed a technology for low-cost pour flush latrines which is simple, affordable and eminently suited to the socio-economic conditions of users living in various geophysical environments.

Dr Pathak laid the foundations of a voluntary, non-profit organization, Sulabh International, (originally Sulabh Shauchalaya Sansthan) in 1974 in Bihar. Sulabh International, with a band of committed workers and under the able leadership of Dr pathak, launched a massive campaign of converting dry latrines into low-cost pour flush latrines (Sulabh Shauchalayas). The traditional dry latrines produced environmental pollution, emitted bad odour and required scavengers. The low-cost Sulabh latrines are practical in use, hygienic, do not need scavengers and, hence, are a viable alternative which has proved to be a boon for users as well as scavengers.

Sulabh International has also set up a number of Sulabh community complexes for public use, providing toilets and baths in busy and commercial areas. They are looked after by the liberated scavengers who work as caretakers. These complexes have gone a long way in saving towns from environmental pollution, besides providing great relief to the people Sulabh International has, within a span of fifteen years, emerged as catalyst, an agent of social change Lakhs of dry latrines have been converted into Sulabh Shauchalayas and hundreds of Sulabh community complexes have been set up throughout the country. As a result, thousands of scavengers have been liberated. Sulabh International has also undertaken the task of training the liberated scavengers in different skills so that they do not suffer due to lack of employment. They are helped to help themselves.

Dr Pathak in this book gives an account of his journey from being an ordinary worker to becoming an action sociologist, the founder and advisor to Sulabh International, which has attracted the attention of State and Central governments, voluntary agencies, municipalities and corporations within the country as well as outside it. He makes an attempt, through scientific techniques and tools, to evaluate the functioning of Sulabh International and Sulabh Shauchalayas, especially in Bihar. At the same time he tries to assess to what extent the task of liberating scavengers and providing relief to the masses has been achieved and what remains to be done.

The work is original in content and scientifically interesting; it is valuable for the general public, academicians, administrators, social workers and social scientists. Written in lucid prose, this is a book worth reading and preserving.

I congratulate Dr Pathak on his monumental work which, I am sure, will inspire many. I wish him success in his noble mission. The book has a clear message for social scientists who are called upon to put in greater efforts in service of the community.

Z. AHMAD
Professor and Head
Department of Sociology
Patna University, Patna

Contents

Acknowledgements

This book is based on my doctoral thesis submitted to Patna University in 1985 for a Ph.D. degree in sociology. The unique feature of this doctoral thesis is the fact that the topic of research was based on a concept developed by the author himself. Since the doctoral work was submitted for evaluation by Patna University, many significant developments have taken place and the programme for liberation of scavengers through low-cost sanitation has crossed national boundaries to become an international venture. Consequently, in writing this book the latest data have been incorporated. The original chapters have been rearranged to suit the book form and the statistical data have been set out in the form of tables in the appendix. The tables have been analysed in Chapters VI and VIII.

I am extremely grateful for the help and encouragement received from my teacher and guide, Prof. Zeyauddin Ahmad, Head, Deptt. of Sociology, Patna University, without which I could not have completed my work. I am also thankful to friends and colleagues like Dr. S.D.N. Singh (Reader, Deptt. of Sociology, Patna University), Dr. A.K. Lal (A.N. Sinha Institute), Shri A.K. Ghosh and Shri Jagannath Sharma for their cooperation and advice during the research and writing of the thesis. From time to time, I also took help from Dr S. Musi Raza (Prof. of Sociology, Patna University) and Shri R.L. Dewan (former Director of Irrigation Research Institute) in completing the book. I am thankful to them for their help and advice.

The wives of busy executives are often sore over the non-participation of their husbands in household affairs, and their working on Sundays to write a thesis or book. I am thankful to my wife who allowed me to write not only my doctoral thesis, but also the present book.

I offer flowers in worship of my mother, Shrimati Yogmaya Devi and father, Dr Rama Kant Pathak, who now rest in heaven. They, despite opposition from neighbours, villagers and relatives, sold their property in order to fulfil my ambition of getting higher education before going into social service. What I am today is certainly because of their scarifices, blessings and encouragement. I wish they were alive today to see their dreams come true.

BINDESHWAR PATHAK

CHAPTER 1

Introduction

THE PROGRAMME for liberating scavengers in Bihar from the demeaning practice of carrying night-soil on the head assumed importance during 1974-84. In the traditional Indian society, a particular section is ordained to do scavenging work. It has been a hereditary occupation and everybody born in the sub-caste of scavenger (*Bhangi*), male or female, is destined to take up this sub-human profession. The members of this sub-caste were bound not only by traditional obligations and customary rules to practise this profession, but mythological sanctions also oblige them to carry night-soil physically for disposal. In the traditional social order, the *Bhangis* (scavengers) were required to perform their job with hands and carry the buckets containing night-soil on their heads through lanes and streets. It was about the worst kind of atrocity committed against any section of traditional Indian society.

These people are hated and shunned for this dirty job. It is clearly a denial of social justice and a manifestation of rank traditionalism. The pathetic conditions of scavengers can further be realized from the fact that there are a number of occupational groups and sub-castes which are described as depressed castes, out-castes or exterior castes. These different terms have been used by different scholars for the same hereditary section. But the complexity of the Indian social structure did not make it clear as to which castes or sub-castes were exterior castes in the country. The regional differences, variations in local traditional sanctions and varying customary rules in different lists of occupational groups or castes were the factors to identify the exterior castes.

But even in this case of differences and variations from region to region, the *Bhangis* were labelled as exterior caste and polluted people throughout the country. The following observations made by Hutton (1981:196) explain the situation clearly: 'For purposes, therefore, of deciding what persons are to be included in the members of the exterior castes, it has been necessary for each province to deal with the problem in its own way and to produce its own list. It is not possible to say generally that such and such caste is exterior to the Hindu society and to apply that dictum to the whole of India. It may be possible to do so in the case of certain castes, such as those of *Dom* and *Bhangis*, but it certainly is not the caste that a caste which is depressed in one part of India is depressed everywhere.' It appears from this observation that the caste of *Bhangi* is that hereditary occupational group which is regarded as exterior at every place in India and scavengers are lowly placed throughout in the traditional Indian society. The caste of scavengers (*Bhangis*) suffered from a number of social disabilities. These social disabilities were not only for *Bhangis*, but also for other exterior castes in different areas. As presented by Hutton (1981:193) on the basis of instructions of the Government of India for taking of the 1931 census, 'I have explained different depressed castes as castes, contact with whom entails purification on the part of high caste Hindus. It is not intended that the term should have any reference to occupation as such, but to those castes which by reasons of their traditional position in the Hindu society, are denied access to temples, for instance, or have to use separate wells or are not allowed to sit inside a school but have to remain outside, or which suffered similar social disabilities.

'These disabilities vary in different parts of India, being much more severe in South India than elsewhere. At the same time, the castes which belong to this class are generally known and can in most parts of India be listed for a definite area, though perhaps the lists for India as a whole will not coincide.' In the light of this remark, it appears that the exterior castes were deprived of a number of privileges and suffered from several social disabilities in the traditional Indian society. But only a few certain castes like *Dom* and *Bhangis* were those which suffered from these social disabilities in every State or Province of the country and, hence, their social sufferings were more acute and deplorable. The saddest aspect of social ranking is the fact that among the exterior castes or hereditary occupational groups of traditional social order, the *Bhangis* were accorded the lowest position. This hereditary group of scavengers was, thus, treated as the 'lowest' of the low throughout the traditional Indian society. The origin and the system of scavenging through the ages have been discussed separately in Chapter 2.

The problem of health and sanitation has also attained high importance in the modern times. A number of international agencies such as the WHO, UNICEF and UNDP are working for improving health and sanitary conditions in the world. These and other agencies of the world have realized the importance of good hygienic conditions for the qualitative development of human population. The programme for the improvement of water supply and provision of an adequate system for the waste disposal have been taken up by different agencies and discussions on various procedures and techniques are taking place at seminars and conferences. The following observations by John M. Kalbermatten (1980:3) throw light on the role of international agencies in introducing improved programmes for water supply and waste disposal: 'The importance of improving water supply and waste disposal, specially for the poor and less privileged, has been repeatedly recognized by the assembled governments of the world in recent years; first at the Habitat Conference in Vancouver in 1976, then at the U.N. Water Conference in Mar del Plata in 1977 and again at the International Conference of Primary Health Care in Alma Ata in 1978. The 1980s (1981-90) have now been declared the 'International Drinking Water and Sanitation Decade' by a resolution of the U.N. General Assembly. The purpose of the decade is to encourage efforts to provide all people with adequate water supply and sanitation in so far as it is possible.' It appears from the above account that a number of international agencies are looking into the problem of sanitation and improving the hygienic conditions in the underdeveloped and developing societies.

It may be stated beyond doubt that the traditional system of service latrines in urban communities (as well as rural communities) of India has been a source of insanitation and pollution of the surroundings in different ways and for different reasons. On the basis of the survey conducted by Kalbermatten (1980:6) in different underdeveloped and developing areas, the investigator came to this conclusion: 'The bucket latrine is judged to be unsuitable for replication. Problems of odour, insects, spillage and generally insanitary conditions et al. . . . and transfer points were ubiquitous in all of the cases surveyed.' The service latrine system is responsible for the breeding of insects and infectious germs not only at the places of disposal, but also on the route through which the human waste is carried by the scavengers either in buckets or trolleys.

The system is also responsible for insanitary conditions in the surrounding areas besides bad smell which causes irritation and restlessness. This system is highly injurious to health and aborts the programme of improving the hygienic conditions of the surroundings. Consequently, the programme to abolish the service latrine system and substitute it for another system is a modern phenomenon. Hence, the scheme of low-cost sanitation, replacing the older and traditional system of service latrines, is rational and modern. This also liberates scavengers from the demeaning work of having to carry night-soil on the head.

The present study analyses the programme of liberation of scavengers and also discusses the low-cost sanitation system which replaces the traditional service latrines. In fact, the twin programmes (liberation of scavengers and introduction of the low-cost sanitation scheme) are concomitant. The *Sulabh Shauchalaya Sansthan* (now *Sulabh International*) is devoted to the implementation of this programme and is introducing the two-pit system of sanitation for disposal of human waste which will liberate scavengers. The two action programmes are being carried out together under this scheme.

It does not, however, mean that liberation of scavengers is possible only through this scheme. The other modern techniques of sanitation and disposal of human waste adopted in developed and developing countries also help redeem scavengers. The sewerage system and other methods are effective substitutes of the bucket latrines. The *Sulabh Shauchalaya* scheme (two-pit system of hand-flush water-seal pit privy) involves the lowest cost compared with others. An evaluation analysis of the different schemes and techniques for the disposal of human wastes in Chapter 4 suggests that the *Sulabh Shauchalaya* scheme involves the lowest cost and can be presented as a programme of low-cost sanitation. The present study is concerned not only with the actual programme of introducing the *Sulabh Shauchalaya* scheme of low-cost sanitation and liberation of scavengers; it is also concerned with the ideas

Depth of degradation: A scavenger cleaning human excreta, bare hand and bare-footed.

Suffering in silence: After manually cleaning dry latrines, excrement is being carried away on the head and in hand-driven trollies.

involved in liberating scavengers. It is this aspect of the study which has a greater sociological significances and leads to the analysis of the social implications of liberation of scavengers. The *Sulabh Shauchalaya* scheme is operating in almost all States of India, but the present study does not cover all the States where the *Sulabh Shauchalaya* scheme is working for liberating scavengers. This study is confined to Bihar where the scheme was initially started and is at present working in different urban communities.

With growing urbanisation in the developed and under-developed countries, different techniques have been adopted for the disposal of human waste. These have been discussed in Chapter 3, in brief, to prove that the Sulabh system is the best of them all keeping in view the traditional, cultural and social values and norms of Bihar. Among the various techniques, two have also been introduced in urban India. These two techniques are known as the sewerage and septic tank systems. But these two systems introduced in different towns and cities of this country are not suited to the economic condition of the people whose lack of space and accommodation is almost proverbial. The sewerage system needs not only a sufficient quantity of running water but its regular supply for the waste disposal. Moreover, the costs involved in developing, constructing and maintaining the sewerage system are immense. Referring to the high cost in the sewerage system, Kalbermatten (1980:3) has made the following observation: 'Among the fundamental problems of increasing sanitation service are the high cost of the conventional solution and the large number of people presently being without such service. Today, around 1¼ billion people in developing countries lack sewerage facility and an almost equal number do not have any access to safe water. If to this number the predicted growth in population up to 1990 is added, over two billion will have to be provided with water and sewerage (or other excreta disposal facilities) during 1980s. A general estimate based on the existing per capita cost indicates that up to $ 500 billion would be needed for conventional (western style) water supply and sewerage. The per capita investment cost for sewerage alone ranges from $ 150-250, which is totally beyond the capacity of the beneficiaries in developing countries to pay'.

It would, thus, be evident that the sewerage system is beyond the means of the common people to adopt. Although the sewerage system has been introduced in some small cities and towns also, this does not cover the entire urban areas.

As of septic tank, it has hardly been adopted even by 10 per cent of the urban population. This system too has its own obvious limitations and problems. On the one hand the septic tank system requires more space to set up the tank and, on the other, it is a costly affair to get it constructed. In this system, it requires at least 10 litres of water per person every time to flush the night-soil from the pan to the tank. For the proper functioning of this system, therefore, it will require a huge quantity of water which is obviously not available in the country, specially Bihar. Therefore, it cannot be adopted by the common man. The gas-pipe attached to the septic tank discharges the gas formed in the septic tank which pollutes the environment. For cleaning the tank, the traditional class or caste of scavengers is needed because the deposit in the tank remains in the forms of digested and raw night-soil and nobody else can do this job.

Cleaning of the tanks can be done through cess pit emptier, but that is not available in Bihar, nor is it possible for municipal bodies to purchase it. Consequently, the septic tank system very much demands the services of a group of scavengers and continuance of the necessity of scavenging. It means that so long as the septic tank system continues to operate, the dream of liberating the scavengers from this sub-human profession shall remain unfulfilled. If the scavengers are to be liberated, if the demand of social justice is to be met and if this demeaning work is to end for achieving the high ideals of a 'Welfare State' in our democratic social order, the system of septic tank latrines cannot be allowed to continue.

In view of these facts, the necessity of developing a low-cost sanitation system was keenly felt in the country. Moreover, the system should be devised in such a way that it not only provides economic relief to the city dwellers, but also serves the cause of social justice, democracy and rationalization of the social structure. For this purpose it is necessary that a scheme should be devised and introduced to help in the liberation of scavengers and manage the disposal of human waste in such a way that scavengers are not needed at any stage of cleaning and disposal. The *Sulabh Shauchalaya* scheme squarely meets these demands. Moreover, the *Sulabh Shauchalaya* scheme is not only economical in nature, but it also needs much less space for the disposal of night-soil. In addition, the night-soil deposited in the *Sulabh* pit or tank does not remain in the same form; it mixes with the soil and turns into manure. Hence, the deposit may be cleaned by any person irrespective of his caste or creed, because it requires clearing only highly enriched manure. In this way, scavengers are not needed for cleaning the Sulabh tanks. Moreover, the manure, thus, taken out from the *Sulabh* pits may be used for increasing land productivity. This way, the human waste acquires value. The technical aspect of *Sulabh Shauchalaya* has been dealt with separately in Chapter 4.

In the light of the above facts, the *Sulabh Shauchalaya* scheme introduced in different urban centres has acquired a considerable importance, compatible as it is with the social and economic conditions of the users, so also with the ideals of social liberty, justice and welfare of the downtrodden. The scheme will very certainly do away the need for scavenging. And the scavengers thus liberated will also find jobs. The *Sulabh Shauchalaya* scheme also helps improve the hygienic condition and sanitation of the surroundings. The dangers of contamination from drinking water, pollution from air or water, in general, and the outflow of excreta on the surface are eliminated by the *Sulabh* scheme. No wonder, the scheme has attained a considerable significance socially and economically.

It is highly desirable at this stage to study the working of this scheme in different urban communities. A sociological probe into the working of the scheme and an in-depth sociological study of the liberation of scavengers through low-cost sanitation have acquired relevance. It is also desirable to know the extent to which the people are responsive to the *Sulabh* scheme of low-cost sanitation; what factors stand in the way of the adoption of the scheme; the experiences of the people, the differences in the attitudes and outlooks of the adopters and non-adopters and the media or sources which are helping the city dwellers in getting themselsves acquainted with the working of the *Sulabh Shauchalaya* scheme. Moreover, the study demands not only a thorough analysis of the attitudes of the scavengers towards the scheme, but also an evaluation of the responses of those who have been liberated, their difficulties in getting alternative jobs and in being rehabilitated, and the efforts being made (or already made) for their rehabilitation.

In addition, the changes in the status of the scavengers after they are liberated are also to be studied. An analysis of all these problems is of vital sociological significance in the changing social life in the country today. The present study is a pioneer effort in this direction which aims at analysing the basic issues involved in the problem and at exploring various avenues for further sociological investigations, economic studies and understanding of the problem through inter-disciplinary projects.

This study is systematic and planned, as it is based on field surveys. And the data thus collected are empirical which may serve as basic materials for deeper analyses. The findings have been systematically discussed relating them to various aspects of the problems. The objectives of the study have been clearly defined and the study design has been discussed in the following chapters before the actual analysis of the data and documentary materials. The investigation has also a theoretical relevance where it examines the traditional social structure, the position of scavengers in the traditional society, the changes taking place in the social and economic condition of scavengers and the problem of their liberation, offering an evaluative analysis of the different techniques of sanitation and disposal of night-soil and the importance of the *Sulabh Shauchalaya* scheme as the low-cost sanitation technology most suited to the existing social and economic conditions of the country.

This theoretical analysis precedes the analysis of the objective of the study, methodology and the field data. In this way, an organised effort has been made for a sociological study of the problem and to find out the social and economic implications of low-cost sanitation and liberation of scavengers in Indian society.

Objectives of Study

The sociological investigation of the problem of liberation of scavengers through low-cost sanitation involves the analysis of social, economic and hygienic aspects of the issue which may be described as a multi-dimensional approach. On the one hand, it demands the analysis of liberation of scavengers from the sub-human job and, on the other, it refers to the evaluation of different methods of sanitation and disposal of night-soil. The evaluation and appraisal of different methods involve the consideration of economic aspect in the context of 'low cost' as well as the safer way of disposing human waste from hygienic point of view. Similarly, the study on liberation of scavengers requires the analysis of facts as well as values. As a matter of fact, the liberation of scavengers refers to the study of the actual efforts being made for the purpose.

As a value, the analysis of the problem demands a deeper sociological insight into centuries old traditional norms and values prevailing in Indian society, declaring the disposal of night-soil as an obligatory occupation for a polluted hereditarty group of society. The very idea of liberation of scavengers militates against the deep-rooted values concerning the hereditary and obligatory division of labour in the caste-ridden Indian social order. Thus, the present study is multi-dimensional in nature for a comprehensive analysis of the problem and may be spelled out in a number of objectives of the study.

The first objective of the present study is the analysis of actual efforts made for the liberation of scavengers in India. Before describing these, it is also significant to point out that manual scavenging is not confined to this country only or to the Indian sub-continent; rather it is still in practice in many underdeveloped and developing countries of the world. The prevalent practice of disposing of night-soil manually in these countries is sub-human that hurts the dignity of man. Night-soil is a dirty object and nobody wants to touch it. But, at the same time, a section of the society is expected to clean night-soil and to carry it on the head to the dumping places. This degrading practice has been persisting for a long time in a large number of countries.

In India, the situation is more pathetic, deplorable and gloomy because a particular class of society is destined and bound to perform this duty on hereditary basis. This hereditary class, or sub-caste, was called *Bhangis, Chandals, Mehtars* or *Halalkhors* (different names in different ages and regions) under the rigid and authoritarian traditional system supported by orthodox religious sanctions and faith oriented values. Consequently, in Indian society, this section has been doing this job irrespective of whether it likes it or not. With the rationalisation of the social structure and propagation of the ideals of social justice, protection of the weaker sections of society and uplift of the down-trodden people, an idea has developed in the present age to liberate scavengers and to help them get rid of this sub-human occupation. In developed countries, the liberation of scavengers has already taken place and alternative methods and systems of disposal of human excreta have been adopted. But, in a country like India the problem still persists and a large number of scavengers are still engaged in this traditional sub-human occupation.

Social reformers, leaders, administrators, and defenders of social justice are in favour of doing away with the evil system of cleaning night-soil manually and carrying it in buckets on the head or in trollies. Besides being degrading, it also affects the health of scavengers. Hence, for solving the problem of public health and sanitation and, also for liberating scavengers, alternative systems for disposing of human excreta are being developed. The author of the book cannot claim to be the first person to present the scheme for the liberation of scavengers. Efforts had been made in the past also. But, the author, who is the founder of *Sulabh International* (formerly *Sulabh Shauchalaya Sansthan),* can certainly claim to be the first person to present a viable scheme, most suited to the social and economic condition of this country. He has also to his credit the innovative achievement of designing and launching a workable scheme which has remarkably succeeded not only in liberating and rehabilitating scavengers, but also in improving environmental sanitation. The innovative low-cost system of sanitation developed by this author in the name of *Sulabh Shauchalaya* has been adopted even by the common people with limited means. In the beginning, upper class families and technical persons like engineers did not attach importance to the scheme. But, later on, not only the engineers, bureaucrats, administrators and upper class families, but also international agencies recognised the relevance of the low-cost sanitation scheme put forward by *Sulabh International.*

In the light of above discussions, the first objective of the present study is the analysis of liberation of scavengers as a fact. For a deeper knowledge of this fact, the study of efforts being made in this direction is necessary. A comparative evaluation of different systems or methods is also desirable to find out the most suitable and workable one for this country. But, at the same time it is important to highlight that any absolute evaluation or appraisal cannot be done in respect of the different methods of disposing of human excreta, because social situations, economic conditions and other circumstances are not alike in all countries. Every evaluation must be in relation to a particular society. Hence, a relative evaluation is needed. It may be stated that the analysis of liberation of scavengers as a fact requires a relative evaluation and comparative analysis of different efforts made in this direction and this aspect constitutes an important objective of the present study.

The objectives also include the analysis of liberation of scavengers as a 'value', which has sociological relevance in the context of the centuries long persisting traditional values making, scavenging an obligatory occupation for a section of society on hereditary basis. The traditional values in respect of scavenging job for *Bhangis* were deeply rooted in society and the very basis of socialisation of the *Bhangis* was loaded with their so-called faith-oriented and sacred values. The development of personality in this section was in the background of the concepts of the sacred and the profane, derived from these values and the *Bhangis* engaged in this sub-human job believed that they were destined to do it. Consequently, they did scavenging without hesitation and protest against this unjust normative value. The sociological significance and relevance of analysing liberation of scavengers as a 'value' also lie in the fact that the rational outlook and recognition of the dignity of man in the present age have developed values contrary to the traditional ones and a phase of value-conflict has arisen as a result of the emergence of the idea of liberation of human beings from the sub-human job of scavenging. In this way, the analysis of traditional values, the emergence of rational modern values and the resultant value-conflict presents the outline for the study of the problem as a 'value'. Moreover, the objective of the present study in the context of value-analysis is also concerned with the value-judgement by the scavengers themselves. How far do they favour the modern values and to what extent do they still want the past practice, based on traditional values to continue? These questions are important to be examined to know the value-judgements of the *Bhangis* themselves.

Another objective of the present study relates to value-judgement, in the context of persisting social order, and to find out the degree of desirability of the scavengers for sticking to the traditional normative patterns and their degree of eagerness to break the traditional bondages for enjoying liberation and emancipation. At this stage, a vital question arises as to what extent the scavengers themselves are willing to get rid of this profession and to have some alternative job. In the traditional structure of Indian society, there have been traditional obligations for different castes and sub-castes, and not only social relations, but the economic ties as well, have been guided by traditional social compulsions. Consequently, the scavengers, who constitute a section of the traditional society, are also influenced by a number of traditional compulsions—social, economic, religious and cultural. The liberation of scavengers means the breaking up of the traditional bondages and developing a new set of social relations in the changed social climate. The degree of loyalty to traditional values and the intensity of willingness to break away from traditional ties matter a lot in the liberation of scavengers. Thus, a change in their social orientation as well as in attitude is important before they welcome the liberated phase of life. From this point of view also, the analysis of 'value-factor', is essential for an in-depth study of the process of liberation of scavengers.

As the views and attitudes of adopters and non-adopters of alternative methods of disposing of night-soil are also crucial in the process of liberation of scavengers, one important objective of the present study is concerned with the values held by adopters and non-adopters of the scheme of low-cost sanitation for the liberation of scavengers. There may be people who might not favour the doing away with the dry latrine system. Their opposition to the change in the system of disposing of night-soil also stands in the way of liberation of scavengers. It is important to point out that only economic reasons are not responsible for the non-adoption of alternative systems of cleaning and disposing of night-soil by the people. There are affluent house holds where the traditional system is still favoured. It is obviously due to the dominance of traditional values and persistence of conservative views. Consequently, the study of liberation of scavengers as a value also demands the analysis of the values held by adopters and non-adopters of other alternative systems, leading to *Bhangi-Mukti*. This analysis of the values leads to include the understanding of the conflict between traditional and rational values in the objectives of the present study.

Along with the analysis of liberation as a fact and as a value, the multi-dimensional nature of the problem also demands the social and economic implications of liberation as an ideology and liberation as a programme of action. The social implication of liberation may involve a conflict between the long persisting practice of cleaning night-soil manually and the alternative ways of disposing it. The privileged section has been enjoying a respectable place in society and the scavengers or *Bhangis,* involved in this dirty and sub-human profession, have been looked down upon by these people. In case the Bhangis are liberated and they are no more involved in cleaning and carrying night-soil they will have to look for some alternative jobs. This occupational mobility will bring out a change in their social status and economic conditions also, generating a change in social relationships. Such a change will obviously weaken traditional ties, resulting in a change of social structure and social system. The traditional bondages will be slowly replaced by rational ties causing social transformation. The privileged section of the traditional society may not favour this change in social climate to protect their dominant positions and they may strive to maintain traditional social ties. In this way, a number of social implications related to conflict between traditional and rational values and the process of social transformation may be found in liberation of scavengers. Consequently, the objectives of the present study also include the analysis of these social implications for a deeper insight into the problem.

The present study also includes the analysis of economic implications of the programme of liberation of scavengers. In spite of being a sub-human profession, scavenging has been the basic means of livelihood for *Bhangis.* Whether they were paid in cash or in kind, their earning largely depends on scavenging. In the traditional social order, the scavengers were also paid in cash or in kind, or both, by the families served by them on certain occasions like child-birth, *Janew* ceremony, marriage, and festivals. This earning was in addition to the wages they were regularly paid. In case of liberation, the scavenging work will stop and the scavengers will be out of job. If they are not provided with some alternative jobs, either they will refuse to give up scavenging, or they will starve. Consequently, simultaneous schemes for their rehabilitation are inevitable along with the programme of liberation to make the programme effective. It is also important to note that the alternative job must fetch at least the same money they got for scavenging. The liberation scheme cannot work successfully without taking this factor into consideration. Hence, the analysis of economic aspect of liberation also constitutes an important objective of present study.

The process of liberation of scavengers involves not only value-conflict, rehabilitation and change in the means of livelihood; it is also closely related to the change in social status and patterns of social relationship. The liberation of scavengers and their rehabilitation involve occupational mobility which is a negation of rigid hereditary system of determining one's occupation. In the caste-ridden Indian society, every caste or sub-caste was associated with a particular occupation under sacred sanctions and the belief in divine decree. Every individual was destined to follow the occupation of his or her own caste and the occupation was fixed, hereditary and unalterable for an individual as well as for a group known as caste or sub-caste. Thus, there was no occupational mobility in the traditional social order. The status of every individual as well as of every caste or sub-caste was also fixed. It is obvious that the occupational mobility following liberation of scavengers will bring about a change in the social status of *Bhangis*. The notion of pollution associated with cleaning night-soil will cease to be operative after liberation from this sub-human job and the liberated scavengers will aspire for a higher social status.

It will inevitably bring about changes in the social relationship between *Bhangis* on the one hand and other *Harijans* as well as the upper caste people on the other. Moreover, the consciousness of being liberated from the demeaning job of scavenging may develop the aspiration for higher status among liberated scavengers and they think themselves to be superior to unliberated scavengers. Consequently, a social cleavage within the hereditary group of *Bhangis* may develop resulting in conflict, social alienation and change of social relationship between liberated and unliberated scavengers. Hence, this aspect of the problem constitute another important objective of the present study.

The present study also includes the analysis of post-liberation phase of the families of liberated scavengers. The process of liberation of scavengers creates a chain of problems. The crisis does not end with the rehabilitation of liberated scavengers. The growing younger generation consisting of the sons and daughters of liberated scavengers poses another kind of problems. The sons and daughters of *Bhangis* did not face any problem of unemployment in the past. Like their parents, they also took up scavenging either under a corporation or municipality or were engaged privately for cleaning household latrines. But the situation has changed with the liberation of scavengers. Their sons and daughters are not essentially to be provided with the jobs given to their liberated parents. In case they do not get other jobs, many of them may revert to scavenging. Consequently, the very purpose of liberation of scavengers will be frustrated and the evil of continuity of scavenging job will persist. Hence, along with the liberation of scavengers, it is also necessary to check the entry of younger generation into scavenging by providing them alternative jobs.

The present study also includes the collection of factual informations on the patterns of social and economic life of the liberated scavengers, their adjustment to the new socio-economic conditions, the gap between their expectation and achievements. It is obvious that the scavengers being liberated have certain expectations and aspirations regarding the liberated phase of their life. They may expect better social dealings, a respectable place in society and improvement in their living standard. In case of a wider gap between the expectations and achievements, they will be frustrated. This frustration is bound to generate social, economic and mental crisis. In this way, the very purpose of liberation may be defeated and the *Bhangis* may not find the liberation movement beneficial for them. Hence, this aspect of liberation process also needs a careful analysis and, thus, highlights an important objective of the present study.

The process of liberation of scavengers is not unilateral. It is not only the manifestation of an agency preparing and launching the scheme and the scavengers accepting the scheme. It is a multilateral and multi-dimensional process, requiring reciprocatory behaviours not only from the *Bhangis*, voluntary and official agencies, but also from the members of the community to be affected by liberation scheme. It is obvious that the people using dry latrines so far will have to adopt the low-cost sanitation scheme for doing away with the old system. Without adoption of low-cost sanitation scheme, the liberation process cannot achieve its goal. Hence, the response of the community to the low-cost sanitation scheme aiming at the liberation of scavengers matters a lot. It is also important to point out that the low-cost sanitation scheme has been introduced in different parts of the country. The responses to the scheme may not be essentially uniform at all places. The degree of acceptability of the scheme is to be determined not only by any one factor; rather, by various forces operating in social life like the educational background, economic condition, degree of religiousity and orthodoxy, caste-orientation, sex, occupation, place of residence and degree of exposure to the media. These factors in different situations may produce different types of responses and may have functional and dysfunctional effects in respect of arousing and promoting positive responses to the scheme of low-cost sanitation. Hence, another objective of the present study is concerned with the analysis of the relevance of different variables to the acceptability and adoption of the scheme in the country.

The mass communication media occupy an important place in the modern age. With the growing urbanization and industrialization and due to high technology, the exposure to external influences is considerable. The increase in the percentage of population being exposed to media has emerged as a global feature, in both developed and developing countries. On the one hand the rise in the percentage of literacy and education has also exposed a higher percentage of India's population to the print media like newspapers, journals, magazines and books, and on the other, the availability of radios and transistors at cheaper rates in the country has facilitated the exposure of a larger section of country's population, both urban and rural, to this media of mass communication. In the recent past, the introduction of television and video in the country and its growing population have provided a very effective medium of communication to the people. More and more people are being exposed to this audio-visual means of communication. A number of sociological studies conducted in different fields and in different societies have revealed that the media of mass communication play a vital role in changing attitudes and outlooks of the people as well as their behaviour patterns and life styles.

The National Government, official agencies, private concerns and voluntary organizations have been using different media for popularising their programmes and for propagating ideologies and ideas. The champions of low-cost sanitation scheme are also utilising these media for wider acceptability of this scheme. Thus in the present study it is highly desirable to find out how far the different media of mass communication are helpful in acquainting the people with the *Sulabh Shauchalaya* scheme of low-cost sanitation. However, it is also important to evaluate the extent of the impact of these media on the people. Hence, the objective of the present study also includes the analysis of the roles of different media of mass communication in popularising the low-cost sanitation scheme and also the evaluation of relative importance of these media in motivating people to accept and adopt this scheme leading to the liberation of scavengers.

Another important objective of the present study is concerned with the analysis of the roles of different channels of communication in the popularization of the scheme and in its actual adoption by the people. Along with the media of mass communication the community leadership, opinion makers and political leadership also constitute the channels of communication in society. Leadership is an integrative institution and a leader acts not only as an organizer, planner, policy-maker or an executive, but also as a model and an example for others. Hence, leadership may prove much effective in persuading the people to adopt the *Sulabh Shauchalaya* scheme. Consequently, the study of the role of different levels and types of leadership in the popularization of the scheme is also included in the objective of the present study.

The present study also relates to the evaluation of the innovational significance of formal organizations in adopting the scheme of *Sulabh Shauchalaya.* It is important to point out that the ideas contained in the innovational scheme of *Sulabh Shauchalaya* have been propagated and supported by a number of formal organizations, like the Planning Commission, Central and State Governments organizations for the welfare of scheduled castes and social welfare organizations in general. The *Sulabh Shauchalaya* scheme aims at the liberation of scavengers and their rehabilitation. It brings about a significant improvement in the sanitary condition of the surroundings and the conditions of scavengers. It is expected that different formal agencies should extend their moral, financial and other types of support to the working of the *Sulabh Shauchalaya* scheme. It is, therefore, also important to find out the extent to which formal agencies are taking interest in the innovational scheme developed by this author for the liberation of scavengers. Hence, the present study also includes the analysis of this aspect of the problem and to assess and analyse this aspect of the problem and assess and appraise the contributions of different formal agencies in the successful working of the *Sulabh Shauchalaya* scheme.

It has been stated above that the *Sulabh Shauchalaya* scheme is in operation and a considerable number of scavengers have already been liberated through it. Along with the liberation of scavengers the implementation of the scheme has also resulted in the adoption of the low-cost sanitation system by the people. Hence, one of the objectives of the present study is to discover various patterns of action-sets activated by the adopters and the beneficiaries to obtain and enjoy the benefits of the scheme. It means that the present study aims at finding out the patterns of actions of the adopters for deriving benefit from this scheme. For this purpose, it is necessary to examine the experiences and action patterns of those who have adopted the *Sulabh Shauchalaya* scheme.

In popularising the *Sulabh Shauchalaya* scheme not only the media and opinion-makers are significant, but friends, relatives and neighbours have also played significant roles. Hence, it also includes the evaluation of the functional role of neighbours, kin, friends and others in popularising the scheme and in motivating and mobilising the non-adopters to adopt this scheme and to switch over from the dry latrine system to the two-pit system evolved and perfected by the author. This aspect of the sociological enquiry is of vital importance in the present study because it facilitates a sociological probe into the working of a social system and the functional and unfunctional aspects of various social institutions and sub-systems.

The scheme of liberating scavengers through low-cost sanitation has been implemented in different parts of the country most specially in Bihar. If on the one hand the scheme has been introduced in big cities like Patna and Ranchi, it has also been introduced in smaller towns like Arrah, Biharsharif, Purnea and Madhubani. The scheme has also been introduced in industrial towns like Begusarai, Dhanbad and Jamshedpur and also in non-industrial towns such as Arrah, Biharsharif and Madhubani. These areas differ not only in ecological conditions and demographic structure, but also in sociological conditions, economic activities and cultural backgrounds. The degree of the impact of the media is also varying. The levels of mobility and mobilisation are not uniform. Moreover, the educational background, occupational patterns, religious orientation, traditional dimensions, extent of modernity and level of rationality are also different in different towns and cities.

It is also important to point out that the population in a particular town or city is also not homogeneous; it reflects heterogeniety in social, economic, educational, ecological and physical conditions. Consequently, the programme of low-cost sanitation through the *Sulabh Shauchalaya* scheme has not attained the same degree of success in different localities of the same town. The extent of adoption of the scheme varies from area to area and from group to group within the same town. These variations are of greater significance and show the relevance of different variables to the adoption of the programme and the success of the scheme.

Hence, the present study also aims at finding out the extent of the adoption of the scheme and the degree of successful implementation of the programme. Such an analysis will also facilitate the discovery of the hurdles standing in the way of implementing the programme which will be of great help in implementing the *Sulabh Shauchalaya* programme. Hence, the inclusion of this aspect of the problem in the objectives of the present study is of vital sociological significance.

It is evident from the above discussions that the present study does not aim at a uni-dimensional analysis of the problem; rather, it covers various problems and may rightly be described as a multi-dimensional study. It is also evident from the above analysis that the liberation of scavengers through low-cost sanitation is important not only from the social point of view, but also for economic planning and development of the country. The nature of the problem attracts the attention of not only sociologists, but also of economic planners, leaders and persons and agencies engaged in welfare activities.

Consequently, the present study covers not only the analysis of attitudes, values, social relationships, patterns of social interaction and the changes in these aspects, but also covers the social implications of the economic aspects involved in the liberation of scavengers through low-cost sanitation. In this way, the objectives of the present study suggest that this survey or social study is comprehensive, multi-dimensional and multifrontal in nature.

In the light of the above discussions, the objectives of the present study may be summarised in the following ways:

1. To study the extent of adoption of various schemes of *Sulabh Shauchalaya.*
2. To prepare a profile of accepters and beneficiaries of the scheme.
3. To attempt a classification of the accepters of the scheme.
4. To obtain a correlation between the degree of adoption and the socio-economic and other variables characterising the adopters and beneficiaries.
5. To study the role of friends, kin and neighbours in the extension of the scheme.
6. To locate various patterns of action-sets activated by the adopters and the beneficiaries to obtain the benefits of the scheme.
7. To study the role of formal agencies in adoption of the scheme.
8. To study the role of channels of communications, opinion leaders, mass media, etc. in the spread of the scheme of *Sulabh Shauchalaya.*
9. To describe the physical and environmental changes ushered through the scheme.
10. To examine the role of variables like sex, education, caste, religion, places of residence, occupation, exposure to media, organizational affiliation in making the scheme popular among the people.
11. To elicit the views and attitudes of the beneficiaries about the scheme to find ways for its effective maintenance.

12. To conduct an in-depth study of the scavengers liberated through the scheme from the fetters of tradition.
13. On the basis of the experience of the study, to suggest gaps in the study of sociology of urban sanitation and to provide insights for improvement in the pattern of analysis and generalization in this field.
14. To evaluate the degree of acceptability of the low-cost sanitation scheme by those who are still having the service latrine system and to analyse the factors standing in the way of adoption of the low-cost sanitation scheme by them.
15. To find out the difficulties or problems faced by the adopters of the scheme and to know the ways for the removal of those obstacles.
16. To find out the best and the most suited system for disposing of human excreta, keeping in view the social, economic, physical and hygienic conditions of Indian society.

The Study Design

It is evident from the objectives of study presented above that the present sociological enquiry is concerned with the analysis of liberation of scavengers through low-cost sanitation. A deeper sociological insight into the problem demands the study of various issues and problems related to liberation process. It is also clear from above discussions that on one hand the objective aspects like family size, family income, education, age of liberated scavengers and places of defecation etc. and on the other, the subjective issues like attitudes, values, patterns of relationship, acceptance and adoption levels and levels of ambitions of the liberated scavengers are included in the objectives of study.

The study is not confined to collection of informations from liberated scavengers, but also from unliberated scavengers, adopters and non-adopters of low-cost sanitation scheme. The survey aims at identifying the factors that facilitate the implementation of low-cost sanitation scheme and also the obstacles in the way of adopting the scheme. Consequently, neither descriptive nor diagnostic or experimental study design was suitably applicable; rather an exploratory study design was to be prepared for conducting the study covering the multi-dimensional objectives in view. For the preparation of an exploratory study design, the objective of the present study was to take a decision on the areas to be selected for conducting field study in order to collect information from liberated as well as unliberated scavengers. The study of those areas will also be done where the actual liberation has taken place and also of the areas where the liberation scheme is yet to be implemented and the scavengers are yet to be liberated. It is obvious that the selection of these two types of areas meant the selection of the areas inhabited by the adopters and non-adopters on the low-cost sanitation scheme. Along with finding out the impact of the liberation programme, the study also aims at the analysis of the factors and forces obstructing the implementation of this programme to facilitate the working of the liberation programme in Bihar as well as in other parts of the country.

In this way an action-oriented research programme and a research-oriented action programme were concerned with the present study and the survey design was to meet both the requirements. It suggests the complexity of the nature of the problem under study which stands at the border-line of empirical sociology and applied sociology. This meeting point of empirical and applied sociology involving sociologists in the actual work of welfare and development provides the breeding ground for 'Action Sociology'—a term coined and developed by the present author and projected in National Seminars and Workshops on 'Action Sociology' at different places in the country. The leading Indian sociologists engaged in sociological researches and teaching work in various universities have accepted the concept of 'Action Sociology' projected by the present author and they have not only attended seminars and workshops on 'Action Sociology', but have also formed the 'Indian Association of Action Sociologists' to promote the concept into a discipline as well as into a programme of action.

The present study covers the State of Bihar. It is also evident from the above stated facts that for collecting informations, the households were to be taken as units because adoption or non-adoption of low-cost sanitation scheme was the concern of a family or household and not that of an individual. In the same way, the liberation scheme is meaningful not only to the individual concerned but to the family of the scavenger. The liberation process carries no meaning, if one person is liberated and other members of scavengers' family, continue to carry night-soil on the head.

Hence, the units in the present study were not the individuals, but the households. But, at the same time, this fact was also to be kept in view that the most important figure in the family or household is the family head. In addition to it, the collection of informations was possible from contacting an individual and not the household. The key person in every household was the family head and, hence, it was decided to collect informations from him or her. In case of non-availability of the family head some other responsible member of the household could provide informations and, consequently, it was decided to contact such a member of the household. The multi-dimensional nature of the present study in Bihar also suggests that the universe is complex. The units of the universe, i.e. the households of liberated and unliberated sca' vengers as well as of adopters and non-adopters also reflect complexity and heterogeneity from different points of view. Moreover, the number of households covering the above stated four categories is quite large and it was not possible to cover all these units of the universe scattered in different towns and cities of the State. It means that the census method of data collection was not practical in the present survey and, hence, it was decided to draw a sample from the universe for conducting the field survey.

For this purpose, a number of considerations are required to be kept in mind, because every part of the universe does not attain the status of a sample. Only that part of the universe which represents it and contains all the important properties and characteristics of the universe in the same proportion may be regarded as the sample of the universe. Goode and Hatt have rightly remarked: 'A Sample, as the name implies, is a smaller representation of a larger whole'. (1952:209). It means that a sample is a smaller section of the universe, representing its chracteristics and properties because the findings drawn from the study of the sample is regarded valid for the entire universe.

'The requirements of a representative sample are that part of the whole and should have in their relative proportions all the significanct characteristics of the larger group.' (Lundberg; 1949:137). In addition to it, 'A sample not only needs to be representative, it also needs to be adequate. A sample is adequate when it is of sufficient size to allow confidence in the stability of characteristics'. (Goode and Hatt; 1952:225). Thus, along with representativeness, the adequacy is also the requirement of a sample and this is attained when the characteristics of the universe present in the sample reflect stability. This stability of the characteristics is not possible if the sample is not adequate in size.

In case of present study, the drawing of sample was more difficult; because the units of study as well as the universes covered by the present study were distinct from each other. From an area point of view the universe was the same in all the four cases, but from the points of view of the nature and type of informations to be collected, the universe is not the same in four cases. In one case, the universe includes the liberated scavengers of Bihar; in the second case it includes the unliberated scavengers of the State and in the same way the adopters and non-adopters of the scheme constitute the two other distinct universes. In this way the universe was really to be divided into four sub-universes and from each sub-universe the units were to be selected for drawing sample. It is also important to point out that in each of the four categories the units are scattered in the towns and cities throughout the State of Bihar.

The complexity of the problem in drawing sample arises from this fact also that the units in each sub-universe are different in respect of educational background, economic status, caste, occupation and orientation to traditional and modern values. In this way each sub-universe was heterogeneous and complex in composition and structure. For drawing a more representative and adequate sample from each sub-universe, it was decided that the units be selected from different urban communities and attention should be paid to the proper representation of different social, economic and cultural properties of the sub-universe.

In view of the complexity of the composition and structure of each universe, it was decided to select units from different towns and cities for drawing a representative sample of adequate size. The towns where unliberated scavengers were in a large number and the liberation work was limited in relation to the requirement, the number of non-adopters was also expected to be larger. It is obvious that in case scavengers are still unliberated in a large number, they are engaged in the traditional job of cleaning and carrying night-soil.

Consequently, in these towns the number of households having dry latrines would also be considerably large, serving a larger number of non-adopters. Hence, it was more desirable to select the units or households of unliberated scavengers and those of non-adopters from the same areas. For this purpose, three urban habitats of Patna, Muzaffarpur and Arrah were selected. These three towns were selected because in each town the *Sulabh Shauchalaya* scheme has been operating for a long time and a considerable number of service latrines have been replaced by *Sulabh Shauchalaya.* Consequently, a considerable number of scavengers in these towns have been liberated. These scavengers have not only been liberated but alternative jobs have been provided to them and, in this way, these liberated scavengers have been rehabilitated. It is obvious that the replacement of the traditional service latrines by *Sulabh Shauchalayas* has been possible only when the citizens of these towns have adopted this scheme. It means that in these three towns, along with the liberated scavengers, a considerable number of adopter households are also found. Those who are still having the traditional service latrines are expected to be acquainted with the innovational scheme of *Sulabh Shauchalaya* and some of them might have come in contact with the adopters of the scheme. Hence, the non-adopters of these towns are expected to be partly or fully acquainted with the experiences of the *Sulabh Shauchalaya* scheme. In the same way, the scavengers who are still engaged in cleaning and carrying night-soil are also acquainted with those who have been liberated and rehabilitated. They are also expected to have come in contact with the liberated scavengers and to be acquainted with the changes in their social and economic modes of life.

Hence, these three towns are inhabited not only by unliberated scavengers and non-adopters, but also by liberated scavengers and adopters. Consequently, it was found more feasible to draw the samples of unliberated scavengers and non-adopters from these three towns. The actual and operational sub-universes for the unliberated scavengers and non-adopters were the populations of these two categories of persons inhabited in these three towns. In case of the liberated scavengers, three other towns, Ranchi, Patna and Purnea, were decided to be selected. These towns were selected for drawing a sample of the liberated scavengers. In these areas, the work of liberation has been done intensively. In this way, the actual and operational sub-universe in this case is the total population of liberated scavengers living in these three towns, Ranchi, Patna and Purnea. For drawing a sample of adopters, the three towns selected in the present study were Patna, Madhubani and Chaibasa where a good number of service latrines have been replaced by *Sulabh Shauchalayas*. Consequently, in this case, the actual sub-universe was the total population of adopters living in the three towns, Patna, Madhubani and Chaibasa.

After selecting the towns for constituting the universe, the next task before the investigator was to decide the size of the sample in each case. For maintaining uniformity in the study, it was decided that equal number of units should be selected for each of the four samples and, thus, to have the same size of sample in all the four cases. It was also kept in view that the size of the sample should be adequate to be really representative of the whole and to generate confidence in the stability of the representative character. But, at the same time, it was also to be kept in mind that the size of the sample should not be very large, because, for a survey of this type, a very large number of units cannot be studied. Consequently, a large size of sample cannot be adequate. Moreover, as no study of this type has ever been conducted in the past and the present study may rightly be regarded as a pioneer work in this field, any definite basis was also not available for the investigator. In such a situation, if a very large size of sample is taken, the complexity of the variables will make the study more complicated and it will be difficult to give a precise finding on the basis of the information collected from different samples and sub-universes. Taking all these facts into consideration, it was decided that the size of the sample should be adequately limited and it should neither be very large nor very small. On this basis, the investigator decided to take a sample of 150 units from each sub-universe and, thus, to analyse a total sample of 600 units selected from the four sub-universes of adopters, non-adopters, liberated scavengers and unliberated scavengers.

In the following stage the investigatoı was faced with the problem of taking a decision about the number of units to be selected from each of the three towns constituting one sub-universe. Here again the uniformity was maintained and equal weight was given to all the three towns of urban communities in each sub-universe. It was decided to select 50 units from each of the three towns constituting one sub-universe and, thus, to select 150 units for each sub-universe. In this case, the technique and principle of 'weighted stratified sample' was adopted by the investigator.

After taking decisions on the size of the sample and the number of units to be selected, the next task was to decide on the procedure for selecting units from the three towns in each sub-universe. In social sciences various methods of drawing a sample and different techniques of selecting units are used. All these techniques and methods are not equally good and valid in each situation. The suitability of a particular technique or method is in relation to the situation under study. Hence, before deciding on the sampling procedure, an appraisal of the prevalent procedures was needed. The most commonly applied sampling method is known as 'random sampling' method. It refers to random selection of the units from the universe.

'A random sample is one which is so drawn that the researcher, from all points of view, has no reason to believe a bias will result. In other words, the units of the universe must be so arranged that the selection gives equi-probability of selection of every unit in that universe'. (Goode and Hatt; 1952:214). The equi-probability of selection is possible only when any unit is not preferred to the other or when the researcher is ignorant about the properties of different units. 'This really means that the researcher does not know his universe sufficiently well to duplicate it exactly in his sample. What he is doing is the attempt to randomise his ignorance in this area'. (Goode and Hatt; 1952:214). This randomisation of ignorance ensures equi-probability of selection and, thus, every unit has some and equal chance of being included in or excluded from the sample drawn. In this way no unit has the zero chance of being selected.

There is no question of intentional selection of any unit. '. . . at random means that no item is given preference. The chance of the selection of any one item is the same as that of any other.' (Chaturvedi; 1947:2). But, at the same time, it is evident that the equi-probability of selection may be ensured only when all the units of the universe are available for selection and the researcher has a complete and up-to-date list of these units. In the present study, the availability of an up-to-date list of units in any of the four sub-universes was not possible because of the spatial mobility among adopters, non-adopters, liberated scavengers and un-liberated scavengers; or, because of the changing phases of the adoption of low-cost sanitation scheme.

The preparation of an up-to-date list was difficult also because the households, constituting the universe, were scattered and likely to shift from one category to the other due to continued efforts for liberation of scavengers through low-cost sanitation scheme launched by *Sulabh International.* Hence, random sampling was not exclusively applicable. The purposive sample method, used in the field of social sciences, refers to the purposive selection of the units. It means that in this case, the inclusion or exclusion of the units is pre-determined and intended. It is possible only when the researcher possesses detailed knowledge about the properties of the units constituting the universe. It is obvious that the present author did not possess complete informations on all the liberated and unliberated scavengers, adopters and non-adopters living in the towns constituting the four sub-universes. Hence, purposive sampling method was also not suitably applicable. The other important sampling method or technique used by social scientists is stratified sampling. This type of sampling technique involves stratification of the universe and selection of units from different strata. 'The basic point involved in stratified sampling is the fact that a homogeneous universe requires a smaller sample than does a heterogeneous universe . . . if a series of homogeneous universes can be sampled in such a way that when the samples are combined to constitute a sample of more heterogeneous universe, then a saving of time and money will result, as well as increased accuracy'. (Goode and Hatt; 1952:221). The system of stratification and the selection of units from each stratum, thus, ensures more accuracy, but the selection of units from each stratum demands application of the principle of random selection.

Keeping the complexity of the nature of the universe in view, the procedure adopted in drawing the sample was also complex. The categorisation or stratification of the universe into four sub-universes corresponds to the principle of stratified sample, because the objective of this categorisation was to have four homogeneous sub-universes, at least on the basis of one significant consideration. The selection of three towns in each sub-universe was purposive, reflecting relevance to the nature of the problem under study. But in selecting the units, the principle of random sampling could not be applied and, hence, the technique of chance selection was adopted for the actual selection of the households in all the four sub-universes. Fifty units or households were to be selected in each category from every town.

The precedence of applying chance selection principle is present in the study of 'rickshaw-pullers of Lucknow' conducted by Herald A. Gould, who himself explained, 'A chance as opposed to random sample was all that could be obtained under the circumstances. There were no statistics available concerning the social composition of this occupation on the basis of which a systematic sample could be constructed' (Gould; 1974:289). An application of the principle of chance selection was necessitated because of non-availability of up-to-date statistics about the rickshaw-pullers in Lucknow. In this procedure, the selection of units was without any pre-determined plan or procedure. The units available were included in the sample. The same principle and procedure were found to be adequate in the present study and the selection of 50 households from each town under each category was based on chance selection.

But care was taken that the households thus selected, reflect the properties of the sub-universe and different cross sections of the society are represented in the sample. Hence, the differences in respect of education, income, occupation, caste, sub-caste, locality and other relevant facts were taken into consideration in selecting the households and in making the sample more representative. In this way 150 units or households were selected in each category and finally a complex sample of 600 household was drawn. The selection of units, in this way, was completed through several stages of selection involving categorisation of universe selection of towns, selection of different classes of people and selection of households as units. The principle of multi-stage sampling was also applied. In this way it appears that the principles of stratification, purposive selection, chance selection and multi-stage selection were adopted by the investigator and hence, the technique adopted for drawing the sample in the present study may adequately be described as the mixed type of sampling.

The next stage was concerned with the adoption of a suitable technique of data collection. As there are different techniques used by social scientists in conducting field survey and in collecting informations from the universe under study, the suitability of a particular technique of data collection in the present case could be determined through a comparative evaluation of different techniques. The frequently applied techniques of data collection are observation, questionnaire and interview and consequently an evaluation of these techniques was desirable. The observation technique refers to the collection of informations through seeing the events and occurrences and watching the activities and behaviours of the people. There is no point of asking questions and collecting informations. 'In the strict sense, observation implies the use of eyes rather than of the ear and voice'. (Moser; 1980:244). The investigator collects relevant data on the basis of his perception. Thus, 'observation is a systematic and deliberate study through the eye of spontaneous occurrences at the time they occur. The purpose of observation is to perceive the nature and extent of significant inter-related elements within complex social phenomenon culture patterns of human conduct.' (Young; 1965:154).

It suggests that the observation technique is applicable for the study of those overt situations and facts which are subject to observation by naked eyes. Moreover, this technique may be used for the study of the present and not the past events and occurrences. In this way, the technique suffers from certain limitations. 'Not all occurrences are, of course, open to observation; not all occurrences open to observation can be observed when an observer is at hand; not all occurrences lend themselves to study by observational technique'. (Young; 1965:154).

It means that observational technique is not applicable to all situations and all types of problems and events cannot be studied through this technique. It is obvious that the present study includes the analysis of attitudes, values, levels of aspirations and underlying causes of adoption or non-adoption of low-cost sanitation scheme. These subjective aspects of the problem cannot be studied through the technique of observation and hence this technique was not suitably applicable in this case.

Another important technique of data collection is questionnaire. A questionnaire is a collection of questions enquiring into various aspects of the problem. This list of questions is administered to the people and their responses in their own hand writings are obtained. 'In general, the word questionnaire refers to a device for securing answers to questions by using a form which the respondent fills in himself'. (Goode and Hatt; 1952:133). Thus, the term questionnaire is used as a tool as well as a technique. Moreover, in case of applying this technique, the questions are not asked by the investigator, rather the questionnaire is administered to the respondents and they fill in the same.

In this way 'the questionnaire is differentiated from the schedule and interview guide by the fact that it is self-administered'. (Goode and Hatt; 1952:170). In fact, it is a technique of self-enumeration through self-administration. 'A questionnaire is defined as a form used in self-enumeration usually mailed to the respondents'. (Young; 1965:177). There is no question of helping the respondent by the investigator in understanding the question or in giving the relevant responses. In fact, 'a questionnaire may be defined as a set of questions to be answered by the informant without the personal aid of an investigator'. (Pope; 63). This technique is, no doubt, beneficial in certain respects. It can be used for collecting subjective as well as objective data from the scattered people. It may also be helpful in collecting information on the present conditions as well as the past occurrences. But at the same time this technique suffers from a major limitation in its application.

'Fundamentally, the questionnaire is a set of stimuli to which literate people are exposed in order to observe their verbal behaviour under these stimuli'. (Lundberg; 1949:183). It means that the questionnaire technique can be used only for the study of literate and educated people. It is not applicable for the study of the community in which illiterate people are also present. In the present study, scavengers and some adopters as well as non-adopters are expected to be illiterate. They can neither read the questions nor can write the responses. Hence, the study of any of the four sub-universes was not possible through questionnaire technique.

As regards the interviewing technique of social survey and social research, it is widely used by social investigators for collecting data from the field. This technique involves face-to-face conversation between the investigator and the respondent. For interviewing the respondents, he goes to the field, asks questions from them and records the responses given by the respondents. In this way, face-to-face interaction between the interviewer and the interviewee takes place in collecting data through the interviewing technique. This face-to-face conversation helps the investigator look into the life of the people covered by the interview. 'The interview may be regarded as a systematic method by which a person enters more or less imaginatively into the inner life of a comparative stranger' (Young; 1965:205). But the mere conversation is not sufficient for collecting data leading to a deeper insight into the problem. 'To ensure that the data are worth analysing, it is imperative to control the processes by which the information is obtained. If it is secured by personal interviews, all significant elements in the interview situation—the interviewer, the surroundings of the interview, the information and the process of questioning and recording—should be so controlled that the resulting record will be a true account of the situation which the survey is designed to describe' (Parten and Mildred; 1950:331).

In this way, a control over the situation is of great significance and relevance in conducting interview for the deep analysis of the problem. The above given facts also reveal that the interviewing technique may be used for studying any group and for collecting informations from any individual, whether illiterate or literate. The respondents or the members of the group or community under study are not required to read the questions and to record their responses. The investigator himself asks the questions and records the responses. Hence, this techique has a wider applicability than the technique of questionnaire. In addition to it, the interviewing technique is concerned with asking questions and recording responses. The informations about subjective as well as objective aspects may be collected through this technique. Moreover, the informations obtained through face-to-face purposive conversation may be related to the present situations and events or to the problems and occurrences of the past. Thus, it appears that the technique of interview is applicable for studying any type of problems concerning present or past and in any group of people. As the present study covers the analysis of not only present conditions but also the problems and conditions of the past and is also concerned with the analysis of subjective as well as objective problems among the four sub-universes, consisting of educated as well as uneducated people, it was found desirable to apply the interviewing technique for collecting relevant data in the present study.

After taking a decision on the data collecting technique it was also necessary to decide what type of interviewing technique should be used in the present study. While structuring interviewing procedure, two broad interviewing styles are found i.e. formal or structured interview and informal or non-structured interview. In case the questions to be asked by the interviewer are already constructed and pre-arranged and the alternative response categories are also pre-determined, the technique is known as formal interviewing technique. The list of already formed questions to be asked in formal interviewing is known as interview schedule. Thus, 'the schedule is referred to as a form filled up during a personal interview.' (Young; 1965:177). In this case the data or responses are conducted in a systematic way and data processing is relatively easier and more systematic. This is why 'formal interviewing, in which set questions are asked and answers are recorded in a strandardised form, is certainly the norm in the large-scale survey'. (Moser; 1980:270).

On the other hand informal or non-structured interview is based upon an interview guide which does not contain specific and already framed questions. It only contains basic points and presents an outline of the study, on the basis of which, the investigator frames questions to ask from respondents. The responses, thus obtained, are not according to pre-determined categories. The investigator is at liberty to ask different questions from different persons, but the data obtained are not systematically arranged. The analysis of scattered and unplanned data is difficult. Hence, in view of the advantages of systematic and relatively easier analysis of data, it was preferable to use the technique of formal interview for conducting the field survey. The technique of formal interviewing has been applied for collecting data from the field.

With the decision of applying structured or formal interviewing technique, the construction of interview schedule was also required. As the present study covers four sub-universes of different types, four different types of schedules were constructed for the purpose of conducting interview. Before finalising the interview schedules, pilot studies were conducted for pre-testing these schedules and for this purpose the four schedules were applied to a few units from the respective sub-universes to find out the shortcomings in the construction of schedule. In the light of the responses obtained and the difficulties in conducting interview, modifications and improvements were made in the four schedules and these were finalised for conducting the field survey in the four sub-samples drawn from respective four sub-universes.

After the schedule is prepared, the actual field work started. As the author is not only associated with schemes of *Sulabh Shauchalaya;* rather the very scheme was innovated and initiated by him and he has a practical knowledge of the condition of the liberated and unliberated scavengers, the level and extent of adoption and non-adoption in different urban communities and problems involved in the adoption of low-cost sanitation as well as the responses of the people to this innovational scheme of low-cost sanitation, the preparation of a plan for conducting the field survery was relatively much easier. The different urban communities covered by the present study were visited by him and different categories of people were personally contacted and requested to grant some time for the interview. The author as an investigator faced some difficulties in getting time for the interview from unliberated scavengers and non-adopters in particular. Only in a few cases the adopters and liberated scavengers showed some reluctance in giving time for the interview. But through persuasion and rapport, the investigator succeeded in arousing confidence among different categories of people and conducted the interview with 150 respondents belonging to 150 households for each category.

Along with using the technique of formal interview as the main technique for conducting the field work, the author also applied the observation technique in studying certain aspects of the problem. The stay of the author in the field helped him observe the behaviours of liberated scavengers, their patterns of rehabilitation, the problems of un-liberated scavengers, adoption of the scheme and the responses of the people to the innovational scheme of low-cost sanitation. The changes in social relationship, patterns of behaviour and life-style of the liberated scavengers and their family members were also observed. In this way, the observation technique was also used for the study of the problem.

In addition to the collection of information and relevant data from primary sources through the techniques of interview and observation, the study design in the present survey also includes the collection of data and information through secondary sources, contained in records and documents on the working of *Sulabh Shauchalaya* and other such schemes, the interest of different formal agencies, policies of the Government and other related informations.

In the writing of this book certain terms have frequently been used by the author. These terms need explanation. The term 'liberated scavengers' has been used for those scavengers who were employed in municipalities or corporations for scavenging, but who have now been assigned jobs other than cleaning and carrying night-soil, such as sweeping and cleaning or disposing of garbage. The term 'unliberated scavengers' has been used for those persons who are employed under municipalities or corporations and are still engaged in cleaning and carrying night-soil. The term 'service latrine' applies to the traditional latrine system in India, which is cleaned by persons belonging to the *Bhangi* caste. The cleaning of night-soil by these *Bhangis* is both manually and mechanically. In the same way the term 'two-pit sytem' is used for *Sulabh Shauchalaya,* which aims at liberating the scavengers and doing away with the system of cleaning human excreta manually. In analysing the problem and in the evaluative discussion of the ways of disposing human excreta, certain technical terms have also been employed by the author who has not only evolved the *Sulabh Shauchalaya* scheme, but has piloted the entire project and programme from the very beginning and is acquainted with the technical aspects of different system. A complete bibliography has also been provided at the end of the book.

CHAPTER 2

Scavenging Through the Ages

Scavenging in India

Indians mainly live in villages. Even today more than 70 per cent of the country's population is rural. In ancient days the percentage was much higher. Being bereft of an enclosed place for defecation inside the house, people generally defecated in open fields, their women using secluded places either surrounded by trees or partly covered with crops or hidden by a raised, grassy mound. The same situation is still prevalent. The people living in towns needed specified places for defecation and, hence, there was need for disposal of night-soil. In this way scavenging was not unknown even in ancient days in India. The scavenging work was done by a particular section of society constituting a caste or a sub-caste.

The sacred scriptures throw some light on the existence of a system for the disposal of night-soil. According to the contents of sacred scriptures and other literature, scavenging, specially the disposal of night-soil by a particular caste or castes of Indian society, has been in existence since the beginning of civilization. One of the 15 duties for slaves enumerated in the *Naradiya Samhita,* was to dispose of human excreta (Nagar; 1980:9). In *Vajasaneyi Samhita* the *Chandals* and *Paulkasa* have been referred to as slaves for the disposal of night-soil (Nagar; 1980:8). During the Buddhist period also, these two names have been mentioned. During the Maurya period *Patliputra* (now known as Patna in Bihar State, India) was one of the five ancient towns where the city mayor as *Nagrak* was the head of the organization entrusted with the task of looking after the civic affairs of the town. The scavengers and sweepers cleaned the city and disposed of night-soil.

During the Maurya period, the sanitary condition of towns was very much improved. Chanakya, known as *Mantri* (principal adviser) to the Emperor, has mentioned that every house should have a kitchen and a bathroom. He had suggested that one, who defecated in the open space must be fined. However, those who defecated due to illness or any disability, must be forgiven (Vachaspati; 1977:305, 350).

Malkani (1960) and other eminent scholars have sought to establish that the *Bhangis* (scavengers) of today are those people who were warriors made captives after they fell to the enemy.

The Muslims had brought with them some women who used the *Burqua* (veils) to cover their faces and they did not like to defecate in the open. The bucket privies were, therefore, designed and constructed for their defecation in *Purdah*. Those made captives were forced to clean latrines like bucket privies and throw the night-soil at distant places. After those captives were released, they were not accepted by their castemen and, hence, they formed a separate caste of *Bhangis* who were re-named as *Mehtar* by Emperor Akbar.

According to Chaturvedi (1980:22, 23) *Kshatriyas* and *Bhangis* have descended from the same source. For, he says, one notices a marked similarity between them. He has cited the following similarities:

BHANGI: Vas, Vasvar, Bir Gujar, Bhadwaria, Bisen.
MEHTAR: Bundelia, Chandal, Chauhan, Nado, Yaduvanshi Kachhwaha, Kinwar Thakur.
RAJPUT: (99) Bundela (48) Bargujaṛ Panna (222) Panna (295) Dajoha or Yaduvansi Gujar Panna (248) Rout.

The people belonging to the *Chandal* caste requested the census officer in 1911 to accord them the status of Brahmin as they had the Brahmin origin. In that respect their customs, rituals and other sacramental roles are identical with those of Brahmins. There is no doubt that the *Chandals* were made to dispose of sullage. These *Chandals* took the initiative to enrol themselves as Brahmins only after they became affluent. Obviously, the castes engaged in the disposal of human excreta were not at all divergent of a single caste (O'Malley, 1913).

Therefore, not only *Kshatriyas*, but also those who were engaged in cleaning night-soil since ancient time, such as *Chandals, Paulkasa* and also those who were made captives in wars either in India or in Jerusalem or other parts of the world, are *Bhangis* and *Mehtars* of today. According to the 1931 Census, the total number of *Bhangis* was estimated at 19,57,460—10,38,678 males and 9,18,782 females in India (Hutton, 1933).

The foregoing account reveals that historical developments led to the emergence of a special class of scavengers in India, known as *Bhangis* or *Mehtars.* This class became a hereditary occupational group with a fixed role and status in the Indian society. The unalterable role and status and the hereditary system made this class immobile and it developed into a caste or a sub-caste occupying the lowest stratum of society. With the allocation of hereditary occupation of scavenging and an immobile position, the caste or sub-caste of *Bhangis* became an integral part of the Indian social structure. This development was not possible without social sanctions.

The scavengers *(Bhangis)* were placed at the lowest rung of the caste ladder. The nature of the job or work traditionally associated with them, or imposed upon them, pushed them to the lowest, stratum of the social hierarchy of exterior castes. The task of cleaning night-soil was the most inferior job because this involved the touching of human excreta by the *Bhangis.* Consequently, they did not get social justice nor the humane treatment. Being economically poor and socially backward, they could not revolt against the unjust sanctions nor could they rid themselves of the scavenging work.

Mahatma Gandhi was the first to serve their cause and struggled for liberating the *Bhangis* from cleaning night-soil. In this way, he initiated the process leading to the liberation of scavengers and raised their status and position in society. Before Mahatma Gandhi appeared, nobody took up the cause of scavengers. When Mahatma Gandhi attended the National Congress Convention in Calcutta in 1901, he asked the volunteers not to engage scavengers. Surprisingly enough, the volunteers expressed their inability to do anything about it. Mahatma Gandhi set the pace by cleaning his own night-soil with the help of a broom (it was impossible for him individually to clean the night-soil of all volunteers).

But it made a great impact on the minds of the volunteers and, thereafter, whenever the All-India Congress Convention was organised, the volunteers themselves had to take up the task of disposing of the night-soil.

In 1918, when Mahatma Gandhi started his *Ashram* at Sabarmati, he advised the inmates of the *Ashram* to tackle the problem of disposal of night-soil themselves and not to engage the professional *Bhangis* for that work. The inmates of the *Ashram* had arranged two buckets—one for defecation and the other for urination and ablution to water and they used to dump it in a trench and cover it with earth which was used as a good manure. Mahatma Gandhi had got this idea of using night-soil as compost in 1908 while he was living at Tolstoy Farm in South Africa. In 1984 Mrs. Indira Gandhi disclosed in the Lok Sabha during the question hour that she herself had to clean night-soil while living as an inmate of the Sabarmati Ashram.

It shows the concern of Mahatma Gandhi about the plight of the scavengers. Once the Mahatma said,

> 'I may not be born again and if it happens, I will like to be born in a family of scavengers so that I may relieve them of inhuman, unhealthy and hateful practice of carrying headloads of night-soil.'

The Father of the Nation asked the volunteers to do social and constructive work simultaneously fighting for the independence of India. It is surprising that whereas in other fields of activity a number of people emerged and engaged themselves in social programmes and other constructive works, only a very few disciples of Mahatma Gandhi engaged themselves in the programme of liberating scavengers.

Notable among such persons were Appa Saheb Patwardhan, Anna Saheb Dastane, Atre Guruje, Dr. B.R. Ambedkar, Jiwan Lal, Jai Ram Das, Kesho Das Sah, Yugal Ram Vaidyave, Mama Saheb Phadke, Thakkar Bapa, Bithal Pharane, Sant Vinoba Bhave, Ballabh Swami, S.N. Murthi, R.R. Diwakar, Rameshwari Nehru, Bhau Narvekar, Viyogi Hari, Jaglal Choudhary, Sarayu Prasad and Rajendra Lal Das. Among all, Appa Saheb Patwardhan kept himself engaged in that pious work till the end of his life. He managed to devise a compost type of latrine, known as *Gopuri,* which has been discussed in Chapter 3.

With the beginning of the Gandhi Centenary period, two prominent social workers of India— Ishwar Bhai Patel of Gujarat and Dr. Bindeshwar Pathak of Bihar (the author) made a tremendous impact on the minds of the planners, administrators, engineers and social scientists, etc., regarding the liberation of scavengers' programme. The third name which has been added recently is that of Govind Narayan, Formerly Chairman, Rajasthan Institute of Local Self-Government.

Notable social organizations connected with the liberation of scavengers' programme in India are:

(a) Harijan Sevak Sangh,
(b) Gandhi Smarak Nidhi,
(c) Safai Vidyalaya,
(d) Rajasthan Institute of Local Self Government,
(e) Institute of Social Studies Trust,
(f) Sulabh International (formerly known as Sulabh Shauchalaya Sansthan).

Gandhiji wanted the scavengers not to carry night-soil on head and advocated the adoption of some safer method for the disposal of night-soil, so that the manual handling of night-soil could be done away with. An attempt was made when at *Sevagram* (Wardha) a trench latrine was constructed, the merits and demerits of which have been discussed separately.

Scavenging in Muslim Countries

The methods of scavenging and the social sanctions related to the scavenging work might be different at different places, but the cleaning of night-soil from the places of defecation and carrying it to the place of disposal were in practice everywhere. Islamic sanctions suggest the presence of the disposal system in the early days of Islam, i.e., the 7th Century A.D. or even in pre-Islamic days. The religious sanctions related to *Bait-al-khola* (latrine) in Islam clearly suggest that the latrine system was existing at that time and, hence, the disposal of human excreta also took place in Arabia. Moreover, the sanctions of *purdah* in Islam imposed a restriction on the free movement of women. In a situation where covering the body and face was a religious duty of Muslim women, it was necessary to have a place of defecation inside the house and also a place for the disposal of night-soil. Defecation outside the house by women involved the possibility of violation of 'purdah sanctions' and was against the concept of *hijab,* essential for every adult Muslim women. These sanctions also lead to the conclusion that there did exist a system for the disposal of night-soil. Moreover the disposal required cleaning of the latrine and removal of the human excreta to some other place outside the habitat, or at a distant place from it. Hence, the scavenging system was in vogue.

Scavenging in European Countries

In the past, even in European countries and America, the disposal of night-soil was done through scavenging. The following extract from 'Scavenger' sheds adequate light on this fact:

'Before the coming of the water closet, the sewage of European cities was disposed of by 'scavengers', men who made nightly rounds of the cities (hence 'night-soil'), collecting the contents of privy vaults and carting them to nearby farming areas. Often the farmer who brought his produce to the city returned home with a load of fertilizer. This was also the custom in America, where the widespread introduction of water closets and the sewerage system occurred only late in the century. But by the mid-19th Century, the scavenging system had broken down in many places. As cities grew, so did the supply of sewage. The laws of supply and demand prevailed and the bottom fell out of the night-soil maker. Farmers living near cities were saturated, while for those living further away transportation costs were too high' (Hamlin, 1982).

This excerpt suggests that the scavenging system was prevalent in American and European countries for the disposal of human excreta before the introduction of the sewerage system. The scavenging system came to an end with the development of higher technology and possibility of water supply in sufficient quantity at all places. The sewerage system for disposing human excreta is now in common practice in the developed countries.

It is also evident that the term 'night-soil' was coined for human excreta, because in American and European countries the human excreta was collected by scavengers from privy vaults at night and was carried to farming areas to be used as manure. The practice of cleaning human excreta at night, therefore, gave it the name of 'night-soil'.

CHAPTER 3

Sanitation and Disposal of Night-soil

WITH THE DEVELOPMENT of human civilization,there cropped up the problem of the disposal of human excreta. In the pre-civilization age or in the early civilization days, there was no such problem faced by human beings because latrines or specified places inside or outside houses were not provided for defecation. The people used open space, river banks and outskirts of habitats for defecation. The night-soil thus deposited on the surface of the earth got converted into soil and there was no need for the disposal of human excreta. But, when the latrine system developed in civilized societies and people desired to have enclosed places for defecation, the problem of disposal of human excreta also arose. The people developed and adopted different systems of disposing of night-soil according to the level of technological knowledge as well as the circumstances and conditions prevailing in their habitats.

In this way different systems of disposal of human excreta developed in different parts of the world. With the advancement of technology and scientific knowledge and the rise in consciousness of the importance of sanitation, health and hygiene, improvements and modifications took place in the system of disposal of night-soil. Climatic conditions, type of soil, water resources, economic conditions and social and cultural heritage also counted in developing and adopting a particular type of latrine system in a society or country. With the development of modern technology and knowledge, further modifications and improvements have been made in the toilet system. At present, different types of toilet systems are in use in different parts of the world. In India itself different designs had been developed during the British days and the post-independence era as well. The most commonly known and prevalent toilet systems in India as well as in other parts of the world are the sewerage, septic tank and the two-pit systems of *Sulabh Shauchalaya* along with the traditional latrine system. In addition to these, some other types of toilet systems have also been developed as descried below.

I. Trench Latrine

After coming back from South Africa, Mahatma Gandhi was concerned about the sub-human practice of scavenging by a separate caste, *Bhangi*, and also about defecation in open places. Whenever a meeting of the All-India Congress Committee was organised, it was a clear instruction by Mahatma Gandhi that the disposal of night-soil would be done only by the volunteers of the Congress and not by the *Bhangis*. In this attempt, a trench latrine was first constructed at *Sevagram*, Wardha Ashram of Mahatma Gandhi.

Trench latrine consists of a shallow pit, 2′ to 3′ deep and 3′ to 4′ wide, either circular, rectangular or square, a wooden plank having a hole in the middle and covered from three sides without roof either by a tin or thatchet. In a trench latrine the users have to put some earth or grass-leaves after defecation. The site of the trench latrine has to be changed after every six months when it is full.

Trench latrine, although better than open defecation, could not serve the purpose. It was very difficult to change its place every six months. Moreover, it could not eliminate fly-breeding and odour. Sometimes bacteria produced in the night-soil used to float on the surface of the latrine. Therefore, this system could not be adopted by the people in general.

II. Bore-hole Latrine

Bore-hole latrine was developed under the joint collaboration of the All-India Institute of Hygiene and Public Health, Calcutta, and the Rockefeller Foundation in pre-independence days. First of all, it was installed in Singur, West Bengal. It consists of a circular hole, usually 40 cm. in diameter, bored vertically into the ground by means of an earth auger to a depth of 6-8 metres. The latrine floor and its super structure are also provided. This is used in the African countries, West-Asia, South-East Asia, Western Pacific and South America.The greatest difficulty in a bore-hole latrine is the collapse or caving-in of the pit walls particularly in alluvial soils. It requires special equipments for its construction and the possibility of water pollution is also very high in this system. Fly-breeding is another serious problem in this type of latrine. Due to these reasons, the bore-hole latrine could not get acceptance on a mass scale (Bhaskaran; 1966:4).

III. Dug-well Latrine

The dug-well latrine was first introduced in Singur district of West Bengal in 1949-50. It is about 30″ in diameter and 10′ to 20′ deep in hard soil. The well is lined to prevent caving-in of the soil and is brimmed with concrete around its entry point. The squatting plate is placed over the pit for defecation with a suitable superstructure for the privacy of users (Bhaskaran; 1966:5).

The dug-well latrine is fairly expensive and it is difficult to construct it at places where the water table is high. The function of a dug-well is the same as that of a bore-hole. If it penetrates ground-water, it carries with it the risk of contamination. Because of these limitations, the dug-well latrine cannot be used in Bihar and so also in most other parts of this country.

IV. Ulta Matka Privy

A large earthen-ware pot (*Matka*) is buried upside down in a pit, at least 0.75 metre below the ground level, which acts as a lining. The *Matka* is about 1.5 metre high. A hole is made to fix a pipe joining the. W.C. for discharging the waste. A layer of horse dung is laid at the bottom in the beginning to accelerate the process of decomposition. Salt water is also flushed once a week to help liquification of the faecal matter. The maximum leaching takes place from the open end at the bottom and a little from the porous side of the *Matka*. The gases produced in the pit are absorbed by the soil. When the *Matka* gets filled up, it is kept closed for about two years and the digested material can be used as fertilizer. During this period an alternate *Matka* has to be provided (Cort;

1981:18-19).

Although the *Matka* privy has been tried in rural areas of Kheda, Gujarat, it has not gained popular acceptance and adoption on account of its very temporary nature.

V. Gopuri

Gopuri is a form of compost latrine provided with two tanks which are constructed over the ground level, instead of being dug in the ground. A movable seat with pan is fixed on the tank in use. The filled-up tank is covered with dry earth, ashes, leaves and domestic waste materials. Gopuri latrine has a permeable bottom and, like other compost latrines, the night-soil filling it up is transformed into compost after a certain period of time. It has a vent-pipe which keeps it reasonably odourless (Bhaskaran; 1966:5).

Although there is no handling of faeces or urine, fly-breeding can be a problem with the Gopuri type. The main disadvantage, however, is the location of its receptacles above the ground level which makes it unsuitable for most of the households in this country (Winblad; 1980:38).

VI. Sopa Sandas Latrine

It is a type of compost latrine which was first introduced in Maharashtra. It consists of (1) RCC or stone slab with cement or mosaic W.C. pan; (2) steep sloping pipe with a tin flap at the upper end; (3) rectangular pit of 4′ × 3′ × 3′ divided into two parts with partial honey-comb brick lining; (4) Y-pipe to connect both pits and (5) a vent pipe to carry away odours from the pit. It has been observed that the tin flap prevents bad odour from entering into the toilet and also prevents the passing of flies, etc. The flap, however, wears out after use and has to be replaced from time to time. The pit is covered with a sheet of tin when full and eventually the human excreta is transformed into compost. It is shovelled from the pit in course of time and spread in the fields to augment the fertility of the soil (Cort; 1981:10).

VII. Hagebu Latrine

This is also a modified form of pit latrine which is dug up to 3′ in the first instance with a diameter of 1′ 9″. The diameter is gradually increased to 4′ at the base, while the depth is extended up to 16′ to 17′. A latrine seat is placed over the pit and a suitable superstructure is also built (Bhaskaran; 1966:4).

This type of latrine was introduced by the Health Department of the State of Mysore and is still found in operation in some parts of that area. Here also, space is a problem as once the pit is filled up, another fresh pit hole has to be dug nearby. The question of its popular acceptance, therefore, does not arise.

VIII. Barapalli Type of Latrine

For the environmental improvement of villages, a pit latrine was developed by Dr. Edwin Abbot in the Barapalli village of Orissa. This type of latrine is 3′ to 5′ deep with a diameter of 30″. About 200 sq. ft. of land is needed for the installation of this latrine. A container of tin or an earthen vessel is provided to store water for flushing and also for washing after defecation. A broom is also provided for cleaning the pan (Bhaskaran; 1966:6).

IX. PRAI Type Latrine

After a number of trials and intensive research spread over a long period, the Planning and Research Action Institute, Lucknow, has designed a hand-flush water-seal latrine with a pan and a trap. Two types were developed—a direct type in which the latrine is placed over the pit and the other type in which the latrine is away from the pit and connected with a pipe. One or two jugs of water are usually sufficient to flush the faeces into the pit. When the pit is filled up with solids, the second pit is made by the side of it, which is connected to the latrine. The contents of the first pit may be used as manure after it is left for a sufficient period. The one-pit system is not very successful as the second pit cannot be constructed immediately after the first gets filled up. Secondly, the cost of the second pit would go up with the passage of time.

X. Ventilated Improved Pit (VIP)

This is based on an improved design of the pit latrine developed in

Rhodesia. Aerobic action takes place in the pit through a cycle provided by air-suction through the toilet seat and up the vent-pipe which is warmed by the sun and thereby draws up the air. It is claimed that the odour emanating from the pit is expelled through the vent-pipe. As flies cannot enter the pit through the flue pipe, chances of fly-breeding in the pit is reduced. Other deficiencies, however, continue to exist. The latrine cannot be constructed at places where the groundwater table is high. When the pit gets filled, a new latrine has to be constructed. However, the VIP latrine is a considerable improvement over the traditional pit latrine (Cort, 1981:13).

XI. Ventilated Improved Double Pit Latrine (VIDP)

The VIDP latrine differs from the VIP in only one respect, viz., that it has two alternating pits. When one is filled up, it should rest at least for one year before it is emptied to ensure pathogen destruction. The operation and maintenance of the VIDP is the same as that of the VIP. Two pits are provided by constructing a separate wall in the VIP pit, or by constructing two separate pits. Thus, the necessity of constructing another latrine, once the pit is full, is precluded. As the VIP and VIDP latrines are designed for use without water, they require good maintenance, which consists principally of keeping the squatting plate and superstructure clean. Otherwise the risk of fly and mosquito breeding is increased. The ventilation system is also to be designed properly to minimise fly and other nuisance.

XII. Reid's Odourless Earth Closet (ROEC)

An alternate design for a VIP latrine is the ROEC. In this latrine, the pit is completely offset and the excrement is introduced into the pit via a chute. A vent pipe is provided as in the VIP latrine. A serious disadvantage of the ROEC, however, is that the chute is easily fouled with the excrement and this may cause fly breeding. The chute is, therefore, to be cleaned regularly by brush.

XIII. RCA Latrine

An appropriate design of latrine for rural areas has been designed under the RCA project. Considerable work in this direction was done particularly by the Poonamallee Centre, near Madras. A composite design was prepared which embodied the salutary features of the earlier designs. The essential parts of this design are: (1) a slab or squatting plate, 3′ square and 2″ thick. The thickness towards the pan declines up to 1½″ paving the way for water to flow down due to its structural slope; (2) a pan measuring 17″ in length, 8″ in width at the rear and 5″ at the front. The depth of the pan at the front portion is 3″. It slopes down to the rear. A trap with 3″ diameter is joined with the pan and its other end is connected with the tank. The recommended depth of water-seal is ¾″; (3) a tank or pit of 30″ diameter or 30″ square with a depth of 6′ to 9′ and (4) a superstructure above the pan and seat. When the first pit is filled up, a second one is made nearby and is connected with the latrine. When the second pit is filled up, the first is emptied and reused.

XIV. Chemical Toilet

The chemical closet consists of a metal tank containing a solution of caustic soda. A seat with cover is placed over the tank, which is ventilated by a flue rising through the house roof. The excreta deposited in the tank is liquified and sterilized by the chemical which also destroys all pathogens. After several months of operation, this spent chemical and liquified matter are drained or removed. This system is quite satisfactory, safe and hygienic. But, the cost of construction and maintenance of chemical toilet is prohibitive which is why this system could not become popular. This system cannot, therefore, be recommended for a large-scale use.

XV. Aqua Privy

The aqua privy consists of a tank filled with water into which plunges a drop-pipe hanging from the latrine floor. The excreta and urine fall through the dropt-pipe into the tank where they undergo anaerobic decomposition as in a septic tank. The digested sludge, which is reduced to about a quarter of the volume of the deposited excreta, accumulates in the tank and has to be removed at intervals (Cort; 1981:21).

In aqua privy, there is no provision of soak pit for the discharge of the affluents. This is, therefore, not hygienic. Secondly, whenever the water level falls below the drop-pipe, the smell comes out of the tank and the entire surroundig is filled with stink. This system could not, therefore, be adopted on a large scale.

XVI. Vietnam Toilet (The Double Vault Latrines)

The double vault latrine consists of two receptacles, each with a volume of 300 litres. The receptacles are covered with a squatting slab which has two holes, foot-rests and a channel for urine. Faeces are deposited in one of the receptacles which can be used for about three to six months by a household of 5-10 persons. Urine is drained away and collected in a jar behind the latrine. The input into the receptacles is, thus, only faeces, ashes and toilet paper. The contents are fairly dry and the decomposition process is basically anaerobic. When the first container is two-thirds full, it is filled with dried and powdered earth, ash or paper and then sealed. The other one is used in its place. When the second vault is nearly full, the first one is opened and emptied. The decomposed exerement, now odourless, provides a good fertilizer. This toilet is known as Vietnam toilet, also because this system has been used in Vietnam on a large scale. Vietnamese health authorities claim that after 45 days in a sealed container, all bacteria and pathogens get killed (Winblad; 1980:29-34).

From health point of view, this system should be acceptable, but it cannot be recommended in India where water is used after ablutions. Moreover, it is built entirely above the ground with the two receptacles placed on the solid floor of concrete. The latrine cannot be constructed inside the house and has to be located far away from it. Hence, this type of latrine is not suitable for use on a mass scale in India, specially in Bihar.

CHAPTER 4

Low-Cost Sanitation and Sulabh Shauchalaya Scheme: An Evaluative Analysis

IN A POOR COUNTRY like India, the scheme for the disposal of night-soil should be affordable. The scheme should also be designed to facilitate the liberation of scavengers. Thus, a scheme of low-cost sanitation leading to the eradication of the evil of scavenging is needed in Indian society. The commonly prevalent systems for the disposal of night-soil in India are the sewerage, the septic tank and *Sulabh Shauchalaya* systems (hand-flush water-seal sanitary latrine), in addition to the traditional service-latrine system which is unhygienic, injurious to health and which involves the sub-human job of physically cleaning the night-soil. This system is quite inadequate and not advisable to be adopted. Hence, an evaluative analysis of the three systems is necessary with a view to finding out the best among them, both from the economic point of view and from the point of view of social justice.

The other system is the septic latrine system. It is commonly used by the urban communities of India. The economic aspect of this system may be understood in the light of its designing and the process involved in the disposal of night-soil. Septic latrines are the rectangular chambers, usually located just under the ground that receive both excrement and flush water from flush toilets. The mean hydraulic retention time in the tank is usually one to three days. During this period, the solid settles at the bottom of the tank where it can be digested anaerobically and a thick layer of scum is found at the surface. Although digestion and volume reduction of the settled solid is resonably effective, yet some sludge accumulates and the tank has to be de-sludged at regular intervals. The effluent from the septic tank is, from the point of view of health, as dangerous as the raw sewage and, if discharged into surface drains or water sources, it emits odour, encourages mosquito breeding and is a health hazard. It is, therefore, ordinarily discharged into soak ways or leaching fields (Kalbermatten; 1980:71).

The main physical features that affect the suitability of the septic tanks are restricted space for drainage fields and high-water service levels. Another main disadvantage is a reasonably high degree of users' attention, as the septic tanks have to be inspected periodically to ensure that neither scum particles nor suspended solids are being carried away with the effluent. Septic tanks and leaching fields are among the expensive forms of household water disposal.

The main advantage of the septic system is its flexibility and adaptability to a wide variety of individual households' water disposal requirements. They may be suitable for houses that have both an in-house water supply and sufficient land for effluent disposal. But, the cost of septic tank installation as well as its periodical de-sludging makes it inappropriate for the people of a developing country. The excessive area required for infiltration field severely limits its application to urban areas (Pathak; 1982:8).

It is evident from the above account that the septic latrine system is also expensive if the entire process and the maintenance and cleaning of the septic tank are taken into consideration. Moreover, the cleaning of the septic tank means the disposal of night-soil deposited in the tank. This operation involves physically carrying the night-soil from the tanks to some other place. Consequently, scavengers are needed for cleaning and disposing of the human excreta. It means that the operation is costly and the scavenging is not abolished as the need for servicing remains there. Hence, from the point of view of liberation as well as its higher cost of installation and maintenance, the septic tank system is not suitable to be adopted on a mass scale.

As of the sewerage system, it has the merit of liberating scavengers because scavenging is not involved in it. This system, not very common in the country, has been partially adopted only at certain places. The high cost involved in the sewerage system does not permit the Government to introduce this system at all places.

Hence, the system is not successfully operating in the country

(Duncan; 1982:19).

In Bihar, like the other States, the sewerage system has not been found successful by and large and even today more than two lakh service latrines exist in the State.

In order to present a comprehensive picture of the status of the existing sewerage system in Bihar, a town-wise study was conducted by the author in 1984. For this purpose a questionnaire was prepared and filled up by competent authorities in five different towns i.e. Patna, Jamshedpur, Ranchi, Bokaro Steel City and Barauni.

In all, eight sewerage plants were investigated—two each in Jamshedpur, Ranchi and Barauni and one each in Patna and Bokaro Steel City.

The sewerage system was first introduced for the central and eastern part of Patna during 1936-39. The sewers, laid by the Public Health Engineering Department, lead to Saidpur where 4 sewage treatment plants of 0.4 m.g.d. capacity were also constructed and commissioned in 1937. Subsequently, the sewerage system was extended to the neighbouring areas and the treatment plant was also augmented from time to time and completed in two phases—phase I in 1946 and phase II in 1972 at Saidpur. Both the old and new treatment plants employed the activated sludge process. The present capacity of this integrated plant is 6.2 m.g.d. which is serving about one lakh people. The cost of the plant was about Rs. 1.2 crores, which has been estimated to be Rs. 9.8 crores on the basis of the price index of 1983-84.

A small sewage treatment plant employing the bio-filterate process was installed in 1951 at Beur. This was designed to treat the septic tank effluents from the whole of old western Patna, mainly Gardanibagh area. However, it became ineffective long ago due to poor maintenance. Moreover, with the increase in population and the resultant increase in sewage generation, the plant could not sustain the excess load beyond its capacity. As such the surrounding area was water-logged with the untreated effluent. To ward off public health hazards and to restore environmental sanitation, a new treatment plant was installed again at Beur in 1968-70. The treated effluent was supposed to be discharged into the Serpentine Nullah and, ultimately, into the river Ganges. Unfortunately, the system could not be commissioned so far.

On the whole the existing state of Patna sewerage system is extremely unsatisfactory. Hardly 11.5 per cent of the population of the city (1,00,000 out of 8,70,940) is served by the sewer network. The sewage is discharged into the river either by direct pumping or through open channels, nullahs and road-side drains, exposing the citizens to considerable health hazards. The level of treatment is not adequate enough to maintain safe chemical and bacteriological standards of the treated effluent because the plant does not function efficiently.

The maintenance of sewerage is far from satisfactory. Due to non-installation of pumping stations at certain points, some of the drains do not function properly. The whole system is in disarray and the situation may not improve in the near future due to the financial constraints of the Patna Municipal Corporation. A total amount of Rs. 1 lakh only is being spent by the Corporation annually on the maintenance of conveyance, collection and treatment of sewage which come to Re. 1 per capita.

In the plateau region, Jamshedpur has two domestic or industrial sewerage systems with secondary treatment for a part of the town. Out of 7,16,450 people, only 1,29,000 (18%) have been provided with this facility.

The first plant at Jamshedpur was installed in TISCO township in 1944 to serve a population of 94,000 at a cost of Rs. 5 crores according to price index of 1983-84. The system was designed to treat 4 m.g.d. of sewage. It is surprising that the TISCO sewage treatment plant, which was set up 40 years ago, is still having the same capacity of 4 m.g.d. The population of TISCO township has risen to 4.1 lakhs and the total quantity of daily water supply is 25 m.g.d. On the basis of this rate of water supply about 20 million gallons of sewage is likely to be generated each day, out of which only one-fifth is treated and the rest is discharged into the river without any treatment. Additional treatment facilities are, thus, to be provided for 16 m.g.d. of waste water to serve a population of 4.1 lakhs for proper sanitation in the town.

The sewerage system of TISCO is being maintained properly. For operation and maintenance of the total sewerage system, Rs. 36.3 lakhs is being spent annually, i.e. Rs. 38.6 per capita.

The second treatment plant at Jamshedpur was constructed by TELCO in 1965. This plant is too small to cater to the needs of the

TELCO township, having a population of 35,000. Treatment facilities have been provided for 2.7 m.g.d. of waste water collected through sewerage. The cost of this activated sluge plant is Rs. 200 lakhs at the price level of 1983-84, i.e. Rs. 571.4 per capita. The supply is 4 m.g.d. on an average as revealed by the questionnaire, which means that 67.5 per cent of the water supply is generated as waste water.

The maintenance of the TELCO sewage plant is quite satisfactory, although the cost of maintenance in this case is also quite high. The TELCO is spending Rs. 12 lakhs per year for the operation and maintenance of the sewerage system which is Rs. 34.28 per capita. This is, however, slightly less when compared with that of TISCO. (This is based on the 1984 figures.)

In Ranchi, two sewage treatment plants are functioning, one for the township of the Heavy Engineering Corporation and the other for the Metallurgical and Engineering Consultants (India) Ltd., in their housing colony. Both the plants were set up in 1981, the former being of conventional type having activated sludge process system while the latter, built by Mecon, having aerated lagoons system (mechanised oxidation).

The sewage plant of the Heavy Engineering Corporation has a capacity of 4.5 m.g.d. to serve a population of 1.25 lakhs, but the volume of sewage being treated is only 1.0 m.g.d., as most of the waste water is intercepted by the local cultivators on the way to the sewage plant for irrigating their fields. The cost of the plant, according to the 1983-84 price index, is Rs. 529.2 lakhs which comes to Rs. 423.4 per capita excluding house connection on the basis of the present population of the township.

Although Rs. 18 lakhs is spent annually for its maintenance and operation, the per capita expenditure being Rs. 14.4, the users generally are not very happy with the system. The covers of manholes are frequently stolen. Scavengers are not easily available to clean the pipes jammed for one reason or another. Ordinary labour is reluctant to do this job because of the presence of human excreta in the pipes. The operation of the plant is often handicapped due to non-availability of spare parts, as some of them have to be obtained from outside the State.

The second plant meant for the township of Mecon is of a very low capacity of 0.44 m.g.d. to serve only 5,500 people. Its process of treatment is by 'aerated lagoons . The cost of its construction is Rs. 50.22 lakhs estimated at the price index of 1983-84. The per capita cost, which is Rs. 913.09, is the highest among the oxidation plants. The expenditure on its maintenance is Rs. 2.15 lakhs per year (Rs. 39.1 per capita), which is the highest among all the plants under study. Its functioning is good and the users are very much satisfied with its performance.

Only a fraction of the population of Ranchi—1.305 lakhs out of 5.38 lakhs (24.3%)—is having the facility of sewerage and sewage treatment.

Bokaro Steel City is the only place where the entire population of 2.8 lakhs is being served by the sewerage system and the sewage treatment plant. It was commissioned in 1968 at a cost of Rs. 10 crores at the price index of 1983-84, the per capita cost being Rs. 357.14. It is also an oxidation plant with a capacity of 20 m.g.d. The total water supply of the residential colony per day is 24 million gallons, of which the generation of waste water treated is 20 m.g.d. (i.e. 83%).

Its operation and maintenance is, on the whole, not unsatisfactory as revealed during the investigation. The main constraints are theft of manhole covers and shortage of scavengers for cleaning. the blocked pipes. The expenditure incurred is Rs. 5 lakhs per year which is very low when calculated on the basis of per capita cost. It is Rs. 1.8 which is higher than that of Patna only.

Barauni has two sewerage plants like those of Jamshedpur and Ranchi. The first plant, commissioned in 1974, served the township of the Indian Oil Corporation and the second, commissioned in 1978, was for the Hindustan Fertilizer Corporation. The process of treatment in both the plants is different. While it is an 'activated sludge' process in the Oil Corporation, there is oxidation system in the HFCL.

The construction cost of the plant at the Indian Oil Corporation is Rs. 256 lakhs and it serves a population of 20,000. The per capita cost is Rs. 1,280.0, which tops all other plants in the State. Although it was designed for a capacity of 1.3 m.g.d. the volume of waste water being treated is only 0.95 m.g.d. against the water supply of 1.3 m.g.d. (73%). The operation and maintenance cost of the plant is also very high. It is Rs. 37.5 per capita, the annual expenditure being Rs. 7.5 lakhs. This plant too suffers from a number of defects in its maintenance, like removal of manhole covers, shortage of spares at times and specially lack of trained personnel for operation of the treatment plant.

The HFCL plant is of the smallest capacity of 0.44 m.g.d. against a water supply of 0.66 m.g.d. The volume of waste water treated in this plant is only 0.29 m.g.d. The per capita construction cost is Rs. 393.3 for a population of 6,000, the total coming to Rs. 23.6 lakhs at the 1983-84 price level. Here again the maintenance and operation cost of Rs. 2 lakhs per year for 6,000 persons is very high. It is Rs. 33.3 per capita which is the second highest among the oxidation plants set up in this State. The users appear to be fully satisfied with its working and no serious complaint was made during the field enquiry.

A population of 26,000 only is being served by both the plants· together which is 43 per cent of the total population of Barauni (60,312).

SALIENT FEATURES

As regards collection, treatment and disposal of sewage the present position is far from satisfactory in Bihar. A summary of information on the state of sewerage in five towns of Bihar, mentioned above, has been provided in Table 1. It is worthwhile to mention that out of 14 Class I and 25 Class II towns of Bihar having a population of 55.6 lakhs (estimated population in 1984 based on the 1981 census), only one town, Bokaro Steal City, having a population of 2.8 lakhs (5%) has full sewage treatment facility. The other four towns, Patna, Jamshedpur, Ranchi and Barauni, with an estimated population of 21.85 lakhs (39.3%), are having only partial sewage treatment facility. The sewerage and sewage treatment facilities are totally absent in almost all the Class II towns of the State.

The result of the survey reveals that out of the 93.3 lakhs urban population of Bihar, 86.65 lakhs (92.8%) are living without any sewerage facility. It is also noticed that no proper facilities exist for collection in most of the towns, let alone treatment of waste water after collection. This appears to be the prime reason for the critical insanitary condition in many towns of Bihar.

TABLE 1
Status of Sewerage Plants in Bihar

Name of town	Township	Population served.	Year of const.	Type of treat.	*Volume of Sewage*		*Cost of const.*		*Maintenance*
					Cap.	Actually treated	(present index) total	price per capita	Per capita per yr. (rupees)
Patna	Patna	100,000	1937 to 1965	Activated sludge	6.2 mgd	6.2 mgd	9.8 crore	980	1.00
Jamshedpur	TISCO	94,000	1944	-do-	40 mgd	40 mgd	5.0 crore	532	38.6
Jamshedpur	TELCO	35,000	1965	-do-	2.7 mgd	2.7 mgd	2 crore	571	34.28
Ranchi	HEC	125,000	1981	-do-	4.5 mgd	1.0 mgd	529.20 lakhs	423.4	14.4
Ranchi	MECON	5,500	1981	Aerated lagoons	0.74 mgd	0.44 mgd	50.22 lakhs	913.09	39.1
Bakaro	Steel City	280,000	1968	Oxidation	20 mgd	20 mgd	10 crore	357.14	1.8
Barauni	Oil Refinery	20,000	1974	Activated sludge	1.3 mgd	0.95 mgd	256 lakhs	1280.0	37.5
Barauni	HFCL	6,000	1978	Oxidation	0.44 mgd	0.29 mgd	23.6 lakhs	393.0	33.3

The cost of sewerage per capita is largely dependent on population density, waste water production, topography, the type of soil through which the sewer is to run and the optimum planning for the sewerage zones. Similarly, the cost of sewage treatment depends on the type and capacity of the treatment plant. The total cost is, therefore, not uniform all over the State, which is given in Table 1 in which the cost figures of different treatment systems in the State have been ascertained through a questionnaire survey.

The summarised table of cost reveals that the total expenditure incurred over the provision of sewerage and sewage treatment facilities is about Rs. 35.38 crores, worked out on the 1984 price index, to serve 6,65,500 people according to 1981 census. The per capita cost is, thus, Rs. 531.6. The cost of operation and maintenance of all the eight plants is Rs. 83.95 lakhs per year which comes to Rs. 12.6 per capita; but all plants are not functioning properly.

As already stated, out of the eight sewage plants in five towns of Bihar, five have the conventional activated sludge system of treatment while the rest three are of oxidation type. The total cost of the former is Rs. 24.65 crores serving a population of 3,74,000 while that of the latter is Rs. 10.73 crores serving 2,91,500 people, the average per capita cost being Rs. 660 and Rs. 368 respectively. Thus, the per capita cost of the conventional system is 50 per cent higher than the oxidation system.

It is evident from the above discussions that the high costs involved in the sewerage system stand in the way of its adoption on a large scale. It, no doubt, liberates the scavengers, but it is not a low-cost sanitation system. Hence, in a poor country like India, the sewerage system cannot be suitable.

SULABH SHAUCHALAYA

As regards the *Sulabh Shauchalaya* scheme, it involves a different set of designing. The components of the system are briefly described below (Pathak; 1981 : 29-38 and Roy; 1984).

Pan

The standard length of the pan is 445 mm (inside). It may,

however, vary from 400 mm to 600 mm. The front and rear portions of the pan are circular having a radius of 50 mm and 125 mm respectively. The maximum depth of the pan is 225 mm. The depth in front is only 25 mm and slopes at an angle of 30° to 35° up to the point of opening into the bottom which is 75 mm in diameter.

The pan can be of ceramic, fibre glass, PVC, mosaic or cement concrete. Ceramic and fibre glass pans are smooth, more aesthetic and require less water for flushing. Of these two, the fibre glass pan is cheaper, lighter and easy to transport. Concrete pans are heavy, difficult to transport and are affected by uric acid. But, initially they are inexpensive. Mosaic pans are cheaper and quite strong. They can be repaired easily and can be moulded at all places on a large scale. The mosaic pan has shown satisfactory performance. It is commonly used in the construction of *Sulabh Shauchalayas.* It is made of white cement, marble chips and marble dust in the proportion of 1:1:¼ and ordinary grey cement and sand in the proportion of 1:2. The mould in the proper size, shape and form is made of clay and husk on levelled ground or a brick platform made for the purpose and left for a day to two to dry up. Wooden moulds can also be used, but with the application of used mobil. A coat of cowdung wash is applied on the mould and left for drying before the casting is done. An admixture of cement, marble chips and marble dust is first laid 12 mm (½") thick evenly on the mould to give it a mosaic finish and then the second layer of 12 mm (½") thick cement and sand mortar in the proportion of 1:2 is laid over it. This is nicely trowelled to have a good finish. A second layer of ordinary cement and sand is provided to make the pan stronger. It is left on the mould to set for a day and then taken out and put in water for proper curing. After a couple of days, it is taken out of water and the mosaic surface is rubbed with different types of carborandum stones to make it even and smooth and then polished to give it a glassy finish. One mould may be used several times after petty repairs, if necessary.

Sulabh water-seal

The Sulabh water-seal has been so designed that a minimum quantity of water, say one litre, is required for flushing. It also prevents bad odour and gases from leaking out of the pit. It has

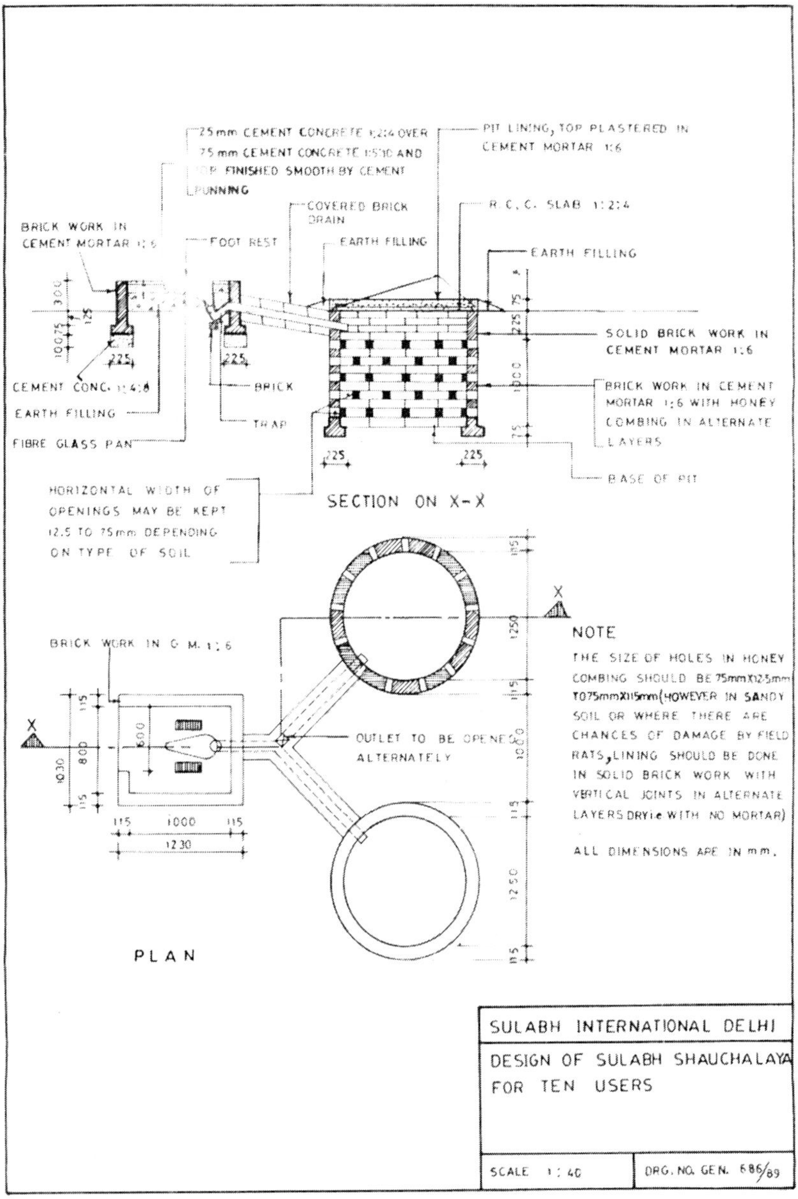

Design of Sulabh Shauchalaya (circular type)

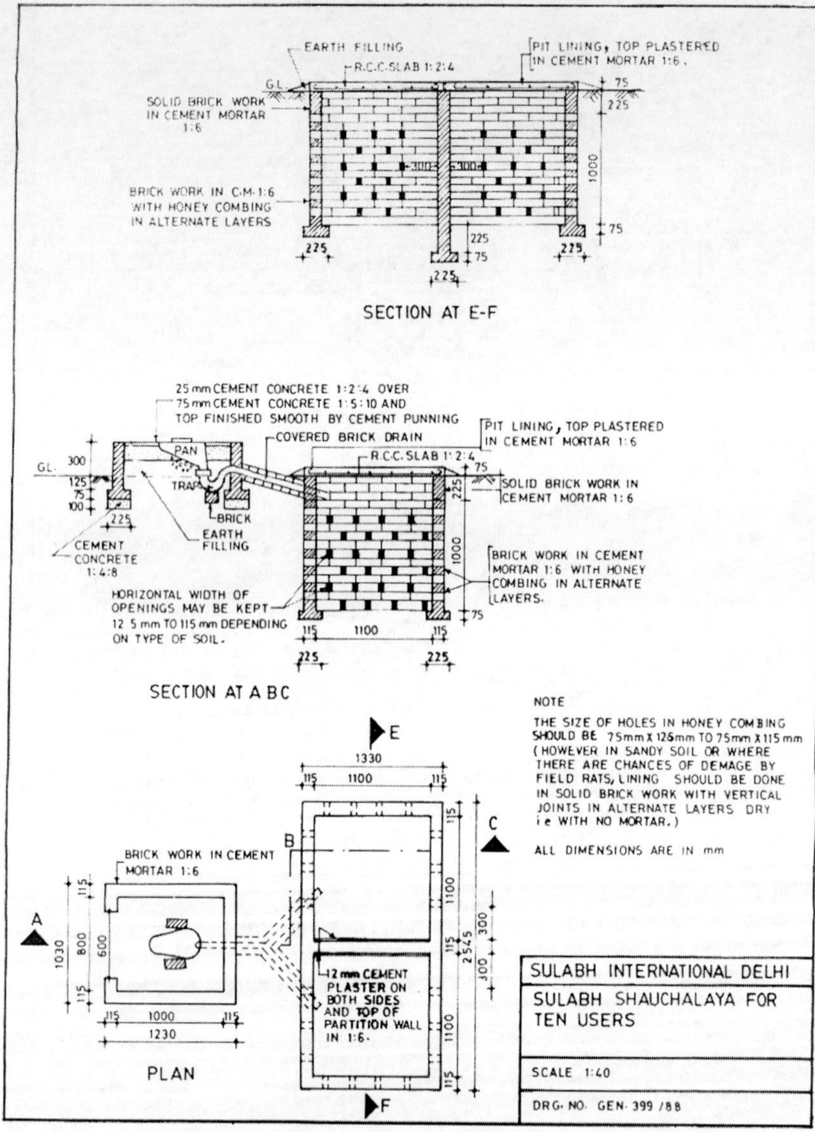

Design of Sulabh Shauchalaya (rectangular type)

been designed to be put just below the pan which has an opening of 75 mm dia in a block of cement concrete 1:2:4. For fixing a china clay or fibre glass pan, a circular groove is made at the top. It has a trapezoidal shape tapering at the bottom from both sides, thereby forming a V-shape. The Jib, which forms part of the water-seal, is protruding below and its lower end, 15 mm to 20 mm, is always dipped in water and is slightly rounded for easy flow of the excreta. The entire inner surface of this water-seal is punned with neat cement and is connected with the covered drain leading to the tank. Between 1974-84, more than 200 million people in India have used pour-flush water-seal latrines.

Platform and Foot-Rest

The platform should be 1150 mm square and 300 mm high from the ground level with the pan located in the middle. The height of the platform can be suitably increased, if required, in low-lying areas. The foot-rests need not be more than 50 mm high from the platform. The platform is plastered in cement mortar 1:3 well punned with neat cement, to give a smooth finish and sloped towards the pan, so that any splash of water may find its way through the pan. The foot-rests are made of bricks cut down so as to make them sloping and are plastered and embedded partially into the platform, the rear end of which is slightly raised. The pan can be fixed on the platform in any direction as desired.

If there is lack of space, the platform can be built over the pit (tank) itself. In this case, the central wall is made 375 mm thick. On this central wall, the pan with the water-seal and the outlet drain is installed to carry the excreta to the tank. The drain in this case too is bifurcated for easy flow of the excreta to the tank. The portion of the bifurcated drain up to the outfall is given a separate cover with necessary lifting arrangements.

The size of the leaching pits depends on the number of users, nature and properties of soil including its permeability characteristics, underground water level, quantity of water used for flushing and cleaning interval. Earlier, it was recommended by Wagner and Lanoix (1958) to provide $0.06m^3$ (2 cft) per person per year for accumulation of human excreta in the pit. Later, studies on sludge accumulation rate were carried out by various research institutes in India and UNDP TAG—India global project and it was recommended by the UNDP (1984) that an effective capacity of 0.045 m^3 (1.588 cft) to 0.05 m^3 (1.76 cft) per capita per year be provided under dry condition; in wet conditions, the capacity has to be increased to 0.067 m^3 (2.36 cft.).

The minimum storage capacity of 4½ to 5 years has been adopted to facilitate cleaning operations, although the pathogens are likely to be killed in two years.

In case the size is limited to 1 m length and 1 m width, the square shape is preferable. In the case of pits requiring higher dimension, circular tanks should be preferred. However, at places where space is limited, rectangular tanks can also be constructed.

In order to avoid seepage of effluent from one pit to another, a gap of about one metre is provided. If this is not feasible due to lack of space, the pits can be separated by a dividing wall which should go at least 300 mm deeper into the foundation as compared to the other walls to prevent seepage of effluent from one pit to another. The bottom of the tank is always earth-based, so that all the water leaches out and helps easy decomposition and transformation of the excreta into organic manure by soil bacteria which are found in abundance in the ground soil. Scientific experiments have shown that excreta, as soon as it comes into contact with earth, starts decomposing and gets smaller in volume as active anaerobic bacteria in millions are developed. This breaks the solid portion of the excreta into organic manure.

Pit Slab

The pit slabs are made separately for the two pits in R.C.C., 75 mm (3″) thick, as a permanent cover with necessary lifting arrangements. The walls on which the slabs are placed are above the ground-level to avoid seepage of rain water, etc., to the tank through the joints of these covers or water-logging. The R.C.C slabs, 75 mm thick, are used to cover the pits. Eight mm or 6 mm rods should be used for reinforcing the slab. M.S. rods of necessary sizes are cut and tied with annealed wire according to the size of the slab and kept ready in advance. The frame or template, to caste the slab, is built on a brick platform. This is either made of bricks and mud mortar or wooden planks securely fixed to the requisite size of the slab.

The admixture of cement concrete for the R.C.C. slab is 1:2:4

(one part of cement, two of sand and four of coarse aggregate, quartz or picked jhama bricks). Five to six gallons of water is used per bag of cement consumed.

The coarse aggregate, sand and cement are measured by volume in the above proportion separately on the brick platform. The cement and sand are first mixed thoroughly and then mixed with the coarse aggregate already spread on the platform. This is mixed dry and spread evenly on the platform. Then water is added in proper quantity and overturned twice or thrice to make a good mix. The concrete thus prepared is laid in the frame already made in a layer 12 mm to 20 mm thick. The reinforcement already made to sizes and tied together is placed over it. The lifting arrangement made either of M.S. rods or iron rings is tied to the rods. The balance of the thickness of the concrete, i.e., 55 mm, is laid over it and well tamped to make a homogeneous and compact slab. The top is nicely finished with a trowel or plastered with cement mortar 1:4. After 24 hours the frame is removed and the slab cured for at least 15 days by sprinkling water over it or dipping it into water or covering it with wet sacks. If required, curing can be restricted to seven days provided quick setting materials are used in the mix.

When perfectly cured, the slabs are placed at the top of the pit with mud mortar on all sides and are made quite air-tight and water-tight by a mixture of cement and sand mortar in the ratio of 1:8 so as to avoid erosion and leakage and can be easily removed at the time of taking out the manure from the pit. The pit covers can be used for household purposes also, like sitting, cooking, washing or taking food.

Adoption on Different Soil Conditions

As already stated, the scheme of *Sulabh Shauchalaya* has been widely adopted in different States of India including Andhra Pradesh, Assam, Bihar, West Bengal, Orissa, Uttar Pradesh, Madhya Pradesh and Jammu & Kashmir. This system has been found suitable to soils with wide variations in genetic and morphological cal, chemical and biological characteristics.

Pollution of Soil and Water

For mass adoption of the Indian hand-flush water-seal toilet, the possibility of soil and water pollution arising from the leaching pits has been the subject of research. Dr. T.R. Bhaskaran and Sampathkumaran (1966:28), have made the following observations:

'If the soil at the bottom of the pit is composed of clay or sand with an effective size of 0.2 mm or less and the velocity of flow of ground water is up to 3 ft. per day, the latrine can be constructed even as close as 20 ft. from the well. If the soil is coarser than 0.2 mm, but less than 0.3 mm of effective size and the sub-soil velocity is greater than 3 ft. per day, a careful study of the conditions must be made in deciding the distance between the latrine and the well. In such extreme cases, one feet to two ft. envelop of fine sand of effective size (0.2 mm) can be placed all round the latrine pit and at the bottom to prevent the ground-water pollution resulting from the flow from the latrine.'

Recently systematic studies have been conducted on the above subject by the World Bank through the UNDP and in collaboration with the Water Pollution Prevention and Control Boards of the concerned States, National Environmental Engineering Research Institute, Nagpur, through their zonal laboratories and State Public Health Research Laboratories. Experiments were conducted in Patna (Bihar) at two sites, where the soil contained an appreciable quantity of silt and the permeability was of the order of 0.032 to 290.5×10^{-5}cm/sec. The study shows that there is no evidence of pollution even in wells eight metres away from the hand-flush latrine pit (UNDP, 1982:2).

It is evident from this analysis that *Sulabh Shauchalaya* is the only low-cost scheme of sanitation. Moreover, as discussed above, the most noteworthy characteristic of the *Sulabh* system is that it neither contaminates the atmosphere nor is there any question of pollution of either the surface or underground water. The *Sulabh* system is also the cheapest among the prevalent conventional systems. It is also easy to maintain. For these qualities *Sulabh Shauchalaya* is the most suited for the Indian conditions and also for other developing countries. The *Sulabh* system also completely liberates the scavengers from the demeaning job of cleaning and carrying night-soil on the head. For that matter, *Sulabh Shauchalaya* is not only a breakthrough in sanitation technology, but a great movement for the liberation of scavengers which is very necessary to achieve for any civilized society.

CHAPTER 5

Efforts Made by National and International Organizations

THE FACTS ANALYSED in Chapter 2 presented a brief account of the social status and pathetic conditions of scavengers in Indian society where it has not only been an occupation, but also a social institution marked by social taboos, religious ostracism and social degradation. The social disabilities pushed scavengers down to the lowest level to get only sub-human treatment. The practices associated with untouchability, in general, and with scavengers, in particular, amounted to a denial of social justice. In an age of rising consciousness for human rights, social sanctions against *Bhangis* cannot have defence. Moreover, the norms of a democratic society and a Welfare State demanded end to such inhuman and unjust discriminations.

Hence, in the post-independence era, social reformers, welfare agencies and the State and Central Governments paid special attention to this problem and made sincere efforts to abolish untouchability and to liberate scavengers from the job of cleaning night-soil; for it was realised that the end of the job of disposing of human excreta and involvement of the people of this section in different jobs will help in improving their social and economic conditions. Various agencies, national as well as international, have been working in the field of sanitation. Although their efforts are aimed at providing good sanitation and not at the liberation of scavengers, yet the consequences of providing sanitary toilets in place of service latrines help in liberating the scavengers. The following account presents, in brief, the efforts made by various organizations and agencies.

NATIONAL ORGANIZATIONS

Perhaps the first organized effort for conducting the latrine construction programme in and around India began with the establishment of health units which were set up first in Ceylon and then in India by the Rockefeller Foundation in 1930. Bore-hole latrines with pre-cast squating slabs were tried at these health centres in Bengal, Uttar Pradesh, Punjab, Bombay, Mysore (then a province) and Madras (then a presidency). These efforts, of course, met with some success, but there were some practical difficulties in getting them installed inside houses and removing the latrines to new locations after the bored hole was filled up. There were also problems of foul smell and fly breeding with this type of latrine as it did not have any water-seal.

After preliminary experiences, the concept of placing a simple water-seal pan directly over a dug pit was developed in Bengal at the Singur health centre. This was certainly an improvement, but the main complaints against the design were that water splashed upon the user and a large quantity of water was needed to flush it. After a few years of trial with this type of water-seal, the Friends Rural Service Project in Orissa thought of making improvements on this design. The shape was modified and the water-seal was reduced. At the same time the construction cost was reduced. The improved design became more successful.

When the Community Projects Administration launched the first Five-year Plan, the bore-hole squatting plates and the dug-pit latrines were officially recommended for rural areas. But, in spite of the efforts made to instal these latrines in the National Extension and Community Development Blocks, the sanitation programme could not be adopted on a large scale.

Although the All-India Institute of Hygiene & Public Health, Calcutta, Environmental Engineering Research Institute, Nagpur, Research-cum-Action Project, Singur, Najafgarh, Delhi and Poonamallee Institute, Tamil Nadu, tried in their own ways to find ways for the proper, safe and hygienic disposal of night-soil, the credit goes to the Planning Research Action Institute, (PRAI), Lucknow, which started its research in 1956 and, finally, got some result. The PRAI, obtained nine designs and carried on its research work. Finally, it developed a separate design of its own having water-seal, squatting plate and two-pit provisions to suit all economic and hygienic conditions. But, the only thing it lacked was that it was recommended for rural areas and instead of two pits it suggested construction of only one pit initially to save the cost and to get the other pit constructed when the first one got filled up. Therefore, the adoption of the PRAI latrine remained confined mostly to rural areas and, as the construction of only one pit was recommended it could not be adopted on a large scale. When the first pit became full, most house-owners dropped the idea of getting constructed the other one. The installation of the PRAI latrine has been done on a large scale in Gujarat, but, mostly in rural areas.

Role of Voluntary Agencies

Before the emergence of Sulabh International as the most effective and dynamic voluntary organization contributing to the liberation of scavengers, a few voluntary agencies did pioneer work in this context in the country. The important among them are the Harijan Sevak Sangh, the Maharashtra Gandhi Smarak Nidhi, Pune, and the Safai Vidyalaya of Ahmedabad. A brief mention of these agencies is also desirable to understand the movement for the liberation of scavengers.

Harijan Sevak Sangh

The national organization of the Harijan Sevak Sangh came into existence in 1932 after Mahatma Gandhi's epic fast in Yarvada prison against the decision of the British Government to separate the so-called untouchables from the Hindus by granting them separate electorates. Gandhiji broke his fast on September 26, 1932 after the British Government's revision of the Communal Award in which the clause of separate electorates for untouchables was deleted. The crisis was resolved, but it made Gandhiji to realise that some concrete steps should be taken to remove the evil of untouchability for saving the Hindu society from disintegration.

On September 30, the same year, it was resolved in Bombay under the presidentship of Pandit Madan Mohan Malaviya that untouchability should be eradicated in all its forms from the Hindu society. To implement this resolution a new-organization named 'Anti-untouchability League' was formed in October 1932, which was later on called the Harijan Sevak Sangh. The entire nation stood in support of this move, morally and politically. Deshbandhu Thakkar Bapa tried to turn it into a national movement and within a few days of its inception, he spread it throughout the country with utmost zeal and devotion.

After some time, Gandhiji made a country-wide tour at the request of Thakkar Bapa, travelling about 12,500 miles between November 1933 and July 1934. This produced great impact on the masses. Millions of people heard the speeches of Gandhiji; thousands of them, inspired by his thought, stopped the practice of treating Harijans as untouchables and started fraternizing with them. The Sangh, constructed schools and hostels throughout the country for Harijan boys and girls and thousands of them were given scholarships. The Harijans secured admission to famous temples, specially in the south, where people practised untouchability in cruel ways. These efforts of the Harijan Sevak Sangh were for the Harijan community as a whole and not particularly for scavengers.

The Harijan Sevak Sangh also struggled for restoring human rights to the untouchables of society. It was realised that for the uplift of the Harijans, improvement in the level of literacy was necessary. It was also planned to educate Harijan youths and training them in technical skills.

Later, moved by extreme poverty, social inequality, inhuman working and living conditions of the scavengers, the Harijan Sevak Sangh took up the work of *Bhangi Kashta Mukti*, which implies betterment of their economic and living conditions, with the ultimate objective of *Bhangi Mukti* which is meant to stop the practice of cleaning the dry latrines manually and carrying the night-soil on the head. This is a revolutionary programme which envisages a society where a particular caste will not be compelled by circumstances to serve as scavengers. The institution has 59 *Sewaks* working under this programme, which includes supply of better implements to scavengers by the municipalities like scrappers, buckets, wheel barrows, hand gloves and rubber shoes etc. as also improvement of dry latrines by providing receptacles.

Besides, the Sangh runs a *Safai Vidyalaya* at the Harijan Ashram, Ahmedabad, for imparting training to the *Bhangi Kashta Mukti* sevaks in modern and scientific methods of scavenging, construction of improved models of latrines and other allied subjects pertaining to cleanliness and hygiene. These persistent efforts of this voluntary organization were a move towards liberation of scavengers. It cannot be claimed that the evil has been eradicated completely, but root had been shaken as was evident in the decline in the intensity of atrocities against this weaker section of the society. Moreover, the reform movement by Sevak Sangh also aroused the social consciousness among the Harijans themselves, in general, and among the *Bhangis* in particular, facilitating the process of liberation.

Maharashtra Gandhi Smarak Nidhi, Pune

The Central Gandhi Smarak Nidhi was established in Delhi in 1956 under the chairmanship of the late Appa Saheb Patwardhan. He was also the founder chairman of the *Bhangi Mukti Samitee* of the *Central Gandhi Smarak Nidhi* set up in the same year for the liberation of scavengers throughout India. Later in 1962, the *Maharashtra Gandhi Smarak Nidhi* (MGSN) was set up as a separate unit. But in the beginning, this State branch tagged its activities with the *Central Gandhi Smarak Nidhi.* The Founder Chairman of this unit was late Mamasaheb Deoginkar. After the Gandhi Centenary celebrations in 1969, the State branch started working as an independent unit. It was engaged in village uplift, propagation of Gandhian philosophy, publication of Gandhian literature and in launching the *Bhangi Mukti Scheme* (liberation of scavengers). The Nidhi has been working to abolish scavenging by converting the service latrines into pour-flush sanitary latrines of *Sulabh Shauchalaya* type and also by constructing new latrines which do not require the services of scavengers. Pioneering experiments in this field were done by the late Appa Saheb Patwardhan in Gopuri Ashram in Ratnagiri district of Maharashtra. Based on his work, the *Nidhi* decided to encourage the construction of two types of latrines, one the *Sopa type* in which the pan is not water sealed, but is provided at the delivery end with a hinged metal plate. The other one is *Naigaon* latrine, which is a modified aqua privy, in which arrangements are made to collect the effluent in containers for use as fertilizer in farms.

The *Nidhi* has established a separate cell, called *Bhangi Mukti Yojna*, for the purpose of propagation and construction of sanitary latrines. The tasks of extension, persuasion and also the construction of sanitary latrines have been undertaken by this cell in a systematic and organized way. The cell launches schemes for motivating the people in rural areas to adopt the programme of latrine construction. For this purpose, different methods like audio-visual methods, films and slide shows, group meetings, exhibitions, *Bhajans*, Kirtans, posters and leaflet distribution were adopted to popularise the scheme in order to achieve the objective of *Bhangi Mukti*.

The *Nidhi* has under its control two-pan manufacturing workshops where pans are manufactured, and water-seal traps cast from cement mortar and marble chips. Training programmes are organised by MGSN for social and municipal workers on its ongoing projects. Each project runs for a week. Regular training camps and lectures are arranged for Govt., municipal and *Zila Parishad* staff at various levels. Besides, the *Nidhi* imparts 15 days' training for latrine construction and 10 days' training for biogas plant construction to local technicians. Stipend is also given to the trainees for the training period.

The *Nidhi* has included in its programme the construction of biogas plants and in this work Dr. Mapuskar has rendered a very valuable service to this organization as an honorary adviser. Initially, the *Nidhi* gave 50 per cent subsidy to farmers. It also has taken up the work of propagating and constructing biogas plants, based exclusively on human excreta (night-soil). Unfortunately, the progress of biogas plants is not as fast as expected. This is due mainly to high initial cost and absence of immediate monetary gain. Repayment of loan also presents a lot of difficulty. Hence, this institution has plans to conduct experiments for low-cost biogas plants.

By 1987 the MGSN constructed 70,000 latrines in 27 districts of Maharashtra and also 500 biogas plants, besides training a large number of field staff of various *Zila Parishads*. Hundreds of training camps had been organised for social workers engaged in different voluntary organizations. A large number of masons and technicians had been given training. The Government of Maharashtra, municipalities and *Zila Parishads* had been rendering full co-operation to the *Nidhi*. They had been directing their administrative and field staff to take up latrine construction work vigorously. Some of them are now subsidizing the cost of construction to the villagers if they adopt the design prepared by the *Nidhi*. The Government of Maharashtra has started giving mosaic pans free of cost to the adopters through *Zila Parishads*.

Safai Vidyalaya, Sabarmati Ashram, Ahmedabad

Safai Vidyalaya, Ahmedabad, a sanitation institution, was set up by the *Harijan Sevak Sangh* at Sabarmati Ashram in 1963 under the. charge of Mr. Ishwarbhai Patel. The building in which the institute is accommodated is named as *Parixit Sadan* to commemorate the memory of late Parixitlal Mazumdar who was one of the pioneers of the Harijan movement in Gujarat. The *Vidyalaya*, in keeping with the objectives of he *Harijan Sevak Sangh*, took up the programmes touching all aspects of scavengers' life—social, economic and educational. Its activity includes training programmes in respect of the method, approach, use of improved implements for cleaning latrines etc., for all concerned, namely junior and senior engineers, mansons, sweepers and scavengers besides sanitary inspectors of primary health centres in rural areas and social workers engaged in the programme of *Bhangi Kashta Mukti*.

Short-term courses for policy-makers and administrators are also arranged at various levels to convince them of the importance of sanitation. The training programme comprised practical demonstration on cleanliness, technique of conversion of dry latrines into water-borne types, construction of new hand-flush sanitary latrines needing no scavenger service, modification of by-laws of local bodies and use of improved implements for sanitation etc. Such training programmes promoted the low-cost sanitation schemes.

The syllabus for training programmes included the methods for improvement of working and living conditions of sweepers and scavengers, their economic, social and cultural development, various types of latrine designs and use of sanitary equipments etc. The *Vidyalaya* has a demonstration plot with various types of sanitary latrines and biogas plants.

Students visit the *Vidyalaya* as a part of their study tours. They are taken round the models and exhibits displayed in the *Vidyalaya*. Films on sanitation and biogas plants are also shown to them. Youths of various organizations like N.S.S are trained in the construction of pour-flush sanitary latrines, soakpits and smokeless ovens. The 1987 figures indicate that about 250 camps were held in villages of various districts of the State which were attended by about 3,000 college students and youths under the National Social Service Scheme.

This institution has been helpful in getting various bye-laws changed and subsidies granted by the local bodies and panchayats for conversion of dry latrines into pour-flush sanitary ones to eradicate the sub-human practice of carrying night-soil as head load by scavengers. There were about 1,70,000 dry latrines when the programme was launched in 1964. Almost all the dry latrines had been converted into pour-flush types in municipal areas with financial assistance of the State Government, municipalities, district panchayats and the contribution by the house-owners themselves. During the conversion, however, two pits were not provided at a large number of places where drainage facilities were available. And, in such cases, the pour-flush latrines were directly connected to the underground drains to facilitate the removal of the night-soil. In this manner, the State has been made almost free from dry latrines and all the scavengers, (about 5,000 in all) were absorbed in other jobs by the municipalities.

The utility of the *Vidyalaya* has been recognised by the State Government, municipalities, district and taluka panchayats and educational institutions, mainly the universities and people in general. They have often been calling on the *Vidyalaya* for organising camps, seminars and conferences. Various national and international agencies and organizations had taken note of the valuable contributions by this institute in the field of low-cost pour-flush latrines and in rural sanitation. For instance, the World Health Organization (WHO), UNICEF, the World Bank and the Government of India have been sending their representatives to study the working of its different wings particularly the training facilities and the methods adopted for implementation of sanitation programmes. Delegations from different countries, like Bangladesh, Sri Lanka, Bhutan, Nepal and Tanzania paid visits to the Safai Vidyalaya and discussed the low-cost sanitation and other related matters.

The impact of the Vidyalaya had been very positive and there was a general acceptability of the technical expertise made available by it to all concerned ranging from community workers to Government employees and engineers working in municipalities, panchayats and government departments. About 1,200 panchayat workers and dozens of chairmen of district and taluka panchayats had already taken advantage of the training programme organised by the *Safai Vidyalaya.* UNICEF has responded favourably to the health and sanitation programme of the *Vidyalaya* by providing a mobile van to the institution with models, charts and arrangement for showing films to be used in rural areas of the State for educating the masses.

In order to help the trainees understand the technical aspects of sanitation, 10 posters on sanitation and *Bhangi Kashta Mukti,* 13 folders on various types of latrines and sanitation guides have been published by the *Vidyalaya.* A booklet on sanitation in Gujarati, coloured posters and folders have been printed with the financial assistance of the State Government. With the help of the Social Welfare Department, a Gujarati version of three important committee reports, namely *Malkani Committee, Barve Committee* and Viyas Committee, have been brought out in which recommendations had been made to improve the condition of scavengers. The Vidyalaya had also helped the Gandhi Centenary Committee in preparing a documentary film *Abhishap*, depicting the plight of scavengers which had tremendous impact on the people.

Government Efforts in Liberating Scavengers

Although during Gandhiji's lifetime efforts were made for liberating scavengers, yet no tangible results could be achieved. First, because India was under foreign rule and the Government did not make any sincere effort at liberating scavengers and, secondly, because there was no technology available to replace the sewerage and septic tank systems.

After independence, the Central and many State Governments started work on liberating scavengers; and they appointed committees to analyse the working and living conditions of scavengers and suggest ways for improving them. The following committees are worth mentioning:

1. The Scavengers' Living Conditions Enquiry Committee constituted by the Govt. of Bombay in 1949, headed by B.N.

Barve (1949-51).

2. The Scavenging Conditions Enquiry Committee, constituted by the Ministry of Home Affairs, Govt. of India, in 1957, chaired by Prof. N.R. Malkani (1957-60).
3. The Committee on Customary Rights to Scavengers, 1969, headed by Prof. N.R. Malkani.
4. Committee on Conditions of Sweepers and Scavengers, appointed by the National Commission on Labour and chaired by Bhanu Prasad Pandya (1967-69).
5. Wage Board for municipal workers constituted by the Government of Kerala in 1971 under the chairmanship of Mr. A.S. Menon.
6. Commission to Enquire into the living conditions of *Safai Mazdoors* employed by local bodies and private scavengers working in Haryana State, appointed in 1969 by the Haryana Government (1969-72).
7. Committee on Improvement of Living and Working Conditions of Sweepers and Scavengers appointed by the Government of Karnataka under the chairmanship of Mr. I.P.D. Salappa (1976).

Although the reports by these committees were important in their own ways, yet the one presented by the Malkani Committee found special favour with the Government. Out of so many recommendations of the Malkani Committee, the following two were very important:

1. *Bhangi Kashta Mukti,*
2. *Bhangi Mukti.*

The Malkani Committee suggested that since it would take time to get all the existing bucket privies converted into sanitary latrines, a programme of *Bhangi Kashta Mukti* should be launched and the scavengers should be provided with gloves, gum-boots and scrapers so that they could be saved from having to touch night-soil. It was also suggested that houseowners be required to have good receptacles so that the night-soil could not disperse over the ground and it could be easy to pour the excreta from receptacles into buckets (containers). It was also recommended that scavengers should be provided proper buckets with trolleys, so that they may not have to carry night-soil on the head.

Various State Governments, including the Government of Bihar, implemented the suggestion of *Bhangi Kashta Mukti* of the Malkani Committee and asked local bodies to purchase gum-boots and trolleys. These were purchased in large numbers by the local bodies, but they vanished soon, as most scavengers sold their gum-boots and the trolleys having rubber covers on their wheels, became dysfunctional. Nor was there any facility to replace and repair them. Due to the miserable condition of the roads, the rubber of the wheels got damaged, making it difficult to push them without the wheel-rubber. Consequently, most scavengers left their trolleys and reverted to the practice of carrying night-soil on the head. A very small number of trolleys are seen in Patna these days.

The next suggestion of the Malkani Committee, (to get the existing number of dry latrines converted into sanitary ones and to ban the construction of new ones) had found favour with Bihar, Gujarat and Kerala Governments but today almost all the States and Union Territories of the country have started making efforts at liberating scavengers from the sub-human practice of carrying night-soil and rehabilitating them and their wards in other occupations after training.

Ministry of Works and Housing

The Ministry of Works and Housing, Government of India, which was earlier a part of the Health and Family Planning Ministry, issued a circular in 1968 directing all the State Governments to get the bucket privies converted into water-borne latrines and to connect them to sewers wherever available; or to a disposal system at the earliest so that scavengers could be freed during the Gandhi Centenary period. It said that it would be the best tribute to *Rashtrapita* Mahatma Gandhi.

Three States, Bihar, Gujarat and Kerala, took up this programme in right earnest. As the number of service latrines was too small in Kerala, almost all the dry latrines were converted there. Only a small number of service latrines were left on.

Gujarat took up the programme of liberating scavengers in a big way and it had tremendous impact. Bihar's programme topped in the country. The Central Ministry of Works and Housing, had the following seminars organised in collaboration of WHO, UNICEF, UNDP and the Governments of Bihar, Rajasthan and Tamil Nadu:

1. National seminar on conversion of bucket privies into sanitary water-borne latrines organised by the Government of India in collaboration with the UNICEF, Patna, May 1978.
2. International seminar on low-cost techniques for disposal of human wastes in urban communities, sponsored by UNDP, Government Project and Government of India, Calcutta, February 1980.
3. Regional conference on low-cost pour-flush latrines, sponsored by the Government of India and the Government of Rajasthan in collaboration with UNDP, Udaipur, August 1982.
4. Regional seminar on low-cost sanitation, organised by the Ministry of Works and Housing, Government of India and UNDP, October 1982.
5. National seminar on integrated development of small and medium towns in New Delhi, 1982.

These seminars not only created an immense impact on the people but also motivated the State Governments to take up the programme for the liberation of scavengers. Now the Ministry of Works and Housing, Government of India, has also started giving loans to small and medium towns under its IDSMT (Integrated Development of Small and Medium Towns) project for the conversion of dry latrines into hand-flush water-seal ones.

The National Building Organization (NBO), under the Central Ministry of Works and Housing, is making experiments on various designs of low-cost sanitation, trying hard to make them popular through the media so that the people may be benefitted and they could be able to adopt the low-cost sanitation programme.

Ministry of Home Affairs

Seeing the success of the liberation of scavengers' programme in

Bihar, the Ministry of Home Affairs, Government of India, also took up the programme under the Protection of Civil Rights Act 1955 in 1980-81. The ministry viewed that out of so many cruelties meted out to Harijans, carrying headloads of night-soil by a particular caste, called scavengers (*Bhangis*) after 37 years of independence, was the most heinous. This was a blot on human civilization. Therefore, the ministry carried on this programme on the 'whole-town-approach' basis, which means that one town should be wholly freed from scavenging and then another should be taken up. Under this programme, the Ministry started giving assistance to the State Governments on the 50:50 basis. The Ministry of Home Affairs is giving matching assistance to the State Governments, i.e. 50 per cent cost of the total project of a town to liberate the scavengers and the rest 50 per cent expenditure has to be met by the State Government. On this pattern, the Ministry of Home Affairs (now Ministry of Welfare) has provided assistance to 19 States and Bihar is one of the beneficiaries of the programme. The Ministry of Welfare is providing financial assistance to the State Governments for making the towns scavenging free. A sum of Rs. 43 crore was released up to March 1989. In all 32 towns out of 166 selected under this programme and were freed from scavenging up to March 1989. In 1989-90 there is a target of 300 towns to be freed from scavenging out of which 130 towns have already been sanctioned. A massive programme for the rehabilitation of liberated scavengers and their wards has been taken up in Bihar and also in other States.

HUDCO Role

The Housing and Urban Development Corporation (HUDCO), set up by the Government of India in 1970 is a premier techno-financing institute in the field of housing and urban development. Primarily moved by the continuing sub-human practice of carrying night-soil as head-load, in 1983 it started financing basic sanitation schemes facilitating the eradication of the evil practice of manual scavenging and leading to the liberation of scavengers. Since then it has been promoting the adoption of two-pit leaching system (*Sulabh Shauchalaya*) for low-cost sanitation. This will help in achieving the targets fixed by the Govt. of India during the current decade declared as 'International Drinking Water Supply and Sanitation Decade'.

According to the arrangement of financing followed so far HUDCO has been extending financial assistance to the extent of 50 per cent of the cost of a latrine unit at 6 per cent interest repayable in 12 years and the balance 50 per cent is arranged by the borrowing agency from its own resources. For the same purpose, the Ministry of Welfare has been separately extending grants to the State Governments for the conversion of dry latrines.

As a special effort towards the elimination of manual scavenging and improving sanitation conditions, it has now been decided to integrate schemes floated by the Ministry of Welfare and HUDCO for better coordination and results. It has been decided that this scheme may be taken up in 300 small and medium towns with less than 5 lakhs population and on a 'whole town' basis in the current financial year. The approach would be through the conversion of dry latrines into low cost water-seal pour-flush latrines and rehabilitation of the scavengers liberated or their dependents through alternative employment and training.

The current system of grants from the Ministry of Welfare to the State Governments for liberation of scavengers is being dovetailed with the HUDCO's loans so that the local body is in a position to extend loans and subsidies for conversion or construction of low-cost sanitation units up to plinth level. The loan and subsidy portion would be based on the income of the beneficiaries as follows:

EWS	— 45% subsidy and 55% loan.
LIG	— 25% subsidy, 60% loan and 15% beneficiary's contribution.
MIG and HIG	— Nil subsidy, 75% loan and 25% beneficiary's contribution.

For all categories, additional loan for the superstructure can be extended by HUDCO to the extent of 50 per cent of the cost not exceeding Rs. 1,000, the balance would have to be met either by the beneficiary or by the concerned State Government.

As to the modus operandi, the HUDCO receives and considers

A Sulabh community complex at Buddhaghat, Patna.

The motif and architectural profile merge with Rajasthan style of house-building in the Sulabh complex at Jaipur.

applications from agencies authorised by the Government to carry out programmes for undertaking basic sanitation facilities schemes like housing boards, slum clearance boards, development authorities, improvement trusts and local bodies etc. The financial assistance is available for the projects for conversion of dry-pit latrines into water-seal pour-flush latrines (*Sulabh Shauchalayas*) or construction of new latrines in the existing houses which do not have such facilities, community latrines, public baths and urinals in the areas where such facilities are not available are also financed under the scheme. The intending borrowers are required to prepare detailed project reports containing description of the proposals like the location, proposed system of sewage disposal supported with drawings, specifications, cost estimates, implementation period and the system of post-implementation maintenance. The proposal for provision of individual latrines or community latrines with disposal arrangements has to conform to guidelines prepared by the Govt. of India.

Up to October 31st, 1989 a loan assistance of Rs. 41.95 crores has been sanctioned for the low-cost sanitation projects, including new constructions, conversion of dry latrines into low-cost pour-flush water-seal latrines with two leaching pits and construction conversion of community latrines. These schemes cover 212 towns in ten states of Andhra Pradesh, Gujarat, Karnataka, Kerala, Madhya Pradesh, Orissa, Punjab, Uttar Pradesh and West Bengal. After successful completion of these shcemes, 146 towns are likely to be free from scavenging.

International Agencies

International agencies like WHO, UNICEF and UNDP have played an important role in sanitation programmes. Although they have worked for low-cost sanitation, the national objective of liberating scavengers was also served.

World Health Organization (WHO)

When in Bihar a controversy was raised by the Public Health Engineering Department on the pollution of the drinking water source, the WHO came to the rescue of the programme; otherwise there was a chance of the whole programme falling flat.

WHO, with the help of the Ministry of Works and housing, Government of India, and UNICEF organized a national seminar in Patna on the conversion of bucket privies into water-seal latrines in 1978, at which, apart from the secretaries of Urban Development Departments and the chief engineers of almost all the State Government, representatives from the *All-India Institute of Hygiene and Public Health, Calcutta,* Environmental Engineering Research Institute, Nagpur, Planning Commission, Director-General of Health Services, World Bank, WHO and UNICEF participated.

The seminar recommended that a two-pit system should be adopted in the hand-flush water-seal toilets. This was a historical seminar and the idea of conversion of dry latrines into hand-flush water-seal latrines started catching up. The recommendation of the seminar was printed by WHO and circulated among the authorities concerned, which really convinced the engineers about the adoption of this technology. Also WHO circulated an article written by Jitendra Tuli, public officer of WHO, which created a tremendous impact on planners, administrators, engineers, etc. An international workshop was organised by WHO on primary health care in 1983, at which low-cost sanitation was discussed thread-bare and it was recommended that sanitation was very much related to health care.

UNICEF

This world agency also played an important role in the sanitation programme of India. It helped in having hand-flush water-seal toilets in schools, besides funding the construction of hand-flush toilets under ICDS (Integrated Child Development Services) programme. UNICEF also involved itself in sanitation programmes in Andhra Pradesh, Orissa, Uttar Pradesh, Madhya Pradesh, Jammu and Kashmir and Bihar. This international agency collaborated with WHO and the Ministry of Works and Housing in the Patna national seminar, and it bore the entire expenditure of the international seminar organised in Calcutta. A national workshop was organised by UNICEF in Sri Lanka in which the author participated as a 'resource person'. UNICEF has hitherto sponsored the visit of experts of different countries, viz., Sri Lanka, Bangladesh, Nepal, Afghanistan, Vietnam, Ethiopia, the U.S.A., Indonesia etc. to Patna to see the low-cost sanitation programme. Apart from this, literature on low-cost sanitation has been distributed by UNICEF and the idea of low-cost sanitation has been propagated through the media of mass communication (slides, etc.). UNICEF has also sponsored the programme for imparting training to masons and engineers in low-cost sanitary toilet.

United Nations Development Programme

UNDP, whose executing agency is the World Bank, started its activities in India in the field of low-cost sanitation in 1978. First of all it got evaluated the programme of low-cost sanitation already being carried out in Bihar and Gujarat. Thereafter, a study on the probability of pollution of the drinking water source from the pit latrine was done in Bihar, Gujarat and Tamil Nadu with the help of the Prevention and Control of Water Pollution Boards of these States. UNDP also assigned the task of preparing a design of the low-cost sanitary latrine to the Central Building Research Institute, Roorkee, in Uttar Pradesh. It took the assistance of the All-India Institute of Hygiene and Public Health, Calcutta, Environmental Engineering Research Institute, Nagpur, Central Building Research Institute, Roorkee, Indian Council of Medical Research, New Delhi, Public Health Institute, Poonamallee and PRAI, Lucknow and finally got prepared a manual on low-cost sanitary toilets for its adoption in South East Asia, Latin America and Africa.

UNDP was requested in 1979 by the Govt. of India to assist in preparing master plans and preliminary engineering and feasibility reports on low-cost water-seal latrines for Assam, Bihar, Gujarat, Maharashtra, Rajasthan, Tamil Nadu and Uttar Pradesh. For this purpose, 20 towns were selected in Uttar Pradesh and 50 towns each of the other six remaining States, in the first instance, by the Government of India. The reports in respect of these States, completed in 1981, covered 110 towns and generated considerably interest in the Central and State Governments. The studies related to the conversion of existing dry latrines into low-cost water-seal latrines, provision of individual low-cost water-seal latrines in houses and provision of community toilets for those households for which individual latrines could not be constructed.

Encouraged by these studies which constituted phase I of the project, the Govt. of India requested UNDP to prepare similar feasibility reports for Andhra Pradesh, Haryana, Himachal Pradesh, Jammu and Kashmir, Karnataka, Kerala, Madhya Pradesh, Orissa, Punjab, Tripura and West Bengal, Goa, Mizoram and Pondicherry. The studies done by UNDP helped the Government launch a centrally-sponsored scavenging elimination programme with 50 per cent grant to convert all the dry latrines in 33 towns in 14 States of Andhra Pradesh, Assam, Bihar, Haryana, Himachal Pradesh, Kerala, Madhya Pradesh, Maharashtra, Orissa, Rajasthan, Tamil Nadu, Tripura, Uttar Pradesh and West Bengal. UNICEF financed some demonstration units in a few States. The State Governments also started putting the low-cost pour-flush latrines both in the project and non-project towns

In the course of preparing the feasibility reports, UNDP organized, supervised and financed, either partly or fully, a number of special studies which included evaluation of ongoing latrine conversion programmes in Bihar, Gujarat and Tamil Nadu, evaluation of the community latrines in Bihar maintained on the 'pay-and-use' basis, design criteria of pour-flush latrines, optimization of technology of pour-flush latrines, sociological study on the impact of latrine conversion on scavengers, institutional, financial and legal studies of 20 local bodies and soil and water pollution studies due to on-site disposal of human excreta conducted in Bihar, Gujarat and Tamil Nadu, as stated earlier.

UNDP has also played a very important role in the diffusion of the concept of low-cost sanitary latrine outside India. Due to the involvement of UNDP in this programme, those engineers, who were rather hesitant to accept this technology, now approve of its installation in urban areas. Also, UNDP got organized an international seminar in Calcutta, a national seminar in Delhi and two regional seminars, one in Rajasthan and the other in Tamil Nadu. In all these four seminars the adoption of low-cost sanitary toilets in urban areas was unanimously recommended.

Author's Role

Incidentally in 1969 the author got himself invovled in the movement for the liberation of scavengers from carrying night-soil as head-load during the Gandhi Centenary period.

The Government of Bihar took a decision to get converted all the existing bucket privies into water-borne latrines and to connect them either to sewers or to leaching pits (now popularly known as *Sulabh Shauchalayas*) to do away with the sub-human practice of carrying night-soil by a section of the people belonging to the low caste called *Bhangi* and *Mehtar* during the Gandhi Centenary period as a tribute to the Father of the Nation. In order to make the programme a success, the Government decided to give 50 per cent of the total cost of construction as grant (maximum for two *Sulabh Shauchalayas:* one for male and one for female in one holding) to the needy house owners who wanted to get their bucket privies converted into *Sulabh Shauchalayas*. It was presumed that those who were having bucket privies were too poor to afford the cost of water-borne latrines. It was the financial constraint that prevented them from having sanitary latrines. In 1968-69, the Government of Bihar made an allocation of Rs. 2 lakhs to various local bodies, including the Patna Municipal Corporation, for the conversion of dry latrines into *Sulabh Shauchalayas*.

The Government of Bihar used to give grants to the Bihar State Gandhi Centenary Celebration Committee for the propagation and demonstration of the leaching pits so that the people might feel attracted to adopt this new technology of two-pit hand-flush water-seal toilets. The efforts of the Gandhi Centenary Celebration Committee in this context were limited to propagation and demonstration alone and the progress in conversion was not at all noticeable. A few house-owners, impressed by the technology of this kind of sanitary latrine, tried to take advantage of the loans and grants from the local bodies, but they found it difficult to obtain financial assitance from local bodies. Some house-owners, who got the required amount, spent it on other items. The time taken in the process of obtaining the loan and grant discouraged even the small number of people who were ready to adopt it. The local bodies also did not show much enthusiasm for the programme, perhaps because the awareness of this new technology had not spread too far. The author tried to convince the then Secretary to the Gandhi Centenary Celebration Committee to allow social workers to directly participate in the programme and engage the organization in the work of conversion of dry latrines into hand-flush water-seal toilets so that the desired result could be achieved and they could create an impact on the beneficiaries for the adoption of this new technology. But the Secretary did not agree to the author's proposal and said: 'voluntary organizations should keep themselves confined to demonstration and propagation only and should not go in for the actual implementation of the programme.' He further said: 'voluntary organizations should not earn money for carrying on their activities; rather they should run their affairs only on donation from the public and grants from the Government.'

The author had a different opinion and he stressed that voluntary organizations should not keep themselves confined only to demonstration; rather they should involve themselves in the actual implementation of the programme and they should earn also instead of living on donations and grants. In this way, the organization could serve a large section of the population (without having) to toe the official line. The institutions in India, which depend on grants are unable to discharge their responsibilities efficiently for want of resources of their own.

This led to the author's departure from the Bihar State Gandhi Centenary Celebration Committee and he set-up an organization named *Sulabh Shauchalaya Sansthan*, (now known as *Sulabh International*) in 1970 with the help of those working with him. The society was registered under the Societies Registration Act XXI of 1860 (*bearing No. 73/70–70*) in Patna. In 1970 the Government of Bihar promulgated an ordinance empowering the executive officers of the local bodies to punish those house-owners who did not get their dry-latrines converted within the stipulated period given by the local bodies.

So after forming the organization, they approached the Government of Bihar to recognise it for the implementation of the programme. In October 1970, the Bihar Gandhi Centenary Celebration Committee was dissolved and Sulabh remained the only organization having the expertise of the leach-pit-type latrines in Bihar. Between 1968–69 and 1974, the Government of Bihar allotted about Rs. 30 lakhs to various local bodies, but no concrete results could be achieved. Most of the funds were diverted to other works of the local bodies and the programme could not gather momentum. The State Government took four years in recognizing *Sulabh International* for the implementation of the programme of conversion of dry latrines into *Sulabh Shauchalayas* and do away with the sub-human practice of carrying night-soil on the head. The State Government made a critical appraisal of the programme made in the past by various local bodies and, finally, it recognised the *Sulabh International* as a catalytic agency to work between the beneficiaries, local bodies and the Government which was convinced that the programme could not be implemented in full and the results could not be achieved within the stipulated period without the help of voluntary organizations. It was observed that the Government and semi-Government organizations could only raise funds, monitor and supervise the work being done by voluntary organizations, but the implementation of the programme could be done only by voluntary organizations, because the workers would have to move from house to house either in the morning or in the evening to contact the beneficiaries.

It was decided by the State Government that the social workers of the *Sulabh International* would move from house to house to convince the owners to get their bucket privies converted into *Sulabh Shauchalayas* because the former are health hazards and sources of many diseases, such as diarrhoea, dysentery, hookworm etc. and also a blot on human civilization. It was also decided that the house-owners, willing to get converted their bucket privies into *Sulabh Shauchalayas*, would simply fill up applications and agreement forms for obtaining loans and grants and hand them over to the neo-social workers (social workers of the *Sulabh International* are termed as neo-social workers) of the organization, who, in turn, would deposit them in offices of the local bodies. After proper verification, the amount for the conversion of bucket privies into *Sulabh Shauchalayas* would not be given to them; rather it would be given to the *Sulabh International* on behalf of the beneficiaries. After obtaining loans and grants from the local bodies on behalf of the beneficiaries, the *Sulabh International* would collect all the materials required for the conversion work and the actual conversion work would also be done by the neo-social workers of the organization. And, this was the beginning of the programme of low-cost sanitation in Bihar in 1974.

Method for Implementation of the Programme

The procedures laid down by the Government of Bihar for the conversion of bucket privies into *Sulabh Shauchalayas* worked well. In this procedure, the beneficiaries are not required to bear the burden either of obtaining loans and grants from the local bodies, or of collecting materials for the conversion of bucket privies. It is very difficult to procure cement at levy rates. Therefore, the beneficiaries feel free because their bucket privies are converted without their having to bother about it. The conversion and construction work is done by the experienced workers of the *Sulabh International* to the full satisfaction of the house-owners. However, if the house-owners so desire, they can supervise the work. In fact, the house-owners are requested by the *Sulabh International* to supervise the work so that it could be done according to their full satisfaction. Due to urbanization and industrialization, most beneficiaries remain engaged in their own work and, therefore, they prefer the conversion and construction work on the turn-key basis, even if they have to pay a little more by way of supervision charges. If the same work is done by the house-owners themselves, they can save a little amount, but they will have to face the arduous task of obtaining loans and grants from the local bodies, arranging materials for the construction and also some skilled masons for the conversion of their bucket privies. Methods for the conversion of dry latrines are so well planned that the workers engaged in the conversion work at the lower level cannot steal the materials or use substandard materials and one has to obtain certificate from the house-owners of satisfactory completion of the work.

Before starting the work, a copy of the directory is given to each house-owner who is requested to supervise the work according to the directory and if the work is not being done properly, the house-owner can stop it and inform the office of *Sulabh International* or local bodies. A utilization card is filled by the house-owner only to determine that the work has been done within the stipulated period and satisfactorily. After the work is over, the social workers of the monitoring cell of *Sulabh International* check the construction by visiting from house to house.

After submission of the report a reply-paid post card is posted to the house-owner to confirm the statement recorded by the social workers of *Sulabh International.*

Thereafter a guarantee card, along with five post cards, is given to each beneficiary. If any defect develops in the construction within five years, it is repaired free of cost. If somebody registers any complaint developed in the construction work he is given a card stating therein the number and date of complaint. The defects are repaired within seven days. This process has worked well and *Sulabh International* has been able to create confidence among the Government, local bodies and the house-owners about the actual implementation of the programme in India.

Experiences through Encounters

To run such type of an organization, the chairman or the Secretary, whoever may be the executive head, should be dynamic in adjusting himself to all the circumstances of society. He must have all the qualities of a politician, a bureaucrat, a psychologist, a neo-social worker, a technocrat as well as of an administrator. Either a politician or a neo-social worker or an engineer or an administrator alone will not be able to show results. A politician does not mean that he should belong to a particular political party; rather he should have access to politicians. Since the future of a country is shaped largely by politicians, for taking up this scheme in priority sector or for raising the yearly budget for conversion of dry latrines, one has to convince politicians and, therefore, one will have to gain access to prominent leaders of all political parties. For example, the total budget of the Government of Bihar in 1968-69 was Rs. 2 lakhs and in 1985-86 it was Rs. 2 crores. So this is not only because of the author, but also because of the policy of the Government of Bihar. But certainly he has played a major role in convincing the politicians and the administrators as well in raising the budget limit from Rs. 2 lakhs to Rs. 2 crores.

A neo-social worker means he should be the Chairman or Secretary of the society registered under the Societies Registration Act. He should be so social that he may sit with the people of all status, may be literate or illiterate, rich or poor, sick or healthy and upper or lower caste people. He should be one who may be able to create confidence among the colleagues that all are at par and none is higher or lower excepting the designations for discharging duty.

A neo-social worker has to possess a good sense of bureaucracy in generating mass confidence in the social movement, otherwise bureaucrats generally believe the social workers as 'khau-pakau' (swindlers).

A neo-social worker has to have the qualities of a good psychologist. He will have to understand and read the minds of the people he meets. They may be either common men, politicians, bureaucrats, technocrats, sociologists, psychologists, beneficiaries or his own colleagues of the organization and accordingly he will have to act so that most of the people should remain happy with his behaviour.

A technocrat has full knowledge of the techniques adopted by an organization as also most of the techniques prevailing in the world. If he has got the technical knowledge, he can be able to convince the engineers, administrators and others about the advantages and disadvantages of different technologies. The executive head of the organization should have ability to run the organization efficiently. As the chairman of an organization becomes the supreme authority, he has to play the part of all the three wings—legislative, executive and judiciary. The head of the organization will have to be a more judicious and upright person to run the administration of a big organization like ours. It is rightly said:

> 'By a little mind, you can't rule over the empire.'

Secondly, the concept of the double-pit hand-flush water-seal toilet is not new, but people, in general, are not aware of the technique of double-pit hand-flush water-seal toilet as they are of the septic tank. Therefore, people have a fear psychosis in adopting a new technology. Generally, the consumers do not want to spend money on experiment. They want a ready-made, fool-proof thing which could satisfy their need.

The International Labour Organization (ILO) has rightly pointed out about the *Sulabh International* that 'the idea of double-pit pour-flush latrines is not new, although some details of the *Sulabh Shauchalaya Sansthan* plans are original; what is new is the success of the scheme, whereby a private organization has built tens of thousands of latrines in a short time'. Although the idea of double-pit hand-flush toilet was available in India, yet all the organizations engaged in this work in the country were advocating construction of only one-pit in the beginning and the other later on when the first one got filled up, to save the construction cost. When the author took up this programme in 1969, he started advocating the construction of both pits simultaneously to save the house-owners from the difficulties of constructing another pit just after the first one got filled up. This idea became acceptable, and in Bihar they started constructing double-pit hand-flush toilet. This idea was confirmed by the participants in the seminar held at Patna in 1978 organised by the WHO, UNICEF and Ministry of Works and Housing, Government of India.

Before the author took up this programme, this type of latrine could not get support from the Government as it should have been for adoption in the urban areas; rather they used to recommend this type of latrines for rural areas. The large-scale installation of *Sulabh Shauchalayas* and their successful functioning found favour with the Government and also by the participants at the said seminar.

In 1977, the Public Health Engineering Department of the Government of Bihar raised questions on pollution of ground-water from the pit latrine and it suggested to the Urban Development Deptt. of the Government of Bihar to issue instructions to stop the conversion of dry latrines into *Sulabh Shauchalayas*, otherwise the entire water supply of Patna would be contaminated and the people would die. The Urban Development Deptt. of the Government of Bihar got alarmed and it sought the author's opinion in this regard. The author suggested to the department to obtain an expert advice on this issue either from the National Environmental Engineering Research Institute, Nagpur, or from the Central Public Health Environmental Engineering Research Organization of the Ministry of Works and Housing, Government of India.

The Government of Bihar referred this matter of NEERI, Nagpur, and it sought their opinion. NEERI reported that if pit latrines were constructed with precautions at a safer distance, there was no chance of pollution of ground water or water pipe-lines. Although it served the purpose and the Government was convinced on this issue, yet the author's mind started itching to get a permanent solution of this problem and he himself went to

Nagpur and had discussions with them. He contacted CPHEERO of the Ministry of Works and Housing, Government of India also. Besides, he contacted the WHO, where he met Mr. A.K. Roy in 1977, who was working there as a sanitary engineer and was later the Resident Manager of the Technology Advisory Group of UNDP in India. At present he is associated with *Sulabh International* as an expert in sanitation technology.

The problem of pollution of water from pit latrines was also discussed in the Patna Seminar in 1978 and Dr. T.R. Bhaskaran, one of the topmost public health engineer in India, participated in the seminar on behalf of the WHO and he explained in detail his research done between 1940 and 1950. The paper presented by Dr. Bhaskaran and the replies given by him to the participants, by and large, satisfied the engineers of Public Health. Later UNDP also did research on water pollution between 1979 and 1982 in three States of India, viz., Bihar, Gujarat and Tamil Nadu and they also confirmed the statement by Dr. Bhaskaran, who was also engaged in this study. Now in Bihar, by and large, there is no apprehension about the technology and proper functioning of *Sulabh Shauchalayas.* The scavengers engaged in cleaning bucket privies also are not scared of unemployment, because the Government has given assurance that they would be given other jobs. In this way, scavengers also did not become an obstacle in the implementation of this programme.

Everyone wants that one's bucket privy should be converted into *Sulabh Shauchalaya*. But people are unable to bear the cost—income level being what it is. Therefore, unless assistance is made available, the programme cannot go ahead. Recovery of the loan may not be a problem if the local bodies want to recover it. Advertisement through the press and news through the media have also played an important role in convincing the house-owners for adoption of the new technology. The author's strong will to defend the work done by *Sulabh International* has also played an important role whenever faced either with the politicians, the press, the technocrates, the administrators or with the national and international agencies involved in similar programmes. The quality of work which is maintained by the *Sulabh International* has attracted the attention of the administrators and everyone wants the services of the *Sulabh International* in achieving the targets of the liberation of scavengers from carrying night-soil by getting all the existing bucket privies converted into *Sulabh Shauchalayas*.

During 1974-88, 1.86 lakh dry latrines had been converted into *Sulabh Shauchalayas* in Bihar alone. And consequently more than 3000 scavengers in 15 towns of the State, namely Biharsharif, Deoghar, Ranchi, Purnea, Saharsa, Chaibasa, Madhubani, Bhagalpur, Daltonganj, Gaya, Chapra, Bettia, Motihari, Patna and Hazaribag..

In fact the non-availability of funds has been the main constraint, otherwise, all the 4 lakh dry latrines would have been converted and the entire State declared 'Bhangi Mukti' by this time.

CHAPTER 6

Unliberated and Liberated Scavengers

I. Unliberated Scavengers

As stated earlier the unliberated scavengers of Patna, Arrah and Muzaffarpur have been included in the present study. From each of these three towns, 50 scavengers have been selected for study. All these 150 unliberated scavengers from the three towns are the employees of Corporation (in case of Patna) or municipalities (in case of Arrah and Muzaffarpur). They are not doing the scavenging job privately and are the regular employees of autonomous bodies. On the basis of the informations collected from these towns, it appears that 100% of these unliberated scavengers are Rauts by caste in Arrah and Muzaffarpur; whereas in case of Patna 88% are Rauts, 10% are Balmikis and 2 % (only one scavengers) are Raiphars (Christian) by caste.

The collected informations about the family structure among scavengers reveal that both joint families and nuclear families are found in all the three towns. In Muzaffarpur, the majority of them (52%) live in joint families, in Patna 28% and in Arrah 32 % are living in joint families It means that in Patna and Arrah most of the families of the unliberated scavengers are nuclear in structure (72% and 68% respectively), whereas in Muzaffarpur only 48% are nuclear families. Hence, the patterns of family structure in Muzaffarpur differ from that of the families of unliberated scavengers in Patna and Arrah. These scavengers live in, different types of houses—owned, rented and government quarters. Only in Patna, the majority of them (70%) live in government quarters, whereas only 18% in Muzaffarpur and 4% in Arrah live in municipal quarters. It suggests that the Patna Municipal Corporation has provided housing facilities to a larger number of its employees than the municipalities in Arrah and Muzaffarpur. Twenty-two per cent unliberated scavengers in Patna, 72% in Arrah and 74% in Muzaffarpur live in their own houses—whether mud-wall houses or hutments or jhuggis. It clearly indicates that in places where the employees have not been provided with residential facilities, most of the them live in their own tenements.

It may be either due to the fact that it is not possible for them to pay the rent of the houses in town areas or because of the social stigma the scavengers do not get a tenement on rent. According to collected information, 8% of these scavengers in Patna and Muzaffarpur and 24% in Arrah live in rented tenements or houses. Hence, it may be interpreted that where the unliberated scavengers have got quarters, they are mostly living there and where the quarters are not available, most of them are living in their own hutments. It is also important to note that those living in rented houses are not actually living in houses, rather in small accommodations like a room, a jhuggi or a tenement.

In some cases two or more scavengers' families share the tenement. Hence, it appears that the housing condition of the unliberated scavengers is extremely deplorable. The information on the kinds of their houses indicates that most scavengers in Patna lived in *pucca* houses because of government quarters provided to most of them. On inquiry, it came to light that some of the scavengers were occupying *pucca* accommodation on rent. It means that the owned tenements or houses have a *kachcha* structure. These findings provide further evidence of the poor housing condition of the unliberated scavengers. They live in congested, and *kachcha* accommodations which are poorly maintained. Information was also gathered about the number of rooms in the houses or quarters in which these unliberated scavengers are living.

It was found that 85 scavengers lived in one-room apartments, 47 in two-room quarters, 12 in three-room houses and another six in four-room houses. The scavengers having 2, 3 or 4 rooms were living either in joint family or they were sharing the houses with other families. In this way, generally one single family of an unliberated scavenger occupied only a one-room tenement. Hence, it appears that the scavengers are not living in spacious accommodations or at least in such houses which provide the minimum accommodation, which is inadequate for a healthy living. This fact is evident from the information about how these scavengers feel in respect of the accommodation they are having or occupying. In all the three towns, majority of them declared that the house was not accommodative. As many as 70% of the cavengers in Patna, 62% in Muzaffarpur and 80% in Arrah had he same opinion. It means that only a small section feels that the accommodation is proper. But the overwhelming majority has complained of improper, inadequate and poor accommodation. Information was also collected about the housing condition and it was enquired whether the houses were provided with electricity or not. On the whole, only 16% in Muzaffarpur, 24% in Arrah and 72% in Patna have power connections. Hence, the worst condition is in the case of the scavengers of Muzaffarpur and the relatively better conditions are found in case of scavengers in Patna. It may be either due to the fact that most unliberated scavengers in Patna are living in government quarters and, hence, they are provided with electric connections at government cost. Hence, a higher percentage has electric connections in Patna.

The second reason may be the fact that the power connection facility is better in Patna than in Arrah and Muzaffarpur because Patna being the capital of the State, there is a better supply of electric power to the consumers. These factors may also be responsible for better condition in Patna in comparison with Muzaffarpur and Arrah. Regarding the source of drinking water, the information furnished by the scavengers suggests that in no case there is any private arrangement for drinking water. It means that no family of the scavengers owns a well or a water tap or a hand pump or a tube-well. This fact speaks of the poor economic condition and absence of modern civic amenities for these scavengers. The informations further reveal that no family takes water from a public well or from a public tube-well. There are only two sources of drinking water, i.e., public tap and public hand pump. In case of the scavengers in Patna, it is found that 100% take water from public taps, but in Muzaffarpur and Arrah, it is 34% and 82% respectively.

The unliberated scavengers were asked to give the place of defecation. The information furnished by them reveals that there are three alternatives used as places of defecation by them. They either defecate in open space or in community latrines or in service latrines. The information also reveals that none of the unliberated scavengers from Patna defecates in an open space and only one scavenger belonging to the income group of Rs. 160—200 declared that he and his family members defecated in service latrines. In 98% of the cases the place of defecation was the community latrine. It means that unliberated scavengers living in government quarters have not been provided with separate latrines in their quarters. The pattern of information gathered from them also reveals that income is relevant to the habit of defecation because, in the three highest income groups no scavenger or his family members defecate in the open and the percentage of response showing defecation in open space has constantly declined with the rise in income in the first three income groups. The relevance of economic factor or family income to the place of defecation is further evident from the fact that zero per cent of the unliberated scavengers in the lowest income group, 42.1% in the next higher income group, 55% in the next higher income group, 50% in the income group of Rs. 1201—1600 and 100% in the two highest income groups use service latrines.

The information from the unliberated scavengers of Arrah indicate that defecation in the open is found both in lower and higher income groups, but the use of community latrines is not found in the last two higher income groups whereas the use of service latrines is found in inconsistently varying degrees in different income groups. Hence, it appears that the place of defecation used by unliberated scavengers in these towns depends on local conditions, availability of service latrines or community latrines and of open space for defecation. A more indefinite pattern has been found in the case of Arrah town than in the case of Muzaffarpur or Patna, and only in the case of the unliberated scavengers of Patna the commonly used places of defecation are community latrines.

The heterogeniety is also reflected in the informations collected about their age-structure, level of education and economic condition. These scavengers in each town belong to different age categories ranging from 20 years to 51-60 years though in varying percentages (Table 2). Some of them (4%) are within 20 years of age and have just entered the service, whereas 6.6% are in the age-group of 51-60 years and are at the verge of retirement. The highest percentage (35.3%) is in the age group of 31-40 years and the second highest percentage (30%) in the age group of 41-50 years. Thus, majority of unliberated scavengers (65.3%) are in the age group of 31-50 years.

The data concerning the level of education suggest (Table 3) that most of the scavengers in each town (70% in Patna, 92% in Muzaffarpur and 86% in Arrah) are illiterate. No scavenger has completed school education and only 4.0% have read up to 7th or 8th class and only 1.3% up to 9th class. It shows the low-level of literacy in this category of scavengers. The above data also reflects educational backwardness in the male section. It is obvious that the condition will be worse in the female section and hence, on the whole the degree of literacy is very low among unliberated scavengers and their families. As regards the economic condition, the data (Table 4) show that the monthly income ranges from Rs. 400 to above Rs. 2000. These income variations are found in each of the three towns, though in Arrah town no family has a monthly income of more than Rs. 1600. On the whole 8.6% of the families have the lowest income of up to Rs. 400 and 32.7% belong to the income category of Rs. 401—Rs. 800. Thus, 58.7% of the families have a monthly income of more than Rs. 800 rising up to more than Rs. 2000. But it does not mean that the earning of an unliberated scavenger is very high. In most families, there are two or more earning members. Both husband and wife are employed in many cases. Moreover, most of these live in joint families. Hence, in view of the family size the income is very low and the economic condition cannot be described as satisfactory. The fact in respect of the presence of two or more earning members in the families of unliberated scavengers is evident from the information collected about the number of male (Table 5) and female adults (Table 6) in each family.

It is found that in most cases one-two male adults as well as female adults are members of the families. As both male and female adults are employed, the number of earning members is bound to be two or more in each family. The informations about the number of male children (Table 7) and of female children (Table 8) with the numbers of male and female adults also suggest that in many cases the families are joint in structure and the size of the family is not very small. Hence, keeping the size of family in view and in the light of the fact that the number of earning hands in most cases exceeds two, the income-range is not higher. The joint structure of the families of these scavengers is also reflected in the data on married male (Table 9) and female members (Table 10). In many cases, the number of married male or female adults is more than one, suggesting joint family structure. It is also evident from the data that no distinct variation is found in family size, family structure and family income in the three towns of Arrah, Muzaffarpur and Patna.

The level of literacy and education is very poor among the families of these scavengers. Of the 150 families in three towns, only 55 families (37%) do not have any illiterate male (Table 11), whereas only 10 families (6.7%) do not have any illiterate female member (Table 12). It indicates that in majority of the cases, the families have illiterate males (63%) and females (93.3%). This is the level of illiteracy among unliberated scavengers in urban areas of Arrah, Muzaffarpur and Patna. It also suggests that comparative percentage of illiteracy is lower among men than women. But this difference does not mean that the male members possess a satisfactory level of literacy. The level of literacy is considerably lower among male as well as female members of the families of scavengers. In case of male members 4.2% are educated up to intermediate stage (Table 13); but in case of female members no one is educated up to this stage (Table 14).

In case of male members, 5.0% in the three towns taken together are matriculates, 9.9% are under-matriculates, 69.4% are educated up to middle stage and 11.5% are illiterate (Table 13). And, among female members 1.7% are matriculates, 1.1% under matriculates, 40.2% are educated up to Middle stage and 57% are illiterate (Table 14). These data reveal that the percentage of literacy is higher among men than women, but the male section of this occupational group is also very backward and scores extremely low in respect of literacy and education. The tables reveal that no significant difference exists in the three towns in respect of the level of literacy. Hence, the educational backwardness is the common feature among scavengers working in different towns. The tables also show the total number of adults (illiterate, literate and educated) in 150 families of scavengers from three towns. The total number of male adults is 262 (Table 13) and of female adults is 179 (Table 14) brining the total figure to 441. In this way there are approximately three adults per family. It shows that even in case of joint structure, the size of the family is not very large. The low literacy level among these families is not confined to the present generation only, but is also likely to persist in the coming generations. The enquiries into the families sending boys and girls to schools have revealed that boys are sent for schooling only in case of 19 (38%) families of Patna, 20 families (40%) of Muzaffarpur and 16 families (32%) of Arrah.

On the other hand, only five families (10%) in Patna, 11 families (22%) in Muzaffarpur and seven families (14%) in Arrah send girls for schooling. On one hand the data reflect that the number of families sending girls for schooling is much lower than that sending boys for schooling and on the other it is found that these educationally, economically and socially backward scavengers do not understand the importance of educating younger generation, though there are facilities for their free education. These facts present a very gloomy picture of the condition of literacy even in the future generation of these scavengers. It is also significant to note that only facilities for free education are not available to this section of society, the government also gives stipends and other forms of economic assistance for encouraging literacy and education among the Scheduled Castes. But, in spite of these facilities only a very small number of boys and girls go to school which indicates lack of social consciousness and absence of realization of the importance of education for the *Bhangi* sub-caste. It is also possible that in certain cases the unliberated scavengers may not be aware of the facilities provided. But it is a remote possibility because the facilities given to the children of Scheduled Castes are so much talked about through media and on different platforms that the scavengers are expected to know about them. It is also possible that these unliberated scavengers think that their children are also to follow their occupation for which education is not at all essential or required. On this basis, unliberated scavengers constitute one of the most socially backward section of the Scheduled Castes (or of the Harijan community). The status of 'the lowest among the lowest' is bound to persist due to very low literacy level and extreme poverty.

The information collected from the unliberated scavengers about the number of boys and girls attending colleges reveals that higher education is almost nil in the case of this section of the Harijan community. On the whole, the boys attending colleges have been found in two families of Patna, two families of Muzaffarpur and one family of Arrah. As regards girls, 100% of the scavengers from each town replied in negative. These data clearly suggest that there is no college education among girls at all and it is negligible in the case of boys. It further reveals the social and educational backwardness of this section of society. It is also important to point out that these unliberated scavengers and their families are not living in rural areas; rather in urban areas and they are expected to be more conscious of their rights, the present trends in the country and the governmental efforts at the social, educational and economic uplift of the poor. They are also more exposed to media than their counterparts in rural areas. Moreover, those living in Patna, capital of Bihar, have greater awareness about trends in the present age, and facilities provided to them by the government. But, these have made no change in poverty status and they still suffer from the same type of extreme educational backwardness.

The information regarding earning of male and female members reveals that in most cases there is only one earning male member in the families of the scavengers from each of the towns. As many as 97 families have only one earning male member while 36 have two in the family. Nine families have three earning male members whereas only two families have four; nine families don't have any earning male member. It means that in such families only female members earn. Of the 130 families, only one female member earns. Only in case of ten families the number of earning female members is two. In case of one family of Patna, three female members are earning. It means that the number of earning hands is not very large in most families in spite of the fact that a considerable number of families have joint structure.

The information provided by unliberated scavengers also throws light on the number of unemployed males and females in their families. It is found that in majority of the families there is no unemployed male or female. As many as 41, 37 and 41 families from Patna, Muzaffarpur and Arrah do not have any unemployed male person. In the same way 34, 32 and 37 families from Patna, Muzaffarpur and Arrah do not have any unemployed female member. It means that employment is not a serious problem because of the nature of the job scavengers do. There is no competing claim on the job. As scavenging is essential in the towns due to the existence of traditional service latrines and the conversion of these service latrines into *Sulabh* system started on a mass scale only in the recent past, the male and female member of the *Bhangi* caste are required for carrying on the profession. Hence, these families do not face difficulty in getting jobs in municipalities and corporations for scavenging work. It may be the most important reason for a lower number of the unemployed among unliberated families of scavengers. They were also asked to furnish information about the males and females engaged in scavenging. In the case of 20 Patna families, no male member is engaged in scavenging whereas only in seven families no female member is engaged in scavenging work. In Muzaffarpur, 100% of the respondents declared that no male member was engaged in the scavenging work and, on the other hand, no family is without a female engaged in scavenging. In Arrah, 27 families do not have any male member engaged in scavenging whereas 32 families do not have any female member engaged in scavenging. It means that only in case of Arrah, the scavenging is done more by men than women; whereas in Patna and Muzaffarpur the number of families having males not doing scavenging work is larger than the number of families having women without the scavenging job.

The information collected from the scavengers about the number of person (male and female) engaged in sanitation work reveals that in Patna 32 families, in Muzaffarpur 12 families and in Arrach 23 families out of 50 do not have any male member engaged in sanitation work; whereas 49 families in Patna, 45 in Muzaffarpur and 50 in Arrah declared that.no female member was engaged in sanitation work. It means that 100% of families in Arrah have women engaged in scavenging work whereas only one family in Patna and five in Muzaffarpur have no female member engaged in sanitation work. On the other hand, 18 families in Patna, 38 in Muzaffarpur and 27 in Arrah have male members engaged in sanitation work. These data also lead to the inference that in comparison to females a large number of males are engaged in sanitation work like sweeping, cleaning of drains and disposing of garbage, whereas the scavenging work is mostly done by women. This situation is not found in only one town, rather, in all the three towns—though in varying degrees.

Information was also collected about the number of family members (both males and females) engaged in non-sanitation work. It was found that in most cases (121), male members of the families were not engaged in non-sanitation work. In case of female members, 100% scavengers declared that no female member was engaged in non-sanitation work. These suggest that only in a very few families of the scavengers non-hereditary and non-traditional occupations have been adopted. It may be interpreted that occupational immobility is still very much prevalent in this section of society which may either be due to illiteracy or difficulty in getting other jobs for illiterate persons. The reservation of jobs has also not helped in occupational mobility because other groups and sub-castes given the facilities of job reservation are also there, and the people from these sub-castes and groups may have a slightly better position in getting the reserved jobs. Thus the general backwardness of the *Bhangi* caste, lack of literacy and education and competition for other jobs may be the reasons for the continuance of the same traditional occupation in this sub-caste of the weaker section of society.

Smoking Habits

The analysis of the lifestyle and habits of the unliberated scavengers and their family members reveal some interesting features. Informations collected about smoking habit reveal that male members of 134 out of 150 families from the three towns are in the habit of smoking (Table 15). That is in 89.2% of these families, the male members smoke. In case of 80% of these families, female members are also in the habit of smoking (Table 16). It is also significant to note that the female members of these families do smoke because they are being modernised or because they have developed this habit as a fashion. The socio-cultural environment in which they live and the traditions they follow are responsible for this lifestyle, which is not admirable for women in the traditional Indian society where smoking has been a habit of male adults. The traditional outlook does not appreciate women developing the habit of smoking. But in spite of this general trend, female members of scavengers' families have the habit of smoking. This aspect of lifestyle adopted by the female adults presents a contrast with the general lifestyle and normative pattern adopted by women in traditional social order. In case a woman smokes, she is condemned or laughed at by members of society. As regards alcoholism (drinking habit) it is not a rare phenomenon among the male members of the families of scavengers in Bihar. The present study also reveals that in most cases, the male members of the families of scavengers are in habit of drinking (Table 17). Only 22% of male scavengers denied being alcoholics. It means that in 78% of the families studied, the male members are alcohol-addict; 26% of the scavengers from Patna, 28% from Muzaffarpur and 12% from Arrah informed that the male members of their families were not in habit of drinking. It suggests that in each town the majority suffers from alcoholism. But among female members, drinking habit is almost absent. As many as 100% of the scavengers from Patna and Arrah, and 96% from Muzaffarpur stated that the women did not drink (Table 18). It means that only two women (4%) from Muzaffarpur town were alcoholic.

In this way, alcoholism is confined to the male section of the community of scavengers and taking alcohol by women is an exception. The observations also suggest that due to economic hardships, scavengers cannot afford to smoke good-quality smoking material—nor can they afford good alcoholic drinks. In most cases, female members smoke *bidis,* which is the cheapest one in the market. The same trend is dominant in case of male members also. There are very few male and female members of scavengers who smoke cigarettes. And those who do are of inferior quality. In the same way, they consume cheap liquor. In most of the cases they are in the habit of taking toddy, or a country-made liquor, which are crude, raw and, hence, cheap. And those in the habit of smoking, male or female, smoke frequently. In the same way those in the habit of drinking do not miss the opportunity, if they have some money in pocket. These suggest that most of these people have become alcohol-addicts and habitual smokers. It is also obvious that the higher frequency of smoking and drinking costs them a good part of their earning.

Hence, the amount spent on essential items like food, clothing and house is much reduced resulting in the lowering of living standard. Moreover smoking of cheaper qualities of cigarettes and *bidis* and drinking of raw alcohol also affect their health. Add to it inadequate or bad food and the reasons for their bad health and low productivity become evident. In addition, the unhealthy living conditions in which they live and the congested accommodation available to them cause health hazard. The economic aspect of drinking and smoking is reflected from the average amount spent by scavengers on these two harmful items. In 30% of the families of these scavengers from three towns, the male members spend more than Rs. 100 per month on these two items (Table 19). As regards the relationship between the level of family income and the amount spent over drinking and smoking, the table shows that in the lowest income group of up to Rs. 400 no family spends more than Rs. 125 per month over these items and only one family (7.5%) spends more than Rs. 100. Moreover, 46.1% of the families spend nothing on these items. In the income group of Rs. 401-800, only 8.1% of the families spend more than Rs. 150 and 16.2% more than Rs. 100. In the next higher income group of Rs. 801-1200, 19.2% of the families spend more than Rs. 150, 29.6% more than Rs. 125 and 40% more than Rs. 100. In the income group of Rs. 1201-1600, 33.3% spend more than Rs. 150 and 41.6% more than Rs. 100. In the income group of Rs. 1600, 33.3% spend more than Rs. 150 and 41.6% more than Rs. 100.

In the income group of Rs. 1601-2000, 66.6% spend more than Rs. 100 over these two items. But in the highest income group, only 25% spend more than Rs. 150 and 75% spend between Rs. 26-50. Excepting the highest income group, there appears to be a significant relationship between the income level and the pattern of expenditure over these two items.

As regards the expenditure on smoking and drinking by female members, it has come to light that 76.9% of the families in the lowest income group spend nothing over these items and 7.7% spend Rs. 16-20, Rs. 21-25 and Rs. 26-30 per month over these habits (Table 20). But in the income group of Rs. 401-800, only 6.1% of the families spend nothing over drinking and smoking by female members; whereas in other income groups the corresponding percentages are higher. On the whole only 20.7% of the families have no expense over these items, and in the majority of the cases (79.3%) some amount is spent.

It is also found that in case of expenses by male members (Table 19) the expenditure range was Rs. 0–151 and above, whereas in case of female members (Table 20), the range is Rs. 0–31 and above. These facts reveal that expenses incurred by female members are much lower than male members. The reason is quite obvious. The expenses by male include the expenses over smoking as well as drinking. But in the case of female, there was only one family in which women also consumed alcoholic drink. Hence, the expenses by female members are only on smoking and a very nominal expense over drinking.

The earlier analysis suggests that the number of families having smoke addict male members is larger than those in which women are in habit of smoking. In addition to it, the number of male members in habit of smoking was also larger than female members. These facts combined together have inevitably resulted in the lower level of expenditure by female section than male section over smoking and drinking.

The analysis of socio-cultural orientation of these unliberated scavengers living in urban areas and also the assessment of the degree of the impact of urbanization on them, have significant relevance to their degree of exposure to mass media. It is obvious that the people more exposed to media are expected to be more influenced by the process of urbanization and modernization and, consequently, the context of socio-cultural orientation is bound to be rationalised. The enquiry into the degree of exposure to newspapers and magazines, etc. (printed media) reveals that these unliberated scavengers have a very poor exposure. The collected informations reveal that only 15 out of 150 (10%) scavengers read newspapers due to illiteracy. It has also been found that nobody reads magazines. The main and basic reason for not being exposed to magazines is illiteracy and very low degree of literacy and education. Reading of newspapers may be possible for an ordinarily literate person, but it is not possible for such a person to read a magazine and to enjoy its contents. These facts clearly suggest that printed media of mass communication (newspapers, magazines, journals and books, etc.) are not much relevant to the socio-cultural orientation of the scavengers. The exposure to printed media of mass communication (newspapers, magazines, journals and books, etc.) are not much relevant to the socio-cultural orientation of the scavengers. The exposure to printed media is very limited and, hence, the Press is not instrumental in arousing consciousness or shaping social orientation. The exposure to radio is of higher degree. The collected informations have revealed that 64% from Patna, 34% from Muzaffarpur and 12% from Arrah listen to radio programmes regularly.

It indicates that only in case of unliberated scavengers of Patna, the majority is exposed to this medium of mass communication. This has also come to light that among 32 (64%) unliberated scavengers of Patna exposed to the radio programme regularly include not only the men but also a considerable number of women. The highest percentage of exposure in Patna may be due to a higher degree of urbanism in the city than in Muzaffarpur or Arrah. Moreover, in Patna town the radio programmes may be listened to not only in a private house, but are heard in a large number of cases at tea-stalls and shops. Besides, locally manufactured inexpensive transistors are available and a considerable number of youths belonging to different sections of the community have these locally made transistors which enable them to listen to radio programmes. In the light of these facts and findings in respect of exposure to radio programmes, it may be stated that socio-cultural orientations of the scavengers in general and of younger generation in particular are expected to be aroused and shaped by this medium of mass communication. Hence, relevance of radio programmes to social orientation is considerably significant.

The audio-visual media appear to be more important than other media including radio and press. The informations suggest that in each of the three towns, the majority is exposed to film, though in varying frequencies (Table 21). Out of 150 scavengers, only 52 (34.6%) do not see films. But this figure refers to the scavengers actually interviewed. However, the members of the families of even these 52 scavengers are also exposed to film. Those who are old generally do not see films. The table also reveals that 30 (60%) scavengers from Patna, 27 (54%) from Muzaffarpur and 41 (82%) from Arrah see films. It is obvious that the degree of exposure to film is higher than other media in each of the three towns. On this basis it may be stated that the most popular and widely cherished medium is cinema which may be instrumental in arousing consciousness and shaping social orientations. These media can be used as an effective agency of publicity by the State and other organizations for changing the attitudes, ideas and behaviours of this backward class and weaker section of society. The popularity of film as a source of entertainment among scavengers and their family members is also clear from the informations furnished by them about the films they see. Out of 150 scavengers 52 (34%) do not see film at all (Table 22). It means that 65.4% of the scavengers are exposed to it. But at the same time it is important to point out that film is seen and enjoyed by family members of those 52 scavengers who are not exposed to this medium of mass communication. Among the 98 scavengers exposed to film, 65 scavengers (66.4%) like to see all types of films whereas 13 scavengers (13.2%) like to see reformative films and 18 scavengers (18.3%) like religious films. The liking for a specific type of films is not of much significance. This liking for films in general is equally significant among males as well as females.

After asking questions about the exposure of unliberated scavengers to the media of mass communication, questions were also asked from them to collect information about their political affiliation, political socialization and political participation. The responses given by them reveal that nobody is the member of any political party. In the same way, all the scavengers informed that they were not associated with any voluntary organization. This section of the community is, thus, not having any organised platform and its members are not conscious of joining any voluntary organization either, may be due to the fact that unliberated scavengers are socially, economically and educationally backward. The social stigma attached to scavenging in the traditional social system does not motivate them to be members of any club or social organization. Illiteracy and poverty again stand in the way of developing an aspiration leading to the membership of any voluntary organization. It also shows lack of political awareness among scavengers. Moreover, the lack of interest in political activities and processes is another reason for non-association of these people with political parties. Low education, poor economic conditions and the nature of work done by the unliberated scavengers may be responsible for the absence of political awareness in this section of the community. They informed that they were members of the trade union of scavengers of the employees of municipality or corporation. It is obvious that they have become members of the trade union not because they have the consciousness of the kind and were interested in union activities, but because they are the employees of municipality or corporation and in these local bodies, unions have been formed by the leaders other than scavengers. All the employees are approached and persuaded by the trade union leaders to become its members. Moreover, the employees feel that their economic interest may be well protected if they are members of the trade unions and this membership provides a safeguard against any sort of exploitation by the employers.

A significant question put to them to know the degree of their political awareness was: 'Do you know that the Indian Constitution has abolished all caste distinctions?' The informations obtained from the scavengers of all the three towns show that 57 of them did not know anything about it. They neither replied in affirmative nor in negative. As many as 60 scavengers declared that they did not know that the Indian Constitution had abolished all caste distinctions. Only 33 said they knew about this provision of the Indian Constitution. This indicates that the majority is not aware of the abolition of the caste distinction under the Indian Constitution.

The political awareness is quite inadequate or superficial in this section of the community. This may be due to lower degree of exposure of scavengers to media. Illiteracy stands in the way of their being exposed to the written media like newspapers, magazines and journals. Those who are exposed to radio are more interested in listening to entertaining programmes. Those who see films are also interested in deriving entertainment and they do not have any objective of gaining knowledge or receiving education through this media.

Another question put to the scavengers in the same context was: 'Do you know that discriminatory behaviour with any caste is a punishable offence in India?' The informations obtained from scavengers of all the three towns show that 57 of them knew nothing about it; 29 declared that they did not know that discriminatory behaviour with any caste is a punishable offence, while 64 of them replied in affirmative and stated that they knew about the legal and constitutional provision in respect of discriminatory behaviour with any caste. It means that the level of awareness about discriminatory behaviour as a punishable offence is higher than the degree of awareness in respect of provision of the Indian Constitution abolishing caste distinction. Hence, it may be interpreted that in this respect the political socialization has been less superficial and less inadequate than in the case of knowledge about the abolition of caste distinction by the Constitution. It may be due to the fact that the provision of the Constitution is a written document which may be taught infrequently whereas the discriminatory behaviour may be experienced in every day life and the reactions and counter-reactions in this respect may be experienced and observed by the people living in this society. Hence, the knowledge about the discriminatory behaviour as a punishable offence may be obtained through happenings and instances in the social surroundings. But it is also important to point out that even knowledge about punishment for discriminatory behaviour is not found in most cases. The same factors, illiteracy, poverty, lower status in society, lower degree of exposure to the media of mass communication, lack of interest in political affairs, traditional womenhood, higher degree of interest in earning livelihood and looking after household affairs, may be responsible for the lower degree of political awareness and superficial political socialization.

Another question put to the scavengers was: 'Are you aware of the facilities given by the State for the welfare of Scheduled Castes?' This question was also asked to find out the degree of political awareness and the level of political socialization. The replies show that 57 scavengers knew nothing about it, 17 of them replied in negative, whereas 76 respondents were aware of these facilities (Table 23).

It appears that 38% of scavengers knew nothing about the facilities given by the State for their welfare; 11.3% of them stated that they were not aware of these facilities, whereas 50.7% of the scavengers were aware of the facilities provided by the State Government for Scheduled Castes. It seems that a high percentage is aware of the facilities provided by the State Government for the welfare of the Scheduled Castes. The analysis of the data on age basis (Table 23) suggests that the lowest percentage of awareness is in the age-group of 41-50 years (42.2%) and the highest percentage in the youngest age-group (83.3%). It does not show a consistent variation in the percentages of responses with the variation in age, but definitely indicates that in the younger age-group the degree of awareness is highei than in the older age-groups.

It has been observed in general that the highest response showing political awareness has been found in the youngest age-group while the lowest in the oldest age-group of 51–60 years. Hence, it may be interpreted that the age factor is significantly relevant to the degree of political awareness and level of political socialization. The younger generation is more aware of the provisions of the Constitution, the sanctions of the law and the welfare activities of the State for the members of the Scheduled Castes. It is also significant to point out that in spite of the fact that most. of the interviewers are illiterate women, who are more interested in earning livelihood, looking after children and managing household affairs, more than 50% of them know about the facilities provided by the State Government.

However, on the whole, the data analysed about the knowledge of the scavengers in respect of constitutional provisions, legal sanctions and facilities show that the degree of political awareness is low among them. In spite of the fact that the scavengers are living in towns, are employed in semi-government establishments and are associated with trade unions, they do not know much about the changes in their status and position under the provisions of the law and the Constitution. The Government provides facilities in different ways, like reservation of jobs and seats in educational institutions, special programmes for coaching to enable the youth of the weaker sections to appear at competitions, stipends and scholarships and free education and hostel facilities for students. But those who are to be benefitted by these welfare schemes are not properly acquainted. This fact is also supported by the finding that a number of seats reserved for the students belonging to the Scheduled Castes in colleges and university departments remain vacant because no application is received for admission or very few applications are submitted. It is obvious that the lack of awareness of these facilities is one of the major reasons for the non-utilization of the facilities provided to the members of this weaker section.

For analysing the degree of political socialization of this section, certain political terms and concepts used in Indian society under the parliamentary system of democracy were put to them and they were asked to state whether they knew their meanings. The findings classified on age basis (Table 24) suggest that on the

(*Top*) *A lonely wait for the bread-winner*: A scavenger, outside a hut which by no imagination can be called a house. But, this is where scavengers live and suffer. (*Bottom*) *From pit into drain*: Having cleaned it from dry latrines, human excrement is being poured into a *nullah* (drain) and, thus, the stink and disease are spread far and wide.

(*Top*) ***The hell revisited***: Most dry latrines are in a state of disrepair where scavengers have to clean excreta with nothing more than flat sticks.
(*Bottom*) ***Suffering together***: Scavengers carry the night-soil on the head sometimes in groups as if to tell that it is the question of a community and not of an individual. (A picture from a colony in Arrah).

whole, 28.7% of the scavengers expressed their ignorance about them. It is also found that the highest percentage of positive response (60.7%) is in case of 'adult franchise' and the second highest (48%) is in case of 'democracy'. The lowest percentage of positive response is in respect of 'mid-term poll', in which only 4% of the interviewers declared that they knew about it. In the same way, the percentages of positive responses are very low in the case of Panchayati Raj (11.3%), Lok Sabha and Vidhan Sabha (27.3%) and 'equality of rights' (36.7%). Hence, it seems that the degree of political awareness is very low and even the terms like 'mid-term poll' and 'Panchayati Raj' are not known to the unliberated scavengers in general. It clearly suggests the persistence of a superficial or low level of political socialization of the people. Even the concept of 'equality of rights' is known only to 36.7% which too shows a poor degree of political awareness. It may be due to the fact that most of the scavengers are illiterate who have been living in poor economic conditions and have been mainly concerned with earning livelihood and meeting the basic needs of life.

The enquiry into political awareness and political participation further reveals that 100% of scavengers participate in elections. But the lone form of their participation in election is as voters. Many of the interviewers were belong 21 year of age, but they also vote in elections. Now after the amendment, 18-year-old persons can vote. It is not because they are politically conscious, but because they are mobilised or pressurised by candidates or their agents to cast bogus votes. In certain cases money plays a significant role in determining the voting pattern. Hence, their participation in election as voters is not an index of active interest in politics. They cast votes either as a ritual or in a mechanical fashion or under some pressure at the time of voting. Lack of political consciousness and active interest in politics is also evident from this finding that 100% of the scavengers do not want to take an active part in election.

These findings indicate that unliberated scavengers are extremely backward from the political point of view. The information gathered from them leads to the inference that they do not understand the importance and innovational significance of political affiliation, political socialization and political participation. They appear to be indifferent to these aspects of the national life in post-independence era. Their membership of the union is not out of eagerness for political. affiliation, but because of the customary practice that the employees become members of their unions. The respondents do not have any type of affiliation with any social, cultural or political organization. It reflects a complete absence of political consciousness and orientation. The factors of illiteracy, poverty, social stigma of the traditional society and lack of contact with the educated and progressive sections of the community are responsible for inadequate political socialization. The absence of political consciousness motivates them to derive only entertainment and enjoyment from the media of mass communication and they are not in a position to realise the importance of these media in arousing political consciousness and in increasing knowledge of the current affairs and problems of the country. As a result, they are not able to appreciate the importance of political participation nor have they developed consciousness about the fact that they play a vital role in the political development of the country. Thus, despite efforts made by the Central and State Governments for generating political consciousness among the weaker sections of society, the unliberated scavengers have not been benefitted so far by these schemes.

The information obtained from scavengers about their background reveal that only 44.0% of 150 scavengers are in this occupation for 15 years or less, whereas 55.9% are engaged for more than 15 years (Table 25). Those engaged in scavenging for more than 15 years have varied periods of scavenging experience i.e. 16-20 years, 21-25 years, 26-30 years and 31 years or more. The percentage of scavengers engaged in scavenging has consistently declined with the increase in the period of experience, but a sizeable section has considerably a longer period of scavenging to its credit. It is also evident from the table that any significant relation does not exist between income variable and the duration of scavenging. It was also gathered from them that they were *Bhangis* by birth and scavenging was their hereditary occupation. It means that nobody adopted the occupation of scavenging because he or she was willing, but because it was a family occupation imposed on them by birth and not choice. The enquiry into the reasons for taking up this occupation reveals that according to 48.7% of the interviewee scavengers, there was no alternative, while according to 40.7% it was the traditional occupation of *Bhangis* and according to 37.3% it was easily available (Tables 26 and 27). All these reasons suggest that scavenging was adopted as an occupation for earning livelihood under compelling circumstances and social values which did not permit them to have a free hand in choosing occupation or to take up an occupation other than scavenging. This generalised finding is valid for all these scavengers irrespective of family income (Table 26) or family structure (Table 27).

All of them said 'no' when asked if they liked this profession. They did not want their children also to take up this occupation. This is quite natural because the sub-human work of cleaning and carrying night-soil cannot be liked by anybody. When they were asked to give reasons for their disliking, most of them replied that it was a dirty job. The second important reason was the lower social status associated with it. Persons doing the scavenging work are hated in society and the other members of the community do not like to have any interaction with them except utilising their services for cleaning and carrying night-soil. Another important reason mentioned by them was also related to lower social status because some of them declared that the occupation did not carry any respect. On the basis of these responses, it may be stated that the scavenging occupation has been adopted by them under compelling circumstances. They neither like it nor regard it as a respectable occupation. They feel that the occupation is dirty and sub-human and it is not proper for a person to clean and carry the night-soil of other persons. The society does not accord any respect or status for performing this important job, rather those engaged in this work are placed at the lowest rung of the social ladder.

Some other questions were also asked from the scavengers on their occupation and the status or position they enjoyed in society. It is obvious from their reply that under this system they are required to clean the night-soil and to collect it in containers from different service latrines. This automatically involves manual handling of the night-soil which is extremely degrading and sub-human. It is a manifestation of the ugliest form of social exploitation and injustice. It is important to note that although untouchability has been abolished under the Constitution of the country, the scavengers have failed to attain the status of 'touchables' as members of the caste society.

When asked: 'Are you allowed to touch persons of other castes while carrying night-soil?', all the scavengers replied in negative. It is important to note that though untouchability has been abolished under the Constitution and the practice of untouchability is a punishable offence, yet the scavengers are not allowed to touch the members of other castes while carrying night-soil. Regarding health hazards the scavengers were of the view that the scavenging profession caused several diseases like cold, cough, cholera and even tuberculosis. This is due to their exposure to unhealthy environments and the highly insanitary condition of work.

The scavengers were also asked: 'Have you made any effort to change this occupation?' The informations obtained from them reveal that 26% of them from Patna, 6% from Muzaffarpur and 18% from Arrah made efforts to change this occupation. It means that a smaller percentage from each town tried to change the occupation, but the majority did not take this step. It is not because the majority was in favour of this occupation, but because it had the impression that the efforts would prove futile and there was no other job which they could get after giving up scavenging. Hence, lack of initiative or effort on the part of the majority of scavengers was due to the realization of the fact that even efforts to this effect would not succeed.

Those who made efforts for changing the occupation were also asked to inform about the steps taken by them. More or less the same reply was given by 25 scavengers from the three towns who had made some efforts. All of them approached the higher authorities for some better job—better not essentially in the sense of economic gain, but in the context of social respect and prestige. Some of them registered their names in employment exchanges and approached the exchanges for suggesting some other jobs. But all these efforts proved fruitless and they neither got and proper guidance from the employment exchange nor did the higher authorities come to their rescue and render help in providing alternative jobs to these scavengers.

To study the degree of desirability of change in occupation, a question put to the scavengers was: 'suppose you are asked to start some business and you are provided with financial help also, are you prepared to leave this occupation?' All of them gave positive reply, which shows an eagerness on thier part to get rid of the scavenging profession and to get some alternative means of livelihood. They were further asked: 'Will you leave this occupation even if you get less income than what you are getting as scavenger?' On the whole, 54% of the scavengers are in favour of change in occupation even if they are losers financially. This view expressed by a majority clearly suggests that they are very keen on changing the present occupation even if it involved economic loss. Hence, economic consideration is important for a sizeable section of the scavengers covered by this question, but the majority desires to get rid of this occupation even at the cost of economic hardship. If the income is lower but the job is respectable, the majority wants to change the present occupation. It shows the importance of social factors and values in the desire or willingness favouring the change of occupation.

It is obvious from the above discussions that the scavengers are not in favour of continuing in the profession. They are doing scavenging because they do not get any other job. Some of them tried to get some other jobs and approached the authorities concerned and the employment exchanges for this purpose, but their efforts were in vain. The analysis also suggests that in case any agency or organization helps them in rehabilitation and provides financial assistance to start some business, they are ready to give up the present occupation and to take up business, 100 per cent unliberated scavengers have this desire and are willing to avail the opportunity of starting business if it is provided to them. More than 50% of the respondents are willing to take up business instead of scavenging even if the former fetches lesser income. It means that the economic factor is not the only consideration; rather the socio-cultural factor and those of prestige, respect and status are also important in determining the attitudes of the scavengers towards the scavenging profession.

They were also asked to express their liking for some other jobs either for themselves or for their children in case they have to give up their occupation. The question put to them was: 'In case you have to leave the present occupation, what other job would you like to take up for you and for your children?' They expressed their liking for different types of jobs like those of peon, sweeper, assistant or clerk, businessman or any suitable job according to their qualifications. A good number of them did not mention any choice for a particular occupation either for themselves or for their children. In case of jobs for the female members, 14% from Patna and 12% from Arrah did not mention any specific job, whereas in the case of children 2% from Patna and 4% from Arrah did not specify any job. It was also found that in case of jobs for female members, the highest percentage of response went in favour of the job of maid-servant mentioned by 44% in Patna, 88% in Muzaffarpur and 80% in Arrah. Other important jobs mentioned by the respondents for the female members are those of peon and sweeper. As many as 28% of the respondents from Patna, 28% from Muzzaffarpur and 24% from Arrah mentioned the job of sweeper; whereas 26% from Patna, 12% from Muzaffarpur and 42% from Arrah mentioned the job of peon for the female members. In the case of children, the highest percentage of response in Patna went in favour of any job according to qualification (56%); in Muzaffarpur the highest percentage of response has gone in favour of the job of peon (48%) and 62% from Arrah have mentioned in job of peon for the children of their families. In this way it appears that the jobs of peon, maid-servant and sweeper have been mentioned by a large number of respondents as alternative jobs. It reflects the realistic outlook and approach of these scavengers. They realise that they are illiterate or lowly educated and their children are also not expected to receive higher education in the existing circumstances. Hence, they have mentioned only those alternative jobs which may be provided to them according to their educational qualification. They appear to be aspirant for better position for their children who may improve their academic status. Hence, they have opined that their children may be given suitable jobs corresponding to their academic performance and educational qualification. Thus, the higher level of aspiration is also not unrealistic and imaginative.

Another question put to the scavengers was: 'What are the difficulties felt by you in the present occupation?' The informations reveal that the total number of respondents is 150 from the three towns, whereas the total number of responses is 258 (Tables 28 and 29). It means that many of them have given more than one response and have mentioned two or more difficulties felt by them in the scavenging profession. It is also evident that 54% of the scavengers are not provided with accessories needed for cleaning night-soil or transferring it from the dry latrine to the bucket. The accessories include hand-gloves, a piece of cloth for covering mouth or face and an equipment for transferring the same from one place to another.

Another important difficulty mentioned by 32% of these employed scavengers is delay in the payment of salary, 26.7% of the scavengers complained against hard duty and heavy load of work. According to them the scavenging work is strenuous and involves a lot of physical labour. Another difficulty pointed out by the scavengers is 'exploitation', social and/or economic, mentioned by 26% of them. The factor of lower salary has been mentioned by a smaller percentage (19.3%) and only 3.3% have mentioned other miscellaneous difficulties. It is also important to note that 16 scavengers (10.7%) do not face any problem in doing the scavenging work.

The analysis of collected data on the basis of income (Table 28) and on the basis of age (Table 29) reveals that neither the income variable nor the age variable is significantly relevant to variations in response patterns expressing difficulties involved in a scavenging profession. Scavengers of different age groups and varying income levels have expressed their problems showing no relevance of income or age.

A number of questions were asked from these scavengers to know the sources from which they came to know about the *Sulabh Shauchalaya* scheme and its importance in liberating the scavengers. The first question put to them was whether they had heard about the *Sulabh Shauchalaya* scheme. All of them gave a positive reply. In reply to another question whether they liked the scheme 100% stated 'yes'. It is obvious that the scheme aims at liberating scavengers and doing away with the sub-human occupation of scavenging and cleaning of night-soil manually. Hence, those who are most concerned with the scheme are those engaged in the scavenging work. Moreover, the scheme aims at benefiting the scavengers and hence their liking for the scheme is quite natural and logical.

They were asked to give reasons for this liking. Their views suggest that the most important reason mentioned by 50.7% is that the scheme is hygienic (Table 30). The second important reason mentioned by 36.7% is that it liberates the scavengers from this sub-human profession. As many as 24% like the scheme because scavenging is not needed, 20.7% of them declared that it made the scavengers as well as the members of the community free from the foul smell of the night-soil, 8% of the scavengers liked it because it was beneficial for the general public whereas according to 4% the scheme was better than the service latrine and according to 2% it is economical. It is also important to note that the total number of responses is 219 whereas the total number of interviewees is 150. It means that some of them have mentioned two or more reasons for their liking of the *Sulabh Shauchalaya* scheme. The table presents the classification of responses on the age basis. It appears that excepting the age-group of 41-50 years, in all other age-groups the highest percentage of response is in respect of the hygienic advantage of the *Sulabh Shauchalaya* scheme. The percentages of response in respect of other reasons do not show any consistent variation with the variation in age.

Questions were also asked from the scavengers to collect information about the caste inter-relation and their levels and types of contacts with other castemen higher or lower. These questions were asked to find out the restrictions and caste sanctions in respect of drinking water, taking food and having personal and friendly relations. The furnished informations indicate that no member of the upper caste accepts drinking water from the scavengers. As regards the acceptance of water by the members of lower castes it is quite interesting to find that even the Harijans (Scheduled Caste people) generally do not accept drinking water from scavengers. It suggests that in spite of the abolition of untouchability and distinctions on the caste basis, the people are not ready to accept drinking water from scavengers. It may be due to the fact that the occupation of the scavengers is dirty and, hence, the people do not like to accept water from them. It clearly indicates that a free and unchecked inter-caste relationship does not exist between scavengers and members of other castes, whether higher, lower or scheduled.

They were also asked to name the castes with whom they could take food. The informations received show that the same restrictions and traditional taboos are found in respect of taking food as in accepting drinking water. No upper caste member accepts food with scavengers. In the same manner in a few cases the members of lower castes or the Scheduled Castes take food with the scavengers, but, in general, scavengers may take food without any restriction only with the members of their own caste. It is also important to note that not only the members of upper and lower castes treat them shabbily rather the members of the Scheduled Castes, other than scavengers, too are not willing to take food with them. Hence, inter-caste dining is very limited in the case of scavengers.

The respondents were further asked to name the castes having friendship with members of their families. It has come to light that only one scavenger from Arrah mentioned friendship with a member of some upper caste; but in all other cases friendship with any member of the upper caste was not found. Although friendship is personal matter and is not guided by group relations or caste sanctions, but the caste prejudices are so strong that even personal relations are conditioned by it. An no scavenger has friendship with any member of the upper caste. The information provided by them reveals that there are cases of friendship with members of lower castes. As many as 30% of the scavengers from Patna, 10% from Arrah and 0% from Muzaffarpur affirmed that members of lower castes had friendship with the members of their families. Thus, the members of the families of scavengers have friendly relations and personal friendship either with the members of their own sub-castes or, in certain cases, with members of different castes. In the light of this finding it may be interpreted that caste distinction is still present in society and there are reservations in the acceptance of drinking water and food from the scavengers. These facts clearly suggest that society has not given a respectable place to scavengers and due to the nature of their occupation they are still looked down upon and are placed at the lowest level of the soceity.

The informations obtained on the question; 'Name the caste of persons who come to your house on ceremonial occasions', reveal that in all the three towns, members of upper caste come to the house of only one scavenger of Patna on ceremonial occasions. In Patna 22%, in Arrah 10% and in Muzaffarpur 0% stated that the members of lower caste came to their houses on ceremonial occasions. In general, the scavengers informed that the members of the same caste or sub-caste attend ceremonial functions at their houses. Even the members of other sub-castes of the Harijan category come to the houses of scavengers on ceremonial occasions in a very low number. Some informants stated that a few members of the upper and lower castes also come. But these persons are exceptional, because they do not believe in caste restrictions. On the whole, the members of superior castes do not like to come to the houses of the scavengers even on ceremonial occasions. It shows a very low level of social intercourse between scavengers on the one hand and upper castes, on the other. It is clear that in spite of constitutional provisions, in actual social life discriminations and distinctions persist. The other side of the picture is important to be presented. In case the members of other castes do not attend ceremonial functions, it is also possible that they were not invited by scavengers at such functions. As the families of the scavengers are socially, culturally, educationally and economically very backward, their social contacts are limited to their own sub-caste or occupational group. They do not interact socially with the people of other castes and their areas of social contact is very limited. Hence, on ceremonial functions they invite only those persons and families with whom they have regular social contact and informal relation. Consequently, they do not normally invite the members of upper and lower castes and hence, there is no question of their coming on such occasions.

The scavengers were asked to name the castes whom they considered socially superior or inferior to them. A list of six castes of *Chamar, Dusadh, Pasi, Musahar, Dhobi* and *Dom* was provided to them for this purpose. In general, the scavengers consider that *Chamar, Dusadh, Musahar,* and *Dom* are socially inferior to them; whereas *Pasi* and *Dhobi* are socially superior. It is important to note that all the six sub-castes are Scheduled Castes and are included in the category of Harijans. The concept of 'superiority' or 'inferiority' in respect of each of these castes expressed by scavengers clearly suggests that a hierarchy exists among the Scheduled Castes or Harijans. It is interesting to note that the scavengers complain of caste discrimination shown by the upper and lower caste people and desire to be recongized as equal. But they themselves possess this concept and consider some of the

Scheduled Castes as superior and others as inferior to them. It means that the discrimination and distinction on the basis of birth and the notion of caste inequality is so deep rooted in the socio-cultural life of the Indians that even the victims of caste inequality believe in socially superior and inferior castes.

Some questions were put to the scavengers on discrimination in an overt form. One question put to them was: 'Is any member of your family subjected to discrimination on account of your being a scavenger?' They were further asked to show any discriminatory behaviour with them or their family members in school or college, in office or getting house on rent. All the scavengers from each of the three towns replied in negative in each case. It is also important to mention that on observation it was found that scavengers do not try to get a house in the area where the members of other castes live. The families of scavengers either live in the hutments built by them or in a Harijan colony or in the official quarters meant for them. Hence, there is no question of being subject to discrimination in getting house on rent. In the office every incumbent has a specific and well-defined role to perform and, hence there is no question of discrimination.

Questions were also asked from them to find out the levels of aspirations in respect of education of their children. In view of the changing social climate, such questions are of great sociological relevance. The responses obtained suggest that only six scavengers did not like to educate their male children. In case of female children, 12 of them declared that they wanted no education for them. It was also found that a considerably large number (94) favoured post-school or college education for male children. In respect of female children, 24 families seek to give college education while most of them (86) have favoured education up to matriculation only. Thus, on the whole, it appears that scavengers, who are mostly illiterate, aspire for better education both for male and female children though the level of aspiration is higher for male than for female children. These findings suggest that even this weaker and backward section of society has developed a favourable attitude towards education and realises its significance in raising the economic condition and social status.

As to the sources of financing the education of their children, the respondents declared that they met the expenses out of their own earnings. It proves that they are realising the significance and importance of education for the younger generation. However, the poor economic condition of this section is the major hurdle in educating their children as stated by them and they want to remove this hurdle in educating their children as stated by them and they want to remove this hurdle through financial grants from the Government—in cash or in kind.

In the light of above stated facts that the socio-economic condition of unliberated scavengers from each of the three towns is miserable, they are backward and depressed not only from economic point of view but also from the point of view of education, social standing and life style. They have developed bad habits of smoking, cheaper *bidis* and cigarettes and of taking coarse and much harmful country-made liquor. The housing condition, the household articles, the clothes they wear and the food they eat are very poor and inferior in quality. Poverty stands in the way of educating the younger generation and improving the living standard. Illiteracy and poverty are two major factors which have put this section of society in miserable conditions. Above all, the social stigma against them has not been done away with so far and the traditional social hierarchy is still in existence. Scavengers realise that the discrimination on the basis of birth is unjust, but they are themselves not free from this social curse. But at the same time a trend of change is also noticed in the socio-cultural life of these people.

They are aspiring for educating younger generation. They are eager to give up scavenging and to take up some other job for earning livelihood. They have grievances against authorities—social, political and bureaucratic, and have complained that their approach towards scavengers is unjust and discriminatory. All these facts definitely provide an index of change in their attitudes, outlooks, ambitions and aspirations.

II. Liberated Scavengers

As stated earlier, the present exercise is designed to study not only the working scavengers, but also those who have left this job and have taken up other occupations. These are liberated scavengers. The term 'liberated' in the present study, applies only to those

BIHAR

TOWNS MADE SCAVENGING FREE

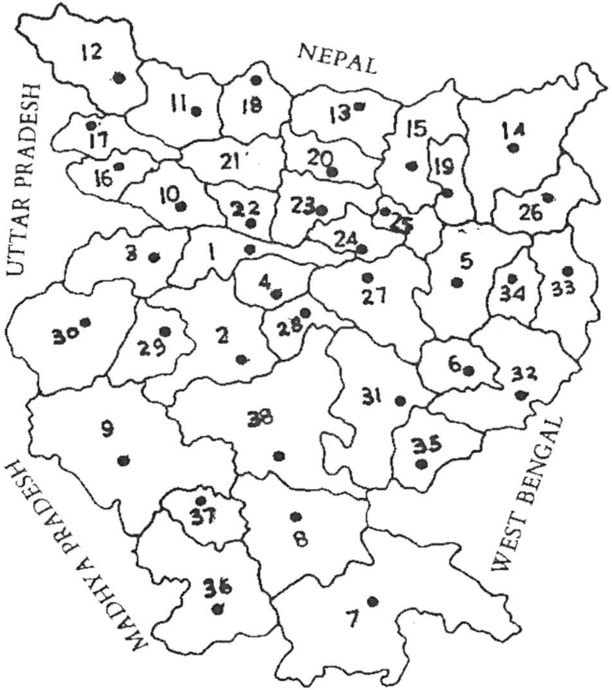

DISTRICTS

1. PATNA
2. GAYA
3. BHOJPUR
4. NALANDA
5. BHAGALPUR
6. DEOGHAR
7. SINGHBUM
8. RANCHI
9. PALAMU
10. SARAN
11. EAST CHAMPARAN
12. WEST CHAMPARAN
13. MADHUBANI
14. PURNEA
15. SAHARSA
16. SIWAN
17. GOPALGANJ
18. SITAMARHI
19. MADHEPURA
20. DARBHANGA
21. MUZAFFARPUR
22. VAISHALI
23. SAMASTIPUR
24. BEGUSARAI
25. KHAGARIA
26. KATIHAR
27. MONGHYR
28. NAWADAH
29. AURANGABAD
30. ROHTAS
31. GIRIDIH
32. DUMKA
33. SAHIBGANJ
34. GODDA
35. DHANBAD
36. GUMLA
37. LOHERDAGA
38. HAZARIBAGH

TOWNS MADE SCAVENGING FREE

PATNA
GAYA
ARRAH
BIHARSHARIF
BHAGALPUR
DEOGHAR
CHAIBASA
RANCHI
DALTONGANG
CHAPRA
MOTIHARI
BETTIAH
MADHUBANI
PURNEA
SAHARSA

scavengers who were employed in municipalities and corporations. After the introduction of the *Sulabh Shauchalaya* scheme and the conversion of service latrines into *Sulabh Shauchalayas* in a number of towns and municipal areas, these persons were relieved of the scavenging work. But, as they are the employees of municipalities and corporations, they have been provided alternative work like sweeping, cleaning of roads and nullas and hauling up garbage. But, there remains the problem for their family members who are not employed as scavengers, but may get their employment in the near future. In case their children or other family members are employed as scavengers, the liberation of scavengers becomes meaningless because in that case the family will not be liberated from the scavenging work. Hence, with the liberation of the scavengers, though the problem of their rehabilitation does not arise, yet the problem of rehabilitation and employment of their dependents exists for the successful implementation of the liberation scheme. As many as liberated scavengers were selected from each of the three towns and information was collected from them about their family life, living conditions, educational background, rehabilitation, impact of liberation and the job and educational requirements of their family members.

Information obtained from the respondents from all the three towns throws light on the types and size of the families of the liberated scavengers. On the whole 40.7% of the families in the three towns are living jointly and 59.3% in nuclear families (Table 31). The number of liberated scavengers living in joint families is lower than those living in nuclear families. It is worth noting that a considerable percentage of the liberated scavengers is still living in joint families although the process of family nuclearization has taken place in a large number of cases. It may be either due to the impact of urbanization or due to individual employment and personal earning as the employees of municipalities and corporations. The trend of nuclearization of families is quite significant because it is responsible for bringing about changes not only in the family structures, but also in social relationship, mode of economic life and concept of individual and joint economy.

Information obtained from the respondents about the size of the family suggests that in case of joint families, the minimum size consists of four to six members except one and the maximum size 13 to 15 members while majority of them (80.3%) have four to nine members (Table 31). The families having nuclear structure have up to nine members excepting one nuclear family from Purnea which consists of 10-12 members. On the whole, 30.3% of nuclear families from the 3 towns are having 1-3 members, 49.5%, 4-6 members and 19.1%, 7-9 members (Table 31). Nuclear families are varying in size, but the dominant trend is in favour of a smaller size.

Informations about housing condition reveal that 46% of the respondents live in their own houses, 10.7% in rented houses or apartments and 43.3% in *government quarters* (Table 32). Thus, the highest percentage of the liberated scavengers have their own dwellings.

It is also found that 55.3% of the house are *kuchcha*, 19.3% *pucca* and 25.3% mixed (Table 33). It is quite significant to note that on the whole 43.3% (Table 32) of the respondents live in government quarters, but only 19.3% (Table 33) are living in *pucca* houses. It means that most of the government quarters allotted to the liberated scavengers are also not *pucca*. Thus the accommodation provided to the liberated scavengers even by municipalities and corporations is not adequated and they are not living in *pucca* houses or quarters.

As regards the accommodation in the houses of liberated scavengers, the collected informations reveal that 80.7% of the families of liberated scavengers are residing in one room dwellings, 14.0% in two-room dwellings and only 5.3% in three-room dwellings (Table 34). In each town majority of the liberated scavengers and their families are living in one-room dwellings.

Keeping the size of families in view, the accommodation appears to be quite inadequate and congested. This fact is also evident from the informations given by the liberated scavengers about the adequacy or otherwise of accommodation.

As many as 83.8% scavengers have declared that accommodation is not sufficient, whereas only 16.3% feel that it is adequate (Table 35). Most of the liberated scavengers have the problem of congestion. But their economic condition does not permit them to have more spacious accommodation and they are compelled by circumstances to suffer from a lower level of living standard.

The information indicated that 34% of scavengers have electricity in their houses while others have not even though they live in urban areas. Nor do they have other civic facilities (Table 36). The collected data show that 60% of liberated scavengers get water from public taps, 21.3% from hand-pumps, 13.3% from wells and 5.3% from tube-wells (Table 37). Very few families own a private source of drinking water. This again proves the poor economic and living condition of liberated scavengers and their families. It is also evident that only 8% of the respondents own private sources of drinking water, whereas 92% take water from public sources (Table 38).

The collected informations further reveal that only 8% of the liberated scavengers have private toilets, 46.7% use community latrines and 45.3% use open space for defecation (Table 39). It is also found that no liberated scavenger uses community latrines in Purnea and most of them (94%) use open space as the place of defecation.

In the light of the above findings it may be stated that the living standard of liberated scavengers is very low. They are not provided with the basic amenities of life even in urban areas.

This fact has also come to light through field enquiry that actual scavenging work was done by women in most cases. Both men and women scavengers were employed, but the task of cleaning and carrying night-soil was done by female scavengers in most of the cases. In the present study only 20% of the liberated scavengers are men and 80% are women (Table 40).

In Ranchi 100% are women scavengers, whereas in Purnea 76% are females and 24% males. In Patna 64% are female scavengers and 36% males. Thus, in Purena and Patna towns most of the liberated scavengers are women.

The liberated scavengers are divided into various age-groups ranging from 20 to 61 years and above (Table 41). There is only one scavenger belonging to the age-group of 61 years and above and she is from Patna town. In the same way, one female scavenger is below 21 years of age and she is from Purnea. Moreover 30.7% of the liberated scavengers belong to the age-group of 31-40 years, 30% of 41-50 years 23.3% to the age-group of 21-30 years and 14.7% of the group of 51-60 years.

As of literacy and education, it appears that a vast majority of scavengers are illiterate. Only 7.3% of them have read up to calss IV and only one (0.7%) up to middle class (Table 42). It is, thus, obvious that the condition of literacy is very poor and, in general, the liberated scavengers are illiterate. This finding clearly suggests that in absence of education they can do only manual work. It has also come to light that the scavengers having primary or middle level education dropped out during the study. They could not give any specific reason except that the poor economic condition of the family did not allow them to study. They started earning and, hence, they left their studies.

An enquiry into their interest in the adult education programme reveals that the interest patterns are not uniform in all the three towns (Table 43). In case of the liberated scavengers of Ranchi town, 62% have declared that they are interested in adult education whereas in Purnea only 28% and in Patna 16% are interested in adult education. It means that most of the liberated scavengers of Ranchi favour adult education while in Patna and Purnea towns the majority is not interested. It is important to note that in Ranchi all the liberated scavengers are women and in spite of belonging to the female sex, they have shown greater interest in adult education.

The table also presents that classification of informations on age basis. In Ranchi the highest percentage of response showing interest in adult education is in the age-group of 21-30 years (92.9%), whereas the lowest percentage (33.3%) is in the age-group of 41-50 years. In Purnea, there has been a constant decline in adult education with the rise in age. Thus, in this town, there is a significant relevance of age to the interest in adult education. In the case of Patna, 100% scavengers in the age-group of 21-30 years have replied in negative whereas 26.7% in the age-group of 31-40 years, 17.6% in the age group of 41-50 years and 9.1% in the age group of 51-60 years have shown interest in adult education. Thus, some relevance of age to the response patterns is found in Patna also. But, in the case of Ranchi, age is not relevant to the interest in adult education.

Informations were also collected about the personal income of liberated scavengers as well as their family income. The enquiry into family income was made with this fact in mind that there are two or more earning hands in the family. The collected facts

Meera Devi goes about carrying bucketful of night-soil without protest, hoping that some day the misery and disgrace will end. (Photo from Patna).

Meera Devi is liberated and provided with non-scavenging work like road cleaning. Her bad days are over.

(*Top*) *After liberation*: Geeta Devi is living happily after liberation with her family members, free from scavenging. Geeta later became a social worker, campaigning for the redemption of other scavengers.
(*Bottom*) *Before liberation*: Before Geeta was liberated, she used to carry excrement on the head along with others. It is Geeta (right), the scavenger, with her mother. (Photo from Patna).

reveal that no scavenger has an income of less than Rs. 100 per month (Table 44). The highest percentage of response is from the income group of Rs. 301-400 (44.7%). The monthly income of the family ranges from Rs. 400 to above Rs. 1600 (Table 45). As two or more persons in most families are earning, the family income is much higher than the personal income of the liberated scavengers.

It is evident from the collected informations that they started scavenging work at different ages; 18.7% in the the age-group of 10-15 years, 7.3% at 21-25 years and 5.3% started scavenging after 25 years of age. The majority of them (68.7%) started scavenging at the age of 16-20 years (Table 46). Hence, it may be interpreted that majority of them started the scavenging work at the proper age of taking up the occupational career. The table also shows that 94% of the liberated scavengers in Ranchi, 60% in Purnea and 52% in Patna took up scavenging in this age-group. Hence, in each town the majority started scavenging in the same age-group. It is also found that scavenging was taken up at an early age by a higher percentage of the wage-earners in Patna (36%) than in Purnea (20%), whereas no one from Ranchi took up scavenging in this age-group. Likewise, 10% of the scavengers from Patna and 6% from Purnea took up scavenging after 25 years of age, but no one from Ranchi took up this job after 25 years. The start of the scavenging career, both early and late, is found in Patna and Purnea, but not in Ranchi. It is also revealed that the scavengers were liberated at different ages and a large number of them (36%) after 40 years of age (Table 47).

The table shows that they worked for a considerable period as scavengers; 20% were liberated in the age-group of 26-30 years, 16.7% in the age group of 31-35 years, 14.7% in the age-group of 20-25 years and 12.7% in the age group of 36-40 years. This difference in age at liberation is not on account of their own options, but because of the stage of time at which the liberation scheme was implemented with the efforts of Sulabh International.

The informations on the period of scavenging before liberation, collected from the three towns, reveal that the highest percentage of scavengers (39.3%) were liberated after working for 21 years or more. Only a smaller section of 9.3% were liberated after less than five years, 18% after 5-10 years whereas 20.7% were liberated after 11-15 years and 12.7% after 16-20 years. Thus, it appears that in most cases the liberation took place after a long period of working as scavengers. The period of scavenging in all the three towns has been considerably long when the liberation took place.

The reason is quite obvious. The liberation of scavengers is not an old movement. This scheme was effectively introduced by *Sulabh Shauchalaya Sansthan* (now *Sulabh International*) and only through this institution the liberation of the scavengers has been possible. As this scheme started working effectively after 1970, the liberation is not very old. Moreover, at the time of liberation, the scavengers belonged to different age-groups and most of them were engaged for a considerably long period of service as scavengers. Hence, the duration of scavenging before liberation has been long in most cases.

On enquiry from the scavengers it was found that scavenging was their traditional occupation. A question was put to them, 'Did you, on your own, try to change your occupation?' In general, the liberated scavengers admitted that they did not try themselves to get their occupation changed. In fact, they were liberated by some other agency. This admission presents the true picture of the situation. It was the *Sulabh Shauchalaya Sansthan* which prepared a scheme for the liberation of scavengers. The *Sulabh Shauchalaya* scheme implemented by this organization under the chairmanship of the present author worked for the liberation of the scavengers in different towns not only in Bihar, but also in other States of the Country.

The service latrines were converted into *Sulabh Shauchalayas*, relieving the scavengers of the inhuman work in areas where this scheme was implemented. But, at the same time, the liberated scavengers were not out of job after the liberation; it was ascertained that they would be given some alternative jobs by the municipalities and corporations and that there would, thus, be no room for their unemployment.

When asked if they were satisfied with the present occupation after liberation, a small section of Purnea and Patna scavengers replied in the negative (Table 49).

However, it appears from this table that all the liberated scavengers from Ranchi are satisfied with their present occupation, which is not scavenging; it is some other job provided by their employers. In Purnea 43 respondents are satisfied, whereas 7 are not. In the same way 37 respondents from Patna are satisfied, whereas 13 have expressed dissatisfaction. It may be due to the fact that the present occupations or jobs held by these liberated scavengers are also lower in status and are not liked by the members of other castes or sub-castes.

The scavengers who expressed satisfaction were asked to give reasons. All of them replied that their existing occupation was better than the previous one, though there was no improvement in their monthly emoluments. The casue of satisfaction is, therefore, not economic; it is exclusively psycho-social. Those who were not satisfied were also asked to explain their dissatisfaction. They gave different reasons. The most important reason for their dissatisfaction was the rather meagre salary they received and more work that they have to do (Tables 50-51). There is no specific variation either in the views given by male and female scavengers (Table 50). But the classification of given reasons on the basis of family income shows that only scavengers from lower income groups have expressed the view that the reason of dissatisfaction is less salary. Moreover, it is also evident that in the second highest income-group no specific reason for dissatisfaction has been given (Table 51).

A few questions were also put to the liberated scavengers with a view to studying the impact of liberation on them. The purpose of asking these questions was to find out if there has been a change in their social status after being liberated. For this purpose certain specific conditions were mentioned and they were asked to give information on them before and after their liberation. The conditions put to them were—(1) visit to temples visited by caste Hindus; (2) engagement of Brahmins to supervise religious ceremonies; (3) invitation by other caste people on ceremonial occasions; (4) taking water from common places along with other caste people, and (5) taking food and catering in hotels and other places.

It appears from the obtained informations that there has been a noticeable change in the social interaction among liberated scavengers and other low or high caste people. Eighty-six of the 150 interviewed scavengers visited temples before their liberation while the number has increased to 120 after liberation (Table 52).

Likewise, 94 of them engaged Brahmins to supervise religious ceremonies in the pre-liberation period, but after liberation, 128 were having the services of Brahmins in their families.

As regards invitation by other caste people on ceremonial occasions, there appears to be a significant impact of the liberation. In the pre-liberation period only 13 persons declared that they were invited by other caste people on ceremonial occasions. But after the liberation 127 declared that they were being invited by other caste people on such occasions.

No less significant is the case regarding taking water from common places along with other caste people and taking food in hotels and other places. In the pre-liberation period there were only 32 who took water from common places along with other caste people and 38 scavengers took food in hotels and other places. But in the post-liberation period the numbers were 142 and 138 respectively.

These furnished informations clearly reveal that there has been a significant impact of liberation on social relationships. The liberation has raised the status of these people in the eyes of the community and the traditional notion of untouchability is not strictly observed in their cases.

The liberated scavengers were further asked: 'Have you ever advised your relatives, who are in this profession, to stop this work?' All of them replied in the negative. Generally, the liberation has taken place through conversion of service latrines into *Sulabh Shauchalayas* and, consequently, where the liberation scheme has been started, the scavengers have been relieved of this sub-human job. There is, therefore, no question of advising the working scavengers to stop scavenging. They were also asked to state whether they were having intimate relations with those who were still engaged in scavenging work. It is significant to note that each of them replied in negative. It must be borne in mind that the respondents were also scavengers in the past.

They have been liberated in the recent past. There has been a change in their job, but their caste or sub-caste has remained unchanged. The scavengers are also from the same caste or sub-caste and have relations among those still unliberated. In spite of this the liberated scavengers do not have any intimate relation with scavengers. In informal conversation and through observation, it was gathered that the liberated scavengers were conscious that they did not do scavenging. In their talks, they declared with a sense of pride that they did not do this dirty job. It is obviously an impact of the liberation which has changed their traditional relations, attitudes, outlooks, approaches, patterns of interaction and social relations.

A few questions were also asked from the liberated scavengers to collect information about the educational status of their family members. One question put to the respondents was: 'Do you send your children to school?' The purpose was to find out the state of literacy and education in the younger genertion as also the changes in the attitude of the illiterate liberated scavengers. The collected informations suggest that in each town the majority has replied in the negative. The highest percentage of liberated scavengers sending their children to schools is from Patna (36%) and the lowest from Purnea (20%) (Table 53). It shows a significant relevance of the degree of urbanization to the favourable attitude towards the education of children. Among the three towns, Patna is the most urbanised and has a higher degree of urbanism, whereas, Purnea is the least urbanised town.

The table provides a classification of responses on income basis, but income does not appear to be a significant variable in determining the number of children being sent to school.

The scavengers who replied in the negative were further asked to give reasons for not sending their children to schools. In all, 96 were covered by this question. All of them stressed 'poor economic condition' or 'poverty' as the basic reason for it. It is also important to note that the Central and State Governments have provided considerable facilities, including free education, for the schooling of children belonging to Scheduled Castes. However, the liberated scavengers do not send their children to school because whatever little was needed was hard for them to give. It shows utter poverty of this section of society.

The people who sent their children to schools were asked how much education they wanted their children to receive. These 54 scavengers (36% of the total) were also asked to give their views separately for male and female. It was done keeping in view the fact that in an Indian society, in general, education of male children is considered more important than that of girls and, in the working section of the Indian society in particular, female education has remained almost 'nil'. It appears from the informations received that except a lower percentage of the scavengers from Patna, all other scavengers attach importance to education of their male children and do not want to impose any limit from their own side. As far as the education of girls is concerned, out of 24 from all the three towns who send their daughters to schools, 7 (29.1%) aspire to educate their daughters up to the matriculation stage, whereas 17 (70.8%) want the maximum possible education to be imparted to them.

The next question related to the availability of adequate facilities for study at home. The data obtained from them are analysed on income basis (Table 54). In each town, the highest percentage of response is negative. Only 18% scavengers from Ranchi, 12% from Purnea and 36% from Patna, said that they were having adequate facilities at home. The highest percentage showing the existence of such facility is in Patna and the lowest in Purnea. This pattern is again consistent with the degree of urbanization. Towns having higher urbanization level and a higher degree of urbanism provide such facilities to a higher percentage of scavengers whereas those having a lower degree of urbanism have such facilities in a lower percentage. The table also reveals the variation of responses in different income-groups, though income has not been found to be a significant and relevant variable in this regard.

The next question put to the scavengers was: 'Do your children study at home ?' The informations given by them reveal that on the whole, according to 36% of the scavengers their children studied at home, while 46.7% replied in the negative. In the case of 17.3% the question was not applicable because their children did not go to schools (Table 55). Thus, a relatively higher percentage of them declared that their children did not study at home. It may be due to inadequate facilitiy or due to lack of environment motivating the children to study at home. As the class of liberated scavengers has remained backward not only from the social and economic points of view, but also from the educational viewpoint and the liberated scavengers are either illiterate or semi-literate, they do not realize the importance of study at home nor are they very serious about it.

The scavengers, whose replies were negative, were further

asked to give reasons for it. This question was put to 70 persons who stated that their children did not read at home. All of them declared that lack of space was the main cause. At the same time, they admitted that lack of interest was the second basic reason for this state of affair. They said that the children could study outside the room, house or hutment in the open field on a mat and with the help of lantern if they had real interest and keen desire for their study. One may, therefore, conclude that poor economic condition and lack of interest among the children of this section of society are the basic reasons for that state of affairs.

Another question the scavengers were asked was about discrimination with their children in class rooms because of their caste. There was only one solitary case of a family in Purnea where discrimination was felt by the wards, whereas in all other cases there was a negative reply. It means that, in general, the children of the liberated scavengers do not experience any discrimination in their classes either from other students or from teachers becasue of their belonging to the *Bhangi* caste. It suggests that discriminatory behaviour on caste basis is not found in schools.

They were also asked to inform about the persons who encouraged their children to continue their studies. One scavenger said that his children were encouraged by relatives and one stated that her children were encouraged by friends, whereas all other scavengers declared that their own family members encouraged their children to study. On this basis it may be interpreted that there is no agency to propagate education in this class or section of the community and the family members themselves take the initiative in sending children to school.

In most cases the liberated scavengers themselves met the expenses over the education of their children. Only in 14 cases out of 49, the facilities provided by the Government have been mentioned as the source of children's education. It suggests that most of them are either not aware of the facilities provided by the Government or they are being deprived of these facilities. It is also possible that they are required to spend something over books and dress for their children for which they do not get any financial assistance from the Government, which is why they are required to meet these expenses out of their earnings. However, the liberated scavengers are not satisfied with the assistance provided by the Government for the education of their children. They feel that the Government should provide adequate financial help, either in cash or in kind, according to their needs and requirements. In case full financial facilities are provided to the section of liberated scavengers, the condition of literacy may improve and the younger generation may receive higher education.

A number of questions were asked to the liberated scavengers about the employment condition and other problems related to employment and job preferences. The number of persons in need of employment in different families were also found out to assess the existing conditions of employment. It is evident from the informations that in the case of families of liberated scavengers from Ranchi 21 declared that only one male member of each family needed employment, whereas six stated that two male members of each family needed it (Table 56). Ten and one respondents said that one and two female members of the family respectively needed employment. It means that in the case of the respondents from Ranchi, 23 families do not face any problem of unemployment for males, whereas 39 are not faced with the problem of unemployment for females. The table further shows that in Purnea town no male member in 39 out of 50 families and no female member in 28 out of 50 families need employment. Hence, also the majority of families are not seriously faced with the unemployment problem. In Patna, out of 50 scavengers 24 said that no male member needed job whereas 21 declared that no woman in their families needed employment. The table reveals that 76.56% of the scavengers' families having job problem for men have only one unemployed male member, 18.75% have two unemployed male members, 3.12% have three and 1.56% have four unemployed male members. In the case of female unemployed members, 69.35% of the respondents mentioned only one female member, 25.81% mentioned two female members, 3.23% mentioned three female members and 1.61% as four female members. Thus, it appears that the problem of unemployment for men and women is more acute in Patna, than in Ranchi and Purnea.

On the whole, the table shows that out of 150 families of the respondents 86 do not have any unemployed male member and 88 do not have any unemployed female member. The problem of unemployment, therefore, exists in the rest of the families. It may, however, be stated that this problem may not exist for those who have been liberated; it is rather for those family members who do not want to take up the scavenging job and are in need of some other employment. The persistence of this unemployment problem in the families of liberated scavengers demands that for eradicating the evil of scavenging the male and female members should be provided with some alternative jobs. In case they are not provided with jobs, they may go to those places where scavenging still exists and they may be compelled by circumstances to take up the scavenging work.

The next question put to the scavengers was, therefore, to find out the nature of employment their family members needed. A list of the types of jobs and occupations was provided to them and they were asked to check up the jobs they felt adequate for them. Their views indicate that the highest percentage of response for male members in need of employment has gone in favour of 'any other' (53%) (Table 57). It shows that these scavengers do not have any clear idea of the nature of the job for the needy family members. As many 48% of the scavengers suggested acceptability of the peon's job for the male members, whereas 44% opted for jobs in an industry. The job of a mechanic or driver was preferred by 25% of them and a job in the police department was preferred by 14%. Only 9% favoured clerical jobs for the unemployed male members of the family. This low percentage in favour of clerical jobs is obviously due to the realization of the fact that only educated persons may get this job and hence, only those mentioned here, are matriculates or above.

The table further shows that in the case of the scavengers of Ranchi and Purnea, the highest percentage of response has gone in favour of 'any other' job whereas in the case of Patna this has gone in favour of the peon's job. The lowest percentage in favour of clerical job is in Patna (2.9%) and the highest in Ranchi (14.3%). The job of a driver or mechanic is most favoured in Patna (40%) and least preferred in Ranchi (14.3%). On the other hand, a job in the Police Department is most preferred in Ranchi (28.6%) and least favoured in Patna (5.7%). Thus, the inherent ambitions of the scavengers from the three towns showing preference for jobs are not alike.

The informations in respect of employment for women show that on the whole the highest percentage has gone in favour of the job of maid-servants (61%). The peon's job for women is preferred by 41% of the scavengers, whereas that of the nurse has been preferred by 27%.

The informations reveal that in Ranchi town 'any other' job is most preferred by men (82.9%), whereas the majority of women in Purnea have favoured the job of maid-servants (70%). In the case of Patna, the highest percentage has gone in favour of the job of maid-servant (82.9%). The least preferred job in all the three towns is that of a nurse. The reason is quite obvious. The nursing profession needs education and professional or vocational training in which the female members of the liberated scavengers are generally lacking. Only those scavengers could opt for the nursing job in whose families the women were educated.

The scavengers were also asked: 'Did you ever try to get jobs for your family members?' It is evident from that 40% of the scavengers replied in the affirmative, 22% in the negative and 38% did not give any definite response (Table 58). It means that less than 50% of the scavengers tried to get jobs for their family members. It shows lack of initiative on the part of most unemployed persons, may be due to illiteracy or lack of information about the jobs. The table further shows that in Ranchi 46%, in Purnea 32% and in Patna 42% of the scavengers or their family members tried to obtain jobs. Thus, it appears that in all the three towns the majority has not taken any initiative for solving the problem of unemployment in the families.

Those scavengers who replied in negative were asked to give reasons for not taking any initiative in this regard. All of them declared that they did not have any *pairvi* and, hence, they did not try. On the other hand, those who tried to get jobs were asked to give details. Almost all the scavengers declared that they were given only false assurances. The frustration of those making efforts for jobs might be, therefore, responsible for developing the impression that people failed in getting jobs because they did not have *pairvi*. This impression stopped others from making vain efforts. It may, therefore, be said that the actual results leading to frustration and disappointment are responsible for stopping others from making efforts for jobs. This situation is very sad. If the occupation of scavenging is to be done away with, special attention will have to be paid to the joblessness of the males and females of the families of liberated scavengers and efforts have to be made for their employment, otherwise they may be compelled by circumstances to take up the scavenging job at some other places.

The above stated facts throw adequate light on employment condition, social life and economy of the liberated scavengers and their families. It is obvious that the process of liberation has not contributed to any significant change in their poor economic condition. The earning has remained unchanged and there has been only a change in the nature of work. Consequently, the living condition is a major obstacle in improving the condition of literacy and education in the younger generation of this section of society.

The extreme educational backwardness even in the younger generation is not only due to poverty, but also due to lack of adequate social consciousness. The scavengers do not realise the importance of education and, hence, in spite of the facilities provided for free education to Harijan youths, it is not being fully availed by them. It also came to light that many of these liberated scavengers are not aware of the facilities provided to them. On the front of socio-cultural life in the community, is has been gathered that a free mixing with caste people is not found, though some healthy trends have definitely developed.

It is also significant to note that the liberated scavengers have shown discriminatory behaviour with unliberated scavengers still engaged in cleaning and carrying night-soil. It means that on the one hand they complain against the discriminatory behaviour of caste Hindus and on the other they are themselves developing similar approach. The findings analysed above further reveal that the liberated scavengers do not want their children to take up scavenging work. They want their children to be provided with any job other than scavenging. They do not aspire for a superior job in an unrealistic way and realise that due to educational backwardness their children can be given low paid jobs.

But the view expressed by them indicate that they want certain vocational training for their children and better rehabilitation. In this way some changes in their thinking and orientation are definitely taking place after their liberation.

CHAPTER 7

Non-adopters and Adopters

I. Non-adopters

THE THIRD SET of schedule was prepared for collecting information from non-adopters of the low-cost sanitation scheme introduced by the *Sulabh Shauchalaya Sansthan*. As discussed in the earlier chapter, the term 'non-adopter' has been used for those who are still having service latrines in their houses and have not adopted the *Sulabh Shauchalaya* system. The non-adopters, covered in the present study are from the three towns, of Patna, Muzaffarpur and Arrah. These were chosen for impact analysis because in all these towns a large number of people have converted their service latrines into *Sulabh Shauchalayas*. However, a sizeable section of society has not yet adopted the *Sulabh Shauchalaya* system and continues to have service latrine which requires scavengers. As many as 50 non-adopters were selected from each of the three towns.

Thus, a total of 150 non-adopters have been covered by the study. Preliminary information was collected about the personality identification of the non-adopters such as name, age, sex, educational qualification, religion, caste, occupation, annual income, marital status, birth place and period of stay in the town. As regards age composition it appears from collected informations from the three towns that only in Arrah there is one non-adopter in the youngest age-group of up to 20 years. No person from Patna or Muzzaffarpur belongs to this age-group (Table 59). On the whole, the highest percentage of non-adopters (28.7%) belongs to the age-group of 41-50 years and the lowest percentage (0.7%) to the lowest age-group and 8% to the age-group of 71 years and above. It means that the non-adopter interviewees are distributed in different age-groups in all the three towns.

In the same way the analysis of sex distribution suggests that 91.3% from the three towns are males and only 8.7% are females

(Table 60). That is because female members from only those families or households were interviewed where male members were not available. This explains why in all the three towns the percentage of male interviewees is very high and only 4%, 12% and 10% from Patna, Muzaffarpur and Arrah respectively are females.

The collected facts also indicate that some of the non-adopters are highly qualified. On the whole, 11.3% from the three towns are illiterate, 32% have read up to the middle standard and are literate; 40.7% are matriculates, 7.3% are intermediates, 7.3% are graduates and 1.3% post-graduates (Table 61). It means that 15.9% of the non-adopters are above the matriculation standard and the reamining 84.1% are matriculates or below this level and educational backwardness cannot be considered as the only factor standing in the way of adoption. Moreover, these non-adopters are both Hindus and Muslims in the ratio of 78% and 22% (Table 62). It is also found that from each town the sample includes both Muslim and Hindu non-adopters. In the case of Patna, the precentage of Muslims is slightly lower (18%) than from Muzaffarpur or Arrah (24%).

It is evident that 37.3% of the non-adopters belong to the upper castes, 56% to the lower castes and 6.6% to the Scheduled Castes (Table 63). No person from the Scheduled Castes is included in the sample from Arrah town whereas the percentage of the Scheduled Castes is the same from Patna and Muzaffarpur towns (10%). The highest percentage of non-adopters from the lower castes is in Arrah (62%) and the lowest in Muzaffarpur (48%).

The non-adopters also differ from each other in respect of occupation and means of earning livelihood 39.3% of them are in business and 33.3% in service (Table 64). In all other categories, the percentages are very less than 8%. Generally, the non-aopters covered by the present study are either in service or in business.

Regarding the income composition of the sample, it has been found that the annual earning of the non-adopters ranges from Rs. 3,000 to Rs. 18,000. The highest percentage (38.7%) is in the income group of Rs. 3,000-6,000 per annum and the second highest percentage (32%) is in the group of Rs. 6000-9000. A small section of 2.7% has, however, an income up to Rs. 3000 per annum.

Of these non-adopters, 90.7% are married, 2.7% unmarried and

6.7% are widows. Thus, they are mostly married. The reason is obvious. Only those persons have been included in the sample who are the heads of the family or perform an important function in the family life. Where such family heads, whether traditional or functional, have not been available, information has been obtained from other family members.

They have also given information about their period of stay in towns. All those persons who were born in towns (91.3%) have been living there since birth. All these non-adopters covered by the present study are exposed to the socio-cultural climate of the city life.

These facts concerning the personal identification of the non-adopters suggest that the non-adopters constituting the sample do not form a homogeneous group by the sameness of their caste, faith, literacy, income or occupation. They belong to different age and income groups. They come from different castes, both Hindu and Muslim. They practise different professions and have varying levels of educational qualification. Hence, the sample of the non-adopters taken from each town is heterogeneous and represents a complex heterogeneous character of the urban community life.

The next question related to the maximum qualification acquired by the members of the families of the non-adopters. It was post-graduate in one family of Patna, two of Muzaffarpur and two of Arrah. Eight from Patna and 14 from Muzaffarpur as well as from Arrah informed that the maximum qualification was graduate. As many as 29 from Patna, 14 from Muzaffapur and 15 from Arrah declared that the maximum educational qualification in the family was matriculation. It shows that the condition of education is not very satisfactory. It was also found that the condition of education was slightly better in families having relatively higher income and belonging to upper castes. In the same way, information about the minimum qualification of familty members reveals that no family in Patna has an illiterate member, whereas only one family each of Muzaffarpur and Arrah has one illiterate member. Forty-nine non-adopters of Patna, 46 of Muzaffapur and 44 of Arrah declared that the minimum qualification was up to middle standard. Hence, it seems that the educational attainment is not high and, in general, most of the family members are only literate.

Information was also collected from them about the number of adults, both male and female, as also of earning members in their families. It was found that three families had 14-18 adult members, both male and female, whereas 6.7% had 10-12, 34.7% had 6-8 and 57% had 2-4 adult members. The informations in respect of the number of earning hands in the family reveal that only in one family there are six or more earning hands, in 1.3% the number is 5, in 4% it is 4, in 14.7% the number is 3; whereas in 27.3% of the families there are two and 52% have only one earning hand in the family. A comparative analysis suggests that all the adult male members are not earning. It may be due to the fact that in most cases only male adults are engaged in some earning job. When the number of male adults and earning hands are taken into consideration, it is found that in 47.3% of the cases there are 1-2 male adults whereas 52% of the families have one and 27.3% have two earning hands. Hence, it may be interpreted that most of the adult members are earning and engaged in one type of job or the other.

Information about the family income per year was also obtained along with the sources of income. The data obtained reveal that 22.7% families have an annual income of Rs. 3,000 to Rs. 6.000; (31.3%), Rs. 6,000 to Rs. 9,000, (16.7%) Rs. 9,000 to Rs. 12,000, (10%); Rs. 12,000 to Rs. 15,000 (5.3%); Rs. 15,000 to Rs. 18,000 and 14% above Rs. 18,000. It means that 29.3% of the families of respondents have an income of above Rs. 12,000 per annum, whereas 70.7% have an income of up to Rs. 1,000. In view of the size of the family and higher cost of living, the income is not very high. In most cases, the source of income is either service or business. As many as 38.3% families have jobs and the same percentage mentioned business as the source. Cultivation was mentioned by 7.4%, labour or wage-earning by 7.9%, whereas 4.8% mentioned house rent and 3.2% mentioned medical or legal practice as the source of income. It is also important to point out that only one source of income was not mentioned by all the non-adopters, rather some of them mentioned two or more sources of income in the family. It may be either due to the involvement of two or more adult members in earning jobs or due to side income in certain cases.

For analysing the family size, information was also collected about the number of children as also those of school and college-going children in the family. It was found that in 47.3% of the cases there were 1-2 male children and in 54.7% 1-2 female children in the family. Only 1.3% of the respondents stated that there were 7-8 female children, whereas 7-8 male children were mentioned by 2.7%. On the whole, most of them mentioned fewer than three female and the same number of male children in their families. But in case the same person mentioned one or two male children and the same number of female children, the total number of children would become two-four. Hence, in a majority of cases the number of children is not very large, though in certain cases it is more than two, both male and female.

The informations about the number of school-going children suggest that in a considerable percentage (36% in case of male children and 42% in case of female children) it was declared that no child was school-going. In 40.7% of male and 46.7% of female children the number of school-going children was 1-2. In respect of the number of college-going male and female youths, 92% and 81.3% of the interviewees informed that no female and male youth was attending college. It clearly suggests that in the case of non-adopters education is not very common and in most of the families higher education is selective. It may be either due to the poor economic condition or social backwardness of the non-adopters in a large number of cases.

The type of houses in which they live also throws light on the living and economic condition of the non-adopters covered by the study. In Patna only 20%, in Muzaffarpur 44% and in Arrah 44% live in *pucca* houses. As many as 38% of the non-adopters in Patna, 22% in Muzaffarpur and 14% in Arrah live in *kutchcha* houses whereas 42% in Patna, 34% in Muzaffarpur and 42% in Arrah live in mixed type of houses. It means that more than 50% of the non-adopters live either in *kutchcha* or mixed type of houses. It is also important to point out that all these non-adopters are not owners of houses, rather in most of the cases they are tenants.

The information about civic amenities reveals that 74% of Patna and Muzaffarpur and 72% of Arrah live in electrified houses, whereas the remaining non-adopters and their families are not enjoying this basic civic amenity even in urban areas. In the same way, the information obtained from them reveals that 46% of the non-adopters of Patna, 52% of Muzaffarpur and 32% of

Arrah have water taps, whereas 8% of Patna, 2% of Muzaffarpur and 12% of Arrah have only wells as the source of drinking water. As many as 8% of Patna, 0% of Muzaffarpur and 4% of Arrah have both water-taps and wells, whereas 2% of Patna, 18% of Muzaffarpur and 14% of Arrah have only hand pipes. It was also found that 36% of Patna and 28% of Arrah do not have either of these facilities. It means that a considerable section of the non-adopters is deprived of this basic civic amenity. Only 10% of the families of Patna 2% of Muzaffarpur and 4% of Arrah lived in newly-built houses whereas an overwhelming majority of the non-adopters and their families lived either in old or very old houses whether ancestral or rented. In all these houses only the service latrine system is operative.

It was also enquired from the non-adopters if they had any knowledge of *Sulabh Shauchalaya*. It came to light that all of them in Patna as well as Muzaffarpur knew about it and only two illiterate non-adopters of Arrah were unaware of it.

The next question asked from them was: 'How did you come to know about the *Sulabh Shauchalaya* Scheme?' A list of possible sources of information was also provided to them. A total of 286 responses have been obtained from 150 non-adopters (Tables 65 and 66). It means that some of them have given two or more sources of information.

It is also found that the highest percentage of non-adopters (66.7%) knew about this scheme through the *Sulabh International*. The next highest percentage has gone in favour of adopters (38%). As many as 32.7% came to know about this scheme through Public *Sulabh Shauchalaya* complex, whereas 23.3% knew it through the mass media like newspapers and radio. Only 8.7% could know it through friends and relatives and 13.3% through neighbours. Thus, the most effective agency propagating the *Sulabh Shauchalaya* scheme is the *Sulabh International* itself and also those who have adopted the scheme in these towns.

The classification of information on the basis of education (Table 65) shows that in all the categories of non-adopters the most important agency is the *Sulabh International* and, hence, the variable of literacy is not significant. In the same way, the classification of responses on caste basis (Table 66) shows that in the categories of upper and lower castes the highest percentages have replied in favour of the *Sulabh International* and only in case of Scheduled Castes the highest percentage of response has gone in favour of adopters (70%) and the second highest percentage (50%) in favour of the *Sulabh International.* Thus, in almost all cases or categories the most effective agency educating people about the *Sulabh Shauchalaya* scheme is the *Sulabh International.*

Another question put to the non-adopters was: 'If you know about the *Sulabh Shauchalaya* scheme, what is your impression about it'? A list of alternative responses was provided to them. The most important impressions expressed by the non-adopters are (1) 'It is economical', (2) 'It does not give foul smell', (3) 'It is better than the service latrine system', (4) 'It gives manure'. And 98.7% of them gave the impression that it was preferable to the service latrine system. As many as 68% held the view that it was economical, whereas 20% declared that 'it gives manure'. On the other hand, 73.3% mentioned that it did not require scavenging and, thus, led to the liberation of scavengers.

The non-adopters were also asked to state the problems they face due to the service latrine system in their houses. It appears from the views expressed by them that 100% realise that the service latrine system is unhygienic (Tables 67 and 68). As many as 74.6% declared that due to irregular scavenging the foul smell sometimes became unbearable. As many as 54.6% of them declared that 'when scavenging is being done there is a very bad smell in the house'. According to 28.7% of the non-adopters 'it gives foul smell'. As many as 9.3% complained of irregular scavenging and 4.7% stated: 'When the scavenger comes, someone of us is to supply water and ashes for cleaning the latrine'. Thus, it appears that the unhygienic condition of service latrines and foul smell on different occasions are two basic problems faced by the non-adopters due to the service latrine system in their houses.

The classification of responses on the basis of occupation (Table 67) does not show much variation in different occupational groups and more or less the same percentage has expressed different types of problems in each category. In the same way, the classification on the basis of the educational level (Table 68) does not show relevance of literacy level. Thus, in all categories the two basic problems of unhygienic condition and foul smell are faced and have been mentioned.

On the basis of different questions the non-adopters were also asked to give their views on the scavenging and cleaning system in different ways. The questions put to them were: (1) Do you think that scavenging is much below the dignity of a human being? (2) Do you agree that scavenging is an evil in the society? (3) Are you in favour of a total ban on scavenging? (4) Do you desire to convert the latrine system of your own house into the *Sulabh Shauchalaya* system? (5) Do you favour the view that scavenging is a negation of social justice? and (6) Do you think that a real welfare society cannot be set up in India so long as the traditional scavenging system persists?

In reply to each of these questions all of them stated 'yes'. It suggests that all the non-adopters are opposed to the scavenging system and regard it as a sub-human occupation. They also realise that scavenging is a social evil and it should be eradicated from Indian society. They also support the view that the ideal of social justice cannot be achieved so long as scavenging persists in society. Moreover, they also agree to this view point that a welfare State cannot be possible in India so long as the scavenging system operates and, in case we want to have a welfare society in the real sense of the term, we must do away with the scavenging profession. Moreover, their expressed views lead to the inference that the non-adopters are also not in favour of the sub-human work of scavenging. But at the same time, they realise that attention should be paid to the rehabilitation of the liberated scavengers. Those who are already in the service of municipalities and corporations are given alternative jobs by their employers, but those who are to become scavengers in future can be stopped from doing the scavenging work only when some alternative is provided and some other means of livelihood is available to them.

The next question put to them was: 'Has anybody in your neighbourhood adopted the *Sulabh Shauchalaya* system?' The furnished informations reveal that in Patna 26, in Muzaffarpur 18 and in Arrah 17 declared that their neighbours had adopted the *Sulabh Shauchalaya* system.

In all the three towns, a sizeable section of people has adopted the *Sulabh Shauchalaya* system doing away with service latrines. The next question put to the non-adopters was if their neighbours had ever complained against this system. It is obvious that this question was applicable to only those 61 non-adopters whose neighbours had adopted the *Sulabh Shauchalaya* system. They informed that there was practically no complaint. The scheme was working satisfactorily and the adopters were satisfied in these three towns.

The non-adopters were asked to give 'reason' for not adopting the *Sulabh Shauchalaya* system. The most important reason mentioned by most of them was that they did not have adequate funds to convert the service latrines into the *Sulabh Shauchalaya* system. The next important reason mentioned by some of them was that they were not fully acquainted with the method of adoption as the scheme was introduced late in their towns.

In the light of the findings from the study of non-adopters it may be stated that the continuance of the service latrine system is not persisting because the people like it or they want to have it. The poor economic condition of house-owners is the main factor for the persistence of the service latrine system. In some cases, the non-adopters do not know the procedure of conversion of the service latrine into *Sulabh Shauchalaya*. Indirectly, it means that they have not been provided any technical guidance or financial assistance, including subsidy. Hence, in such cases this factor has also been responsible for the non-conversion of service latrines into *Sulabh Shauchalayas*. However, all the non-adopters know about *Sulabh Shauchalaya* and realise that this system is preferable to service latrine. These non-adopters also admit that scavenging is a sub-human job and negates the principle of social justice. They favour the idea of liberation of scavengers and want the dry latrine system to go.

But due to lack of adequate knowledge about the technical know-how and poor economic condition, they have not adopted the sanitary latrine system. In case they are provided with necessary technical and economic assistance, they may adopt *Sulabh Shauchalaya* scheme. Hence, it appears that neither in ideology nor in value context, they are opposed to the adoption of low-cost sanitation scheme and the non-adoption is due to some hurdles which are beyond their control. It is, therefore, evident that *Sulabh Shauchalaya* Scheme is known even to these non-adopters and working of *Sulabh International* has proved significantly instrumental in popularising the low-cost sanitation scheme.

II. ADOPTERS

The fourth set of the sample covered by the present study includes the adopters of the *Sulabh Shauchalaya* scheme. As already stated in the chapter on the Study Design, the three towns selected for the study of adopters are Patna, Madhubani and Chaibasa. From each town 50 adopters have been selected and, thus, a sample of 150 adopters from the three towns has been covered by this study. The information collected from the adopters on the basis of an interview schedule is concerned with their personal identification, details about family life, social and economic conditions of the families and problems related to the knowledge and adoption of *Sulabh Shauchalaya* and their experiences about it.

As regards the adopters, it may be stated that the sample from each town and also as a whole is heterogeneous when persons differ in age, sex, education, religion, caste, occupation, marital status, personal income and the period of stay in town. From all the three towns the respondents belong to different age groups, ranging from 21-30 years to 71 years and above. Only in the case of Madhubani, 8% are in the age group of up to 20 years. But in most cases the adopters are above 40 years. It is because efforts were made to contact the heads of families for conducting interviews and collecting information. In case the male family head was not available, female family heads were contacted.

In some cases other responsible members of the families were interviewed. Hence, in Patna 34% and in Chaibasa 22% are females whereas in Madhubani 100% are males. It means that in the case of Madhubani the patriarchs or male adults were available and, hence, the female adults were not interviewed.

The information obtained reveals that the adopters include educated, semi-educated, literate and illiterate persons. As many as 4% of Patna, 20% of Madhubani and 10% of Chaibasa are illiterate whereas 60%, 32% and 30% respectively of these towns are educated up to the middle standard. In the same way, 22% of Patna, 24% of Madhubani and 40% of Chaibasa are matriculates and 2%, 10% and 14% respectively are educated up to intermediate stage whereas 12% and 6% are graduates. Only one person from Madhubani was holding the post-graduate degree,

(*Left to Right*) Shashillaya Devi and Jhamni Devi after liberation. (Photo from Patna)

Shashillaya Devi and Jhamni Devi, when they were scavengers in Ranchi, carrying night-soil on the head. There is no measure of their miseries.

(*Top*) *Liberated folks*: These are the liberated scavengers of the Ranchi Municipal Corporation.
(*Bottom*) *The liberated women*: They were scavengers before liberation. And, now settled in families practising other professions. (Photo Ranchi, Bihar).

but no such degree was possessed by any adopter of Patna or Chaibasa. On the whole, 19.4% of the adopters of the three towns are having intermediate or above qualification and the remaining 80.6% are either illiterate, literate or having educational qualification up to the matriculation standard.

In Patna, the adopters are divided into three religious communities of Muslims (8%), Hindus (24%) and Sikhs (68%), but in the case of Madhubani and Chaibasa only Muslims and Hindus are included as adopters in the sample. On the whole, 32% of the adopters are Muslims, 45.3% Hindus and 22.7% Sikhs. It is also important to note that in Patna, most adopters are Sikhs. In the same way, the adopters are divided into different castes. On the whole, 40% belong to upper castes, 57.3% to lower castes, 2% to Scheduled Castes and 0.7% to Scheduled Tribes. There was only one Scheduled Tribe adopter in Chaibasa. There was no Scheduled Caste adopter in Madhubani, whereas there was one such adopter in Patna and two in Chaibasa. The adopters included in the sample are also heterogeneous from the point of view of occupation. Whereas 17.3% are in service, 42.7% in business and 7.3% are working as labourers, 6.7% of them are retired and 18.7% are housewives. Only 2.7% are engaged in cultivation and 4.7% are having no engagement.

Thus, the sample includes persons from different occupational categories. The personal income of the adopters differs from up to Rs. 3.000 to above Rs. 18,000 per annum. On the whole 25.3% have practically no income. It includes those who are either housewives, unemployed or retired with no post-retirement benefit, i.e. pension. But with the rise in the income level the percentage of adopters has declined.

The adopters are also subject to classification on the basis of marital status. On the whole, 90.7% are married, 5.3% are unmarried and 4% are widowed. The reason is quite obvious. As care was taken to select the head of the family for the interview, the percentage of married persons was bound to be high. The information obtained from these persons also reveals that they have different periods of stay in town. Only 2.7% of them are staying for a period up to 10 years whereas in all the other cases the period of stay is more than 10 years and in most of the cases it is more than 30 years. Hence, it appears that either the adopters are living in urban areas since their birth or early days of life or they have lived there for a considerably long period.

In the light of the above findings it appears that the sample covered by the present study is heterogeneous not only from the social and economic points of view, but also in respect of the age structure, sex and the marital status. Thus, the adopters of the *Sulabh Shauchalaya* scheme are not confined to any particular income or occupation group or to any particular caste or community, rather persons from different castes and communities and having different occupations and levels of income have adopted the scheme. Moreover, the adopters are not only educated, but also semi-educated and uneducated. Hence, it may be stated that the *Sulabh Shauchalaya* scheme is being accepted and adopted not by any particular section of the society, but by different sections and groups from the point of view of social, economic and cultural background.

Reports collected from the adopters regarding their family life suggest that the families of the adopters included both literate and illiterate members. But, the collected facts clearly suggest that the number of illiterate adopters is considerably lower as compared to those of literate adopters in all the three towns. This fact is further strengthened by the information about the number of educated members in the family. In Patna, 34%, in Madhubani 48% and in Chaibasa 12% of the adopters declared that there was no educated member in the family. It means that in all the three towns more than 50% of the families of the adopters have educated members. In Chaibasa, a tribal area, Christian missionaries have been working for a long period for educating people and, hence, education is relatively more common in this town than in Madhubani or in Patna.

Along with asking questions about the personal income, informations were also collected about the total family income and its sources. The information furnished by the adopters suggests that family income also ranges from Rs. 3,000 to above Rs. 18,000 per annum. As many as 22.7% of the families of the adopters earn more than Rs. 12,000 per year. It means that this percentage has an income of more than Rs. 1,000 per month, whereas 77.3% have Rs. 1,000 per month or less. Hence, it may be stated that their economic condition is not satisfactory. The most important source of income in the three towns appears to be business, because, on the whole, 52.3% have mentioned business as the source of family income.

The next important source appears to be service, mentioned by 30.5%. As many as 7.5% have mentioned cultivation as the source of family income whereas 6.3% have informed that labour or manual work is the source of family income. Only 2.3% have mentioned house-rent and 1.1% medical and legal practice as the source of income in the family. It is also important to point out that the total number of adopters is 150 whereas the total number of responses has been found to be 174. It means that some of them have mentioned more than one source as the sources of family income. It may be either due to two or more earning hands in the family or side income through house-rent or cultivation.

The information about the number of earning members, reveals that according to 50.7% there is only one earning member, whereas according to 32% there are two earning hands. As many as 12% of them informed that there were three earning members in their families, whereas only 5.3% declared that there were four earning hands. It means that in majority of cases only one person is earning and he is to support the family, but in a considerable percentage there are two or more earning hands. It is obvious that in case there are two or more earning hands, the income may be relatively higher and there may be more than one source of income also in the family. Keeping in view the number of more than one earning hand in 49.3% of the cases, it may be stated that the earning or family income is not very high. Hence, it may be interpreted that those who are engaged in service or business do not earn a sizeable amount and either they are doing petty business or are engaged in services with low income or salary.

Informations were also collected from the adopters of the *Sulabh Shauchalaya* system about their association with the scheme, their knowledge about it, the reason for adopting the scheme and the after-effects of adoption. The first question put to them in this regard was: 'Is any member of your family associated with the *Sulabh International* in any capacity?' The purpose of asking this question was to find out whether they adopted the scheme because someone in their family was associated with the *Sulabh International* or they adopted the scheme due to some other reason. In response to this question, all of them replied in negative. It means that in no case the adopter had any prior relation with the *Sulabh International*.

The next question put to them was: 'which of the following systems did you have in your house before adopting the *Sulabh Shauchalaya* system?' On the whole, it appears from the informations furnished by the adopters that 78.7% had service latrines and 4.7% had *Sandas* before adopting the *Sulabh Shauchalaya* system (Table 69). As many as 10% had no latrine in their houses and used open space for defecation, whereas 4.7% used community latrines. Hence, in general the adopters were having the service latrine system or they did not have any place for defecation in their houses prior to adopting the *Sulabh Shauchalaya* system. The percentage showing the septic latrine system is very small and does not serve as a basis for giving any interpretative analysis. As there is no specific variation in response patterns, the analysis of the significance of any variable is not required. But this much can be stated that in the case of Scheduled Caste and Scheduled Tribe adopters, no family used open space or community latrine.

The next question put to them was: 'How did you come to know about the *Sulabh Shauchalaya*'? Along with asking this question a list of alternative sources of information was provided to them.

It is evident from the informations that the adopters came to know about the *Sulabh Shauchalaya* system through various sources. The most important source among these is the *Sulabh International* agency which has been mentioned by 94.7% of the adopters (Tables 70 and 71). The second important source of information is the adopter, mentioned by 34.7%. As many as 8.7% came to know about it through friends and relatives 5.3% through municipalities, 4.7% through mass conversion or mass media and 0.7% through technical experts. In popularising the *Sulabh Shauchalaya* system the most effective role has been played by the *Sulabh International* agency and the mass contact as well as the education imparted by it has proved most significant in the adoption of the *Sulabh Shauchalaya* system. It is also important to note that the total number of responses is 230, whereas the total number of adopters is only 150. It means that a considerable number of adopters have mentioned two or more sources through which they came to know about the *Sulabh Shauchalaya* system.

The classification of responses on occupation basis (Table 70) suggests that excepting categories of labourers and businessmen, in all other occupational categories 100% mentioned the *Sulabh International* as the sources of information. In case of labour adopters 72.7% and in case of businessmen 94.2% mentioned this source. Hence, it may be stated that in all occupational categories the most important source has been the *Sulabh International* agency. There was only one businessman who mentioned technical expert as the source of information about *Sulabh Shauchalaya*. In all the occupational categories a considerable percentage mentioned the adopters also as the source of information. Except the category of service-holders, the second important source has been adopters in all other categories.

Hence, occupation does not appear to be a significant variable in this regard. In the same way, the classification of responses on the basis of literacy and education (Table 71) reveals that in all categories the highest percentage of response is in favour of the *Sulabh International* agency and the second highest is in respect of adopters. The literacy variable also does not appear to be significant in this regard.

The next question put to them was: 'Please mention the reason for abandoning the previous system operating in your house'. It would appear from the obtained informations (Tables 72 and 73) that the total number of responses is 333. It means that more than one reason has been mentioned by a considerable number of adopters. As many as 80.7% of them declared that the previous system was unhygienic; 32% said that they were faced with scavenging problem and, hence, they abandoned the previous latrine system; 44.7% had pointed out that there is no sewerage system and, hence, they had abandoned the previous system and adopted *Sulabh Shauchalaya*. As many as 26.7% declared that the previous system was costly because it involved regular expenses over cleaning whereas 14.7% have abandoned the previous system because of foul smell of service latrines and *Sandas*. It means that in most cases the troubles arising from the service latrine system have been responsible for adopting the *Sulabh Shauchalaya* scheme.

The given reasons suggest that the experience of the service latrine system or *sandas* is not pleasant and with a suitable alternative provided in the form of *Sulabh Shauchalaya* at relatively lower cost, they adopted it. Hence, along with other merits of the *Sulabh Shauchalaya* system its feature of being a low-cost sanitation scheme has been most instrumental in the adoption of this system.

The classification of responses on caste basis (Table 72) and on literacy and education basis (Table 73) do not present any specific variation in response patterns on the basis of either of the two variables and, hence, the variables are not significantly relevant to the reasons for adopting the scheme.

The following question asked from them was: 'In what way did you adopt the *Sulabh Shauchalaya* system?' A list of alternative ways was provided to them and the informations given by the adopters reveal that 78.7% adopted the *Sulabh Shauchalaya* system by converting service latrines into *Sulabh Shauchalaya* (Table 74). And 14.7% constructed Sulabh Shauchalayas for the first time whereas 4.7% converted the *sandas* system into the *Sulabh* system. It means that those who defecated in the open o: used community latrines constructed *Sulabh Shauchalayas* in their houses and these were new constructions. It is also found that the construction of new *Sulabh Shauchalayas* has been in the highest percentage in categories showing a low level of education. The reason is quite obvious. In the case of families of educated adopters one or the other type of the system was already existing and, hence, they did not have new constructions in most of the cases whereas in the families of illiterates and semi-literates, no system was operating in the houses and hence the percentages showing new constructions are higher.

Another question asked from them was: 'What inspired you to adopt the *Sulabh Shauchalaya* system?' A list of alternative response categories was provided and they were asked to check whatever applied in their cases. It would appear from the furnished informations that the total number of responses is 588 (Table 75). All the adopters declared that the *Sulabh Shauchalaya* was hygienic and, hence, they adopted this system. As many as 83.3% have adopted it because this system does not give foul smell. According to 78.0% this system does not require scavenging. And 61.3% hold the view that the *Sulabh* system is the best system in the absence of sewerage facility; 33.3% were inspired by the subsidy or economic assistance given for construction of *Sulabh Shauchalayas*. These facts suggest that the most important reasons inspiring people to adopt the *Sulabh Shauchalaya* system are concerned with the demerits of the service latrine system and the merits of the *Sulabh Shauchalaya* system. The economic factor has also been mentioned by some of them. The absence of sewerage facility is also an important consideration for a considerable number of adopters, but this consideration goes along with considerations reflecting the merits of the *Sulabh Shauchalaya* system. Hence, it may be stated that the bad experiences of the service latrine system and the merits of the *Sulabh Shauchalaya* system inspired the adopters to switch over to this system and this inspiration was further strengthened by the consideration of economic subsidy or assistance and absence of proper sewerage facility in these towns.

The adopters were further asked: 'Did you face any trouble after adopting the *Sulabh Shauchalaya* system?' The informations reveal that two adopters of Patna and three of Chaibasa have mentioned some troubles in this system. It shows that in Patna and Chaibasa a very small number of people have pointed out certain difficulties. But in Madhubani not even a single adopter has mentioned any defect. However, there is one adopter in Madhubani who reported that the pan of *Sulabh Shauchalaya* got choked at times during use. (This is actually not a defect as choking is generally caused by adding some foreign material during use. It means that in this town *Sulabh Shauchalayas* have been working effectively and satisfactorily).

The adopters have also mentioned different types of difficulties experienced by them after adopting this system. According to one adopter in Patna (2%) there are some defects in the pits of *Sulabh Shauchalayas*. The same number has mentioned some minor general constructional defects. Only two adopters in Chaibasa reveal that there are minor cracks in the floor whereas the leakage in the slabs of *Sulabh Shauchalayas* was mentioned by only one adopter (Table 76).

In the light of the above findings it may be stated that the *Sulabh Shauchalaya* system adopted by the respondents does not show any significant defect. The minor defects pointed out by five adopters only seem to be insignificant and could have been rectified without any difficulty, had the adopters informed the complaint section of the *Sulabh International* about it. The *Sulabh International* has all the necessary arrangements in towns, where the scheme is functioning, for looking into such defects as and when reported. It may also be mentioned that the minor defects reported are due to negligence on the part of the users themselves.

CHAPTER 8

Summing Up

IN THE PRECEDING chapter, the informations collected from the four sets of samples of unliberated scavengers, liberated scavengers, non-adopters and adopters have been analysed in an interpretative manner, throwing light on the profile of different categories of interviewers, their family life, size of the family and family structure, economic condition, occupation, condition of employment and unemployment in the family, personal and family income and the views and attitudes towards social values, traditional practices and sanctions. The information also throws light on the problems of scavenging as a profession, the place of scavengers in society, the desirability of doing away with the scavenging job, liberation of scavengers and their rehabilitation, degree of acceptability of the *Sulabh Shauchalaya* system and the relative preferences for the different types of system of disposing of human excreta in the context of the climatic conditions and economic position in the country.

Scavenging has been existing in India for a long period and the persons engaged in cleaning, carrying and disposing of night-soil have been known as scavengers or *Bhangis.* The occupation of cleaning and carrying night-soil has not been open to all sections of society, rather the caste sanctions and traditional dictates made it obligatory for a section of society to do scavenging and the class of persons working as scavengers were known as *Bhangis*. They constituted a hereditary sub-caste. The scavenging became hereditary and all the male and female members born in the family of a *Bhangi* were bound to take up the scavenging work. Under traditional mythological sanctions, it was a religious duty or *dharma* of the *Bhangis* to take up scavenging. The traditional sanctions not only dictated a particular hereditary group to do scavenging work; rather the place and position of this occupational group were also fixed and were declared unalterable under the normative sanctions of the traditional society.

This sub-caste or occupational group was placed at the lowest level and was labelled as 'untouchable' in the traditional social system. The scavengers were not included in the caste society; rather they were treated as the polluted out-caste because they clean night-soil. They were not allowed to touch the high caste people and, hence, all types of social interactions were forbidden for this sub-caste of scavengers. The demeaning and sub-human occupation of scavenging was their fate under the traditional system and they were not permitted to take up any other job according to their likings, merits and capabilities. The dominance of caste sanctions continued for centuries in Indian society, but with the development of science and technology, revolutionization of ideas and ideologies in the western world, in particular and in the human society, in general, a considerable impact was produced on the traditional ideas and practices. Moreover, the reform movements launched in India also started a rationalization of attitudes and ideas. The introduction of the system of secular and democratic education also contributed to the development of creative thinking and produced significant changes in the attitude and outlook of the people. The assimilation of tradition under the impact of conservative, sacred and authoritarian education in the past did not continue with the same intensity and breaking of traditional sanctions and deviations from traditional practices became significant.

Moreover, the impact of western culture and ideology during the British rule and in the following years brought about significant changes in manners, customs, habits and behaviours of the people in the Indian society. The concept of caste as a divine sanction became less and less operative and the caste system was considered as a social product. Along with these developments, the scientific and technological achievements, the processes of urbanization, industrialization, democratization, secularization and westernization contributed to the dynamics of the Indian society and a process of tradition rationality-continum emerged. Scientific world-view and rational outlook dominated and the unjust practices of the traditional society became the subject of open criticism. In the present age, the concept of the hereditary system of division of labour has lost its significance and free choice of occupation is becoming dominant and more acceptable to the society. This wind of change in Indian society had its impact on different aspects of the social life and consequently scavenging also came under its impact. The people having rational outlook started mobilising forces against the humiliating treatment to the scavengers and protested against the denial of social justice and just human rights to this section of the society. Moreover, with the passage of time, the scavenging work itself was considered sub-human.

Hence, the idea of liberation of scavengers also came to the surface. The simultaneous developments taking place in other parts of the world also strengthened the idea of doing away with the system of manual cleaning of night-soil by human beings. The idea did not come into effective and actual practice for a considerable number of years. The first effective step in the direction of doing away with the scavenging work and liberating the scavengers was taken by the *Sulabh Shauchalaya Sansthan.* The present author initiated the actual programme of liberation of scavengers. In the beginning, the programme was initiated and started in Bihar and certain areas were selected for the purpose. The success attained in the implementation of the programme, caught the attention of the government and other agencies interested in the service of mankind. Gradually, the programme of liberation of scavengers was extended to different urban areas of Bihar and then to other States of the country. Now the programme has been internationally accepted as an effective method of liberating scavengers through low-cost sanitation system. The *Sulabh Shauchalaya* scheme aims at abolishing scavenging and liberating scavengers through the low-cost sanitation system so that the poor countries of the world may adopt it.

It is important to point out that liberation of scavengers is highly significant in a traditional society, specially in view of the ideals of democracy and Welfare State. The Indian Constitution has abolished all distinctions on the basis of caste, creed, race or faith. But the constitutional safeguards are not sufficient to eradicate the evil in actual practice. The *Bhangis* are engaged in scavenging, because this is the only means of livelihood easily available to them. In case they give up this job, they will be jobless and starving. Hence, the scheme of abolishing the scavenging system and liberating the scavengers is meaningless if the problem of rehabilitation of scavengers and provision of alternative jobs to them are not taken into consideration. The liberation of scavengers involves not only putting an end to this sub-human occupation, but also to find out ways for the rehabilitation of persons engaged in this work. Moreover, the ideals of equality, equity and distributive justice can only be achieved when this type of evil is eradicated. Hence, the liberation of scavengers is also significant from the point of view of developing a society characterised with equality, social justice and good for all. It suggests that the scheme of liberation of scavengers is important from the social, political and humanitarian points of view. On the other hand, the problem of low-cost sanitation is also quite significant.

India is a country where most of the people still live below the poverty-line. The different systems of disposing of night-soil found in developing countries are costly which a country like India cannot afford. The sewerage system involves heavy expenditure and hence, it cannot be adopted on a large-scale. The septic latrine system is also a costly affair in view of the poor economic condition of the people. Moreover, under the septic latrine system the need of cleaning night-soil continues to persist for cleaning the tank and hence, the task of scavenging remains there. The ideal of doing away with the scavenging system cannot be achieved if the septic latrine system is adopted. Under these circumstances a system was needed to be developed which is not costly and which helps in abolishing the scavenging work and there is no need for disposing of night-soil at any stage of the system. The *Sulabh Shauchalaya* scheme meets all these requirements. It is inexpensive and requires no manual handling of night-soil, and the night-soil deposited in the pit turns into manure to be used as organic fertilizer.

The present study is, therefore, not uni-dimensional; it is multi-dimensional because it involves social, economic, political, humanitarian and cultural aspects. The multi-dimensional nature of the study is justified by this fact also that the study covers not only the scavengers, but also the adopters and non-adopters. In the study of the scavengers, both liberated and unliberated, have also been included. The problem of, both liberation and sanitation, have been analysed in detail on the basis of the informations obtained from them. The study of adopters helps in understanding the circumstances leading to the adoption of low-cost sanitation scheme, whereas the study of non-adopters reveals the reasons for their not adopting the scheme so far. Thus, the factors promoting and obstructing low-cost sanitation programme come to light. In the same way, the study of unliberated scavengers throws light on the problems faced by them on account of doing scavenging work; whereas the collection of informations from liberated scavengers helps in analysing the changes experienced by them in the post-liberation phase of life. The liberated scavengers are expected to give a comparative account of their living conditions in the pre-liberation and post-liberation phases. Hence, different aspects of the problem have been included in the present study making it multi-dimensional from this point of view also.

The informations obtained from the unliberated scavengers and analysed earlier suggest that persons still engaged in the scavenging work belong to different age groups. The unliberated scavengers are poor and they may be placed in the lowest class economically. In proportion to the number of members in the family, the income is very inadequate. Hence, it may be concluded that the unliberated scavengers live at the lowest level of subsistence and their economic condition is not at all satisfactory. Moreover, the observation of the life style of unliberated scavengers and the informations obtained from them also lead to the conclusion that they are in the habit of smoking and drinking. A considerable amount of their income is also spent on smoking and alcohol, magnifying their economic hardship. In addition to it, the personal observations of the author reveal that these people are also in the habit of gambling and some amount of earning is spent over it. Consequently, with a limited income and with these expenses, they are not in a position to provide adequate amenities to the family members. Their foodstuff is very poor in comparison with their hard physical labour and, in most of the cases, the unliberated male scavengers are semi-clothed and the female scavengers are deprived of proper clothing. In many cases it is not possible for a female scavenger to change her dress after doing the scavenging work and she is compelled to perform her domestic work in the same clothes. Consequently, the infection caused by

Sulabh Institute of Research, Training and Rehabilitation, Patna.

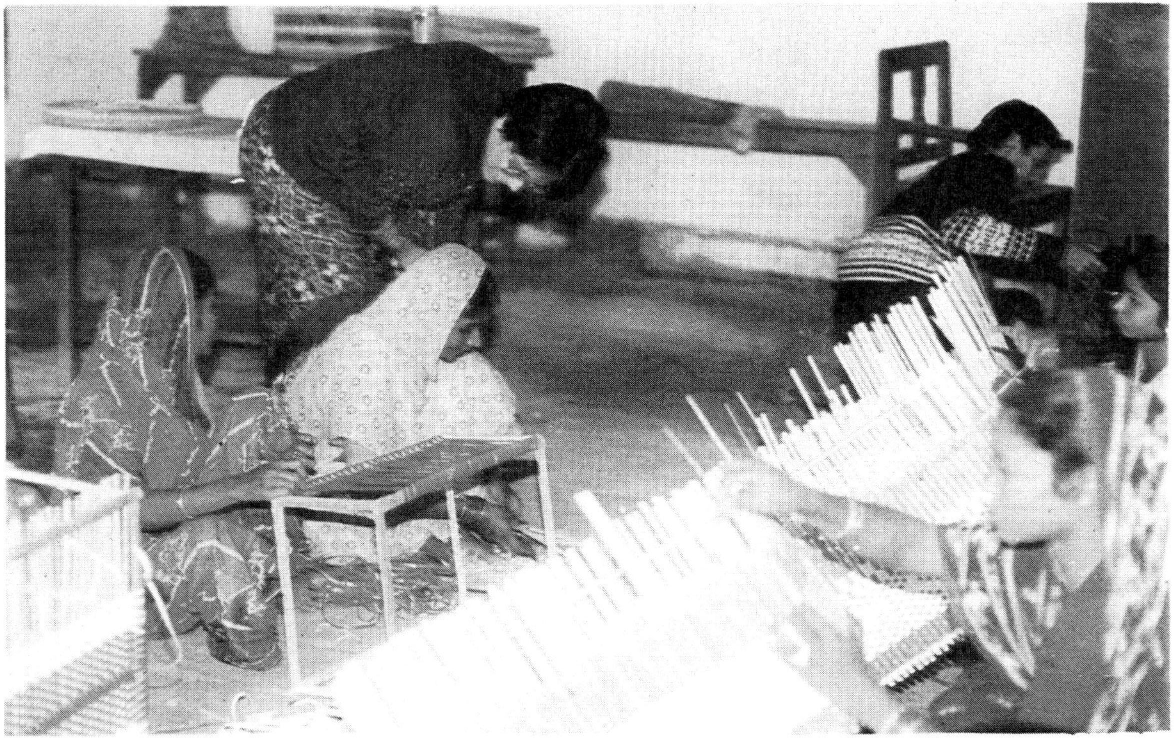

Weaving is one of the many trades in which liberated scavengers and their wards are trained at Sulabh Training Institute, Patna.

carrying night-soil is also transmitted to the home through these clothes and that affects the health of scavengers and their families.

The information obtained from the unliberated scavengers also reveals that most scavengers are illiterate. The information about the literacy condition in the family leads to the inference that not on the scavengers themselves are illiterate, rather, in general, the family members are also illiterate and, in a few cases, some of them are literate or semi-literate. It means that this section of society is extremely backward from the educational point of view. In spite of facilities for free education even the younger generation is not sent for schooling in a considerable number of cases and female education does not appear to be at all important.

The economic and educational backwardness of the unliberated scavengers has deprived them of a number of social privileges in the society. As they are poor and illiterate, they do not enjoy any membership in a socio-cultural organization. There is no question of their attending libraries, reading newspapers, books and journals. Moreover, on the one hand the traditional stigma on the scavengers and, on the other, their economic and educational backwardness are responsible for the lack of their social interaction with other members of the community. As scavengers, they come in contact only with other scavengers. Even on the occasion of social festivities, they are not allowed to participate along with other members of the community. In this way the educational, economic and social backwardness has placed this section at the lowest stratum of society. In spite of the constitutional safeguards and the legal sanctions in favour of equality and equity and against all types of discrimination on the basis of birth, creed and religion, in practical life the unliberated scavengers still suffer from the evils of social injustice and exploitation.

It is also important to note that their social backwardness is responsible for lack of awareness and consciousness of this community with regard to its legal rights and facilities provided under the Constitution and implemented by the Central and State Governments. Only in a few cases, they know about the reservation of jobs, reservation of seats in educational institutions and other such facilities for the uplift of the downtrodden and weaker sections of society. Moreover, those who know about these privileges do not get the same because the facilities are not

As stated above the habit of alcoholism and smoking deepen their poverty. Information suggests that scavengers and their families are also in the habit of seeing films, which involves certain expenditure and additional burden to their low income. The younger generation is more interested in films and, consequently, a considerable amount is spent on this means of entertainment. The films liked by them are not of any specific type, rather, in most of the cases, the people like all types of films—religious, romantic, reformative, detective or Bhojpuri. This liking for all types of films is responsible for an increase in the expenses over seeing films, because there is no specific choice for entertainment and enjoyment. As a result, the other requirements of life are not adequately met and the means of subsistence is quite low.

Information collected about political socialization and participation of the unliberated scavengers has revealed that they are not politically conscious. Most of them are not aware of the fact that the Indian Constitution has abolished caste distinctions. Similarly, a considerable number of scavengers do not know about the facilities given to the Scheduled Castes and they are also not aware of the punishment for discriminatory behaviour with any caste or sub-caste. These facts reveal lack of social and political consciousness among the unliberated scavengers. Majority of the unliberated scavengers know about democracy and adult franchise; but, most of them do not know about equality of rights, the meaning of mid-term poll, the Lok Sabha, Vidhan Sabha and Panchayati Raj. It means that because the talk of democracy and adult franchise is frequent in society, specially on the occasion of general elections, the scavengers have also come to know about them, but they do not know the meaning of other political concepts expected to be known by every citizen in a democratic society. It leads to the inference that the political socialization of the unliberated scavengers is highly inadequate and of a low degree. It is obvious that the backwardness in education and social life and check on free social interaction with other sections of the community have been responsible for a lower degree of political consciousness and lack of adequate political socialization. It may be stated that for India where democracy has been practised for more than 40 years and where a number of general and mid-term polls have been held, this low level of knowledge about common political concepts is an index of extreme backwardness in the sphere of social, political and educational activities.

The data obtained from the unliberated scavengers have also revealed that they did not take up this occupation in the present generation; rather it has been a traditional occupation in most of the cases. Moreover, even those who wanted not to follow this traditional occupation had to adopt it because of poverty and failure to get any other job. Majority of the unliberated scavengers declared that they took up this job because of unavailability of other jobs and because their poor economic condition did not permit them to remain without a job for a long period. As the scavenging job was easily available, they took it up. This pattern of response leads to the conclusion that all persons engaged in scavenging do not have a liking for this job; rather they have been compelled by social and economic circumstances to continue in this occupation. On this basis, it may be concluded that in case some other job is provided to them, scavengers will gladly accept it. In other words, the unliberated scavengers have also started realising that they are being looked down upon in society because they are scavengers. For an improvement in their social condition it is necessary that they should give up this job and engage themselves in some other occupation. It is obvious that this realization by scavengers themselves is an index of the development of social consciousness in this regard.

In case the scheme for the liberation of the scavengers is implemented with the objective of doing away with this work and providing alternative jobs to the liberated persons, this section will respond positively and cooperate in changing the present system in which a particular section of the society is compelled to do a job which is not meant for a human being.

The information obtained from them has also revealed that the unliberated scavengers are also aware of the *Sulabh Shauchalaya* scheme and they not only know about this scheme; rather they have expressed their liking for it. This is because the *Sulabh Shauchalaya* scheme is hygienic in nature, leads to the liberation of scavengers, does not involve the need for scavenging at any stage and is free from foul odour. All these reasons explained by the scavengers are mostly concerned with their own experiences. Hence, it may be concluded that the unliberated scavengers also feel that the *Sulabh Shauchalaya* scheme is beneficial to them. It not only liberates them from the scavenging work, but also saves them from adverse and unhygienic effect on their health. In other words, the unliberated scavengers, through their experience, have expressed their desire for being liberated and have indicated that the *Sulabh Shauchalaya* scheme is the only scheme which can do away with the scavenging work.

The findings presented and analysed in the preceding chapter further reveal that the unliberated scavengers are not engaged in this job because they like it or because they earn more. Circumstances have compelled them to remain in the scavenging job. They are not only eager to change the occupation; rather they also tried for the same in the past. They approached higher authorities for some other job, not only for themselves, but also for their families. But in almost all cases, they met with disappointment. All of them have expressed their disliking for the scavenging job as multi-dimensional.

Apart from social stigma, the other reasons for disliking the job is the involvement of hard physical work. Scavengers also realise that the nature of the job is very dirty and is not desirable for human beings. They also feel that the sanction of untouchability in the traditional society against the *Bhangi* caste is mainly due to cleaning and carrying night-soil. They admitted that they were not allowed to touch any person while carrying night-soil. In other words, the untouchability of scavengers carrying night-soil is still in practice even in urban communities. The scavengers have also complained of exploitation by other members of the society at different levels because of doing the scavenging work.

Hence, it may be concluded that scavenging is very much disliked by the scavengers themselves due to the social, economic, hygienic and psychological problems faced by them in doing this work. They are conscious of the fact that several diseases are caused to them because they carry night-soil and perform scavenging. They are not willing to do scavenging, but they are compelled to do it as they have no alternative. The disliking for and aversion to the occupation of scavenging is further revealed from this fact that no one likes this profession for his or her children. The views expressed and the informations given by them have also revealed that they made efforts at changing the occupation. In certain cases the names were registered in employment exchanges and the higher authorities were approached. But all these proved futile. According to their own estimation of the account they do not get some other job because they do not have any *pairvi*.

Their eagerness to get rid of this occupation is also reflected from the fact that they favour the idea of giving up this job and taking up some business, provided they get some financial assistance. They are willing to take up some other jobs even if they fetch less income. It means that even despite financial loss they would prefer some other job to carrying night-soil on the head. In the light of this fact it may be concluded that liberation from scavenging is eagerly desired by those still involved in the work. It clearly suggests that in case the scheme for the liberation of scavengers is implemented, it will receive the whole-hearted support of scavengers and they will cooperate in the successful implementation of any such scheme. Consequently; it may be stated that the *Sulabh Shauchalaya* scheme for the liberation of scavengers is fully acceptable to them, if some alternative means of livelihood is provided.

The facts collected and analysed earlier also lead to the inference that the scavengers recognise their limitations and shortcomings. They are conscious of the fact that they and their children are illiterate or semi-literate and unskilled. Hence, they do not aspire for a higher or superior post carrying handsome salary and bestowing status and authority in case they have to leave this occupation. The occupations they have suggested for themselves and their children are those of peon, sweeper, driver, mechanic and, in a few cases, the job of teacher or clerk for males. The occupations suggested and desired for females are those of maid-servant, sweeper, female peon and the like. In other words, they aspire for the job they deserve. It is also significant to note that the same jobs have been suggested for their children. The jobs of teacher and clerk have been mentioned with the expectation of their sons attaining the requisite qualifications. Hence, it may also be concluded that the level of their ambition and aspiration is not high. They are more interested in getting rid of the scavenging work and being employed in other jobs of the same cadre. It shows the intensity of their desire for liberation.

The social and economic backwardness of the unliberated scavengers is also reflected from their lower degree of exposure to the media of mass communication, like newspapers, magazines and T.V. programmes. They are exposed only to radio broadcasts and film shows and that too for entertainment. The educative and informative aspects of these media do not appear to be significant to them. It means that their exposure to mass communication is not meaningful from the educational point of view. Moreover, the lower frequency of seeing films and listening to radio programmes speaks of their poor economic condition and economic strains. This finding clearly suggests that exposure to the media of mass communication is not instrumental in rousing their political consciousness and social awareness.

As regards inter-caste relations, the traditional sanctions are still in operation though the rigidity of the past does not exist. The scavengers did not complain of any discriminatory behaviour with their children or family members in schools, offices and in getting house on rent. But at the same time, they have pointed out that in general, only the members of the same caste or sub-caste attend ceremonial functions at their houses. Even the members of other sub-castes of the Harijan category come to the houses of the scavengers on ceremonial occasions in a very low number. It is, thus, significant to note that on the one hand the unliberated scavengers have complained against discriminatory behaviour by the upper caste people and want the abolition of all such distinctions; but, on the other, they themselves suffer from such feelings as is evident from the distinctionary behaviour of the various sub-castes of Harijans and their belief in the existence of the sub-caste hierarchy.

The scavengers, in most of the cases, described their sub-caste as superior to the sub-castes of *Dom, Dusadh, Musahar* or *Chamar;* whereas the sub-castes of *Pasi* and *Dhobi* have been ranked higher. This very ranking suggests that they also recognise the inter-caste distinction among themselves. In the light of these facts it may be concluded that inter-caste relations are not free from the traditional caste norms, though a considerable degree of relaxation is also reflected. These relaxations show the process of the weakening of the traditional caste ties and caste stigma under the impact of the constitutional safeguards as well as the processes of urbanization, democratization and secularization.

The information obtained from the liberated scavengers, and analysed earlier, has revealed that both male and female scavengers have been liberated in the three towns of Ranchi, Purnea and Patna. Among the liberated scavengers females outnumber males. The information about their personal identification has revealed that they are backward not only from the economic and social points of view, but also from the educational point of view. For most of the liberated scavengers, literacy is a rare phenomenon. The findings have also shown that the liberated scavengers are living in single as well as joint families and are having relatively large-size families.

Moreover, the liberated scavengers form a heterogeneous group in respect of their age and family income because in certain families there is only one earning hand whereas in other families the number of earning hands is two or more. But the total family earning is inadequate in proportion to the size of the family and the number of dependent members. Consequently, the liberated scavengers are also living at the poverty-line or just below or above it. This poor economic condition, as informed by them, has been one of the basic reasons for discontinuing their education. According to them the poor economic condition of the family did not permit them to study further and many of them had to drop out and some of them were not sent for schooling due to the social and economic backwardness of their families.

The findings also lead to the conclusion that they took up scavenging because it was their traditional occupation, and no initiative was taken by them to get out of it. Even if they tried to change their occupation, they could not succeed. It was the *Sulabh Shauchalaya* scheme which came to their rescue and took steps for their liberation from the scavenging work through installing *Sulabh Shauchalayas* which did not require scavenging. As all the liberated scavengers were employed either in Purnea or Ranchi municipalities or in Patna Municipal Corporation, there was no problem of providing an alternative job. They were the employees of the corporations or municipalities and after liberation their services were not terminated; rather they were given some alternative jobs like sweeping, cleaning and disposing of garbage.

Hence, these liberated scavengers did not face unemployment

and did not require any scheme for rehabilitation. The *Sulabh Shauchalaya* scheme was introduced in these towns with the understanding that the scavengers thus liberated will be given other jobs by their employers. At this stage, it is also important to point out that the liberation of scavengers could take place only after the conversion of service latrines into *Sulabh* latrines. This conversion process needed the cooperation of the citizens having service latrines. In case the citizens were not willing to adopt the *Sulabh Shauchalaya* system, the conversion was not possible and hence, the liberation of the scavengers could not take place. For receiving the cooperation of the citizens in the liberation of the scavengers it was, therefore, required to introduce a scheme which might be attractive to the people having service latrines in their houses. The *Sulabh* institution was aware of the fact that persons with low or very low income were still having service latrines and the economic hardship stood in the way of switching over to any costly scheme. Hence, any scheme imposing economic burden upon the people was not expected to yield the desired result. A low-cost sanitation scheme was needed, which was provided by *Sulabh Shauchalaya.* Moreover, economic relief in the form of subsidy was provided to the adopters for converting their service latrines into *Sulabh Shauchalayas*. In this way the liberation of scavengers and adoption of low-cost sanitation went side-by-side and hence, the programme of liberation of scavengers could operate successfully. This contribution of the *Sulabh Shauchalaya Sansthan* is not only in favour of the scavengers or adopters of the scheme, but also in favour of the general people and the community from the points of view of sanitation, hygienic condition, lesser probability of infections and pollution of the environment.

The collected facts also lead to the inference that most of the liberated scavengers are satisfied with the present occupation in which they are now engaged. They are satisfied because they have been relieved of the scavenging work and manual cleaning of night-soil. The work assigned to them after liberation is better than the previous one and, hence, they are satisfied. But there does exist the problem of providing jobs to their family members who are unemployed. Unless this is solved, there is every possibility of some of their children taking up the scavenging work under compulsion which may defeat the very purpose of the programme. It is also important to note that like the unliberated scavengers, the ambition of liberated ones is also not very high. The jobs they have preferred for their unemployed children are of unskilled, semi-skilled and, in a few cases of skilled categories. It clearly suggests that the liberated scavengers are conscious of their limitations and shortcomings and realise that with the existing qualifications of their children, they cannot hope to secure better jobs for them. Hence, they are realistic in their approach and want to improve the status of their families under the existing circumstances.

The information showing the impact of liberation on the scavengers which has been presented in the preceding chapter, reveals that there has been some impact of liberation on the liberty and social prestige enjoyed by the liberated scavengers, in respect of visit to temples, engagement of *Brahmins* to supervise religious ceremonies, invitation by other caste people on ceremonial occasions, taking water from common places along with other caste people and taking food in hotels and other places. It proves that their liberation has enhanced their social prestige and, hence, they are paying visits to even those temples which are visited by high caste *Hindus*. In the same way, in respect of engagement of *Brahmins* to supervise religious ceremonies, in Patna a considerable number was denied this privilege in the past, but now all of them are enjoying it and in Purnea the number of scavengers enjoying this privilege has doubled after the liberation. It means that liberation has brought higher status and respect to scavengers. A remarkable impact is found in respect of invitation by other caste people on ceremonial occasions in all the three towns. A very low percentage from each of the three towns was invited by other caste people in the pre-liberation period whereas quite a high percentage is now being invited by other caste people after the liberation. The same is the position in respect of taking water from common places and taking food in hotels in all the three towns. The so-called scavengers, after being liberated, are taking food like high caste Hindus and are being invited by other caste people on the occasion of ceremonies and rituals.

It indicates the positive impact of liberation and enhancement in social prestige and position of this downtrodden section of the traditional society. It is important to note that the liberation has taken place very recently and only a few years have passed since attitude of high caste people are beginning to accept *Bhangis* into the mainstream of social and community life.

In the following generations, on the basis of the trend of change, it may be expected that this section will be like other sections and the social barriers and stigma against them will vanish in due course. On this basis it may be stated that the *Sulabh Shauchalaya* scheme is not only liberating the scavengers and is not only doing away with the sub-human work of cleaning night-soil; rather it is initiating the process of attainment of the stage of equality, equity and distributive social justice. Hence, it is not only a scheme to improve the lot of the existing generation, but also to improve the condition of the coming generations and its contributions are of greater value to the development of a society characterised by the ideals of democracy, social justice and eradication of social exploitation.

The findings analysed earlier also lead to the conclusion that there has been a change not only in the attitude and outlook of other caste people, but also in the attitude and outlook of the scavengers themselves who have started realising that they are liberated and that they should no more be engaged in scavenging work. The author noted on different occasions that these liberated scavengers declared with a sense of pride and prestige that they were no more engaged in scavenging. The way in which they expressed this fact indicated that they also regarded cleaning of night-soil as a humiliating work. Moreover, most of them made it clear that they were not having any interaction with those persons who were still engaged in the scavenging work. In the light of this finding also, it may be concluded that liberation has produced a profound impact not only on their actual behaviour and way of life, but also on their attitude, outlook and approaches. Thus, it may be concluded that the liberated scavengers are developing a consciousness of being liberated and not being engaged in the scavenging job.

The economic and social backwardness of the liberated scavengers has adversely affected the education of their children. The data reveal that in most of the families the children are not attending schools and they are not receiving even primary education in spite of the fact that free education is imparted to the children and youths of this section of the community. Those scavengers whose children are studying also admitted that there was no adequate facility for study at home and the children did not regularly do home work. It means that the facility of space and light needed for the study at home are not available in most of the cases. The author observed that most of these liberated scavengers and their family members were living either in one-room tenements or in hutments. It is obvious that in this type of living accommodation there cannot be a separate space for the study purpose. Hence, the children of the liberated scavengers did not get adequate facilities for study. It does not mean that the children are not interested in studies, because most of the respondents whose children are attending schools have declared that they are interested in their studies. Hence, it may be concluded that in spite of being interested they are not studying because of lack of proper accommodation and adequate facilities. It clearly speaks of the economic hardship on the part of the families of liberated scavengers. Moreover, the lack of enjoying the facility of free education by a majority of liberated scavengers reflects their social backwardness and lack of realization of the importance of education for the younger generation. Those sending their children to schools declared that they met the expenses of education out of their own earnings. It means that they are not aware of the facilities of scholarship. Moreover, some of them have expressed the view that the assistance provided by the Government is inadequate and does not help them to prosecute the study of their children.

In the light of these it may be concluded that, on the one hand, economic backwardness is responsible for the low percentage of literacy in the younger generation and, on the other, social backwardness and lack of social consciouness are responsible for the low percentage of children attending schools. When the school-going children are fewer, it can be well understood that higher education will be a rare phenomenon among *Bhangis*. Hence, along with liberation, it is also necessary that scavengers should be educated on importance of education, the facilities available to them for education and the role of education in the uplift of social, economic and political condition of the community.

The information obtained from non-adopters from Patna,

Muzaffarpur and Arrah, and analysed earlier, leads to the inference that the non-adopters are mostly from lower or upper-lower class of the society from the economic point of view. The annual income of the families of the non-adopters ranges from Rs. 3,000 to Rs. 18,000 and above per annum. But the number of families having an income of Rs. 18,000 per year is very low and those having an annual income of Rs. 12,000 or below constitute the majority of the non-adopters. On this basis it may be concluded that the families of the non-adopters having a monthly income of less than Rs. 1,000 are living at the lowest level of the poverty line because of the high cost of living and considerably large size of the family. This suggests that one important reason for the continuance of service latrines in the houses of the non-adopters is the economic reason. They cannot afford to convert the service latrine system into the *Sulabh Shauchalaya* system and hence, the old system continues.

Along with the poor economic condition of the non-adopters, this fact has also come to light that majority of the non-adopters are matriculates or below matric, and, in certain cases, even illiterate. It is also important to point out that the non-adopters come from different castes and religions. But, according to the analysed facts only a smaller section belongs to the upper caste and the majority of the non-adopters come from lower or Scheduled Castes. On this basis it may be further interpreted that in comparison to the members of upper castes, those belonging to lower or Scheduled Castes are relatively more backward from the economic and educational points of view. Their social backwardness is linked with economic and educational backwardness. The reason for not adopting the *Sulabh Shauchalaya* system appears to be economic. The facts have revealed that the non-adopters are aware of the *Sulabh Shauchalaya* scheme and in most of the cases they have come to know about this scheme through the *Sulabh International* and the agencies or organs working under it. In a very few cases the non-adopters have come to know about this scheme through their friends, relatives or neighbours. It means that the most effective agency acquainting the people with the *Sulabh Shauchalaya* system is the agency of the *Sulabh International* itself. It shows the significant and vital role played by the agencies associated with the *Sulabh International*.

The views expressed by the non-adopters about the *Sulabh Shauchalaya* system reveal that they have a positive attitude towards this scheme and they are acquainted with multi-dimensional benefits of *Sulabh Shauchalaya*. They have declared that *Sulabh Shauchalaya* is good and preferable as it does not require scavenging. In the same way the majority also holds the view the *Sulabh Shauchalaya* is economical and it may be constructed with the investment of a lower amount in comparison to the septic latrine and other systems. The non-adopters have also felt that *Sulabh Shauchalaya* is suited to the existing environmental conditions and requires less space and gives best service. The absence of foul smell and the benefit of obtaining manure out of the *Sulabh* system have also been mentioned by them. These views expressed by them lead to the inference that the non-adopters are acquainted with the environmental suitability, economical nature and hygienic conditions under the *Sulabh Shauchalaya* system. In other words, they accept the merits of the system, but they have not adopted it because of the circumstances prevailing around them. Most of the non-adopters made it clear that they could not convert service latrines into the *Sulabh Shauchalaya* system because they did not have money for it. On this basis it may be concluded that either the non-adopters were not provided with economic subsidy or they were not in a position to spend the amount needed for the conversion. In the light of this finding it may be concluded that the main and basic factor responsible for the continuance of the service latrine system has been the poor economic condition.

In case economic subsidy is provided and they are approached properly, the service latrine system may be converted into the *Sulabh Shauchalaya* system. In case the non-adopters are tenants, the house-owners may be approached and, with their permission and cooperation, the purpose may be achieved. On the whole, it comes to light that the non-adopters are not opposed to *Sulabh Shauchalaya*, rather they have not been in a position to adopt the system under pressing circumstances. The majority of the respondents have categorically declared that after abandoning the service latrine system they will prefer *Sulabh Shauchalaya*. The higher degree of acceptability of the *Sulabh Shauchalaya* system is further revealed by the fact that majority of the non-adopters declared that in case they constructed their own houses, they would prefer the *Sulabh*

Shauchalaya system to any other system. This categorical preference for *Sulabh Shauchalaya* shows the eagerness of the non-adopters for the system and their desirability to switch over to the low-cost sanitation scheme. Hence, it may be concluded that the services rendered so far by the *Sulabh Shauchalaya* system have resulted not only in the conversion of service latrines into *Sulabh Shauchalayas,* but also in mobilising the opinion and attitude of the citizens in favour of the *Sulabh Shauchalaya* scheme.

The education imparted through *Sulabh Shauchalaya* agencies has proved effective and fruitful in the sense that even those who are not enjoying the benefits of the *Sulabh Shauchalaya* system have developed a favourable attitude towards it and have categorically preferred this system to other systems. Hence, it may be concluded that the partial adoption of the *Sulabh Shauchalaya* system in these three towns and the working of *Sulabh Shauchalaya* agencies have produced positive results and the non-adopter section of the society is also willing to abandon the service latrine system and to adopt *Sulabh Shauchalaya*. On this basis it may be stated that the scheme of *Sulabh Shauchalaya* is not only favourable to the scavengers who are to be liberated, but also to citizens who are to switch over to a new system. It clearly suggests that the aspect of liberation involved in the *Sulabh Shauchalaya* scheme is attractive for the scavengers whereas the aspect of low-cost sanitation including the benefits of improved hygienic condition is attractive for the people in general. The ideal of liberation of scavengers through low-cost sanitation put forward by the *Sulabh Shauchalaya* system has a multi-pronged effect on the society and is beneficial not only to the scavengers or to the adopters, but to the whole community from the social and economic points of view as well as from the medical, hygienic and humanitarian angles of vision.

The adopters covered by the present study have been selected from Patna, Madhubani and Chaibasa to constitute the sample. These adopters, as the data analysed earlier suggest, do not belong to any one particular community. They are from Muslims, Hindus and Sikhs though the Sikhs adopters are only in Patna. Moreover, these adopters belong to different income groups and occupations. As regards the occupational composition, they are engaged in service, wage-earning jobs, business and farming. Most female adopters are housewives and some adopters are either retired or jobless. The personal income of the adopters varies from Rs. 3,000 per annum to Rs. 18,000 or more. The family income of the adopters per annum also varies within the same range with the difference that in case of family income slightly higher percentages are found in higher income groups. In view of the size of the families, they cannot be placed in the category of rich or well-to-do families. In most of the families the income is inadequate and does not suffice all the needs and requirements of the family members. But in comparison to the non-adopters their economic condition appears to be slightly better. The educational aspect of the adopters and their family members shows that illiterate as well as literate and educated persons are found in their families and in most of the cases the adopters are not highly qualified. Only a smaller section has received college education and most of them are educated either up to the matriculation stage or below it.

The information obtained from the adopters and analysed earlier reveals that before adopting the *Sulabh Shauchalaya* system in most of the houses the service latrine system was in operation. In some other cases the adopters did not have any latrine in their houses and the place of defecation was either open space or community latrines. It suggests that the adoption of *Sulabh Shauchalaya* by the adopters has, in most of the cases, resulted in the conversion of service latrines into the *Sulabh Shauchalaya* system. The information given by the adopters has also revealed that they came to know about *Sulabh Shauchalaya* through different sources. But in most of the cases the adopters knew about *Sulabh Shauchalaya* through the *Sulabh International* agencies. In a considerable number of cases they came to know about this scheme through those persons who have already adopted the same. The other sources mentioned by the adopters are relatives and friends, municipalities, mass media and mass conversion campaign. But these sources do not appear to be much effective because very few persons have mentioned them. In fact, the most effective source in acquainting them with the *Sulabh Shauchalaya* scheme is found to be *Sulabh Shauchalaya* agency. Hence, it may be concluded that the *Sulabh Shauchalaya* agency is not only working for the conversion of service latrines into *Sulabh Shauchalayas*, but it is also instrumental in popularising the scheme and educating people on the benefits of *Sulabh Shauchalaya*. In other words, the adoption of the *Sulabh*

Shauchalaya system is mainly taking place due to the working of the *Sulabh* agencies and, thus, the major contribution to this aspect has been made by the *Sulabh International* itself.

The reasons for abandoning the previous system by the adopters have also been analysed in the foregoing chapter. The reasons mentioned by the adopters reveal that they were conscious of the unhygienic conditions developing from the service latrine system and this unhygienic effect of the service latrine system appears to be the most important reason for converting it into the *Sulabh* system. The other important reasons mentioned by the adopters are the scavenging problem and lack of the sewerage system. They have also declared that the other systems are costly and, hence, they cannot afford them. It clearly suggests that the adopters also knew about the low-cost *Sulabh Shauchalaya* system and, hence, they preferred this system to other expensive systems. In other words, the benefit of low-cost sanitation also attracted the adopters to the *Sulabh Shauchalaya* system. In most of the cases service latrines were converted into *Sulabh Shauchalayas*, but in some cases the *Sandas* system was converted into the *Sulabh* system and, in certain cases where there was no system in the house, the *Sulabh* system was adopted for the first time.

The adopters appears to be conscious of the advantages and benefits of the system they have adopted. All of them do accept that the system is hygienic and an overwhelming majority hold the view that it does not give foul smell. Likewise a major section of the adopters declared that *Sulabh Shauchalaya* did not require scavenging and was cheaper. Some adopters declared that the subsidy provided for adopting the system also acted as an incentive for them whereas, according to a considerable number of adopters, *Sulabh Shauchalaya* is the best system in the absence of adequate sewerage facility. This opinion of the adopters is quite significant because only under the sewerage system there is no need for scavenging or manual cleaning of night-soil. Even under the septic latrine system scavenging is required to be done for cleaning the septic tank and somebody is needed for manual cleaning of human excreta and carrying the same to dispose it of. Hence, the objective of abolishing scavenging at all levels can be achieved only through switching over to the sewerage system or through adopting the *Sulabh Shauchalaya* system. The sewerage system is highly expensive and is unthinkable in a poor country like India. Hence, in case scavenging is to be done away with, the only alternative left to the Indians is to adopt the *Sulabh Shauchalaya* system.

Consequently, this view of the adopters that in the absence of the sewerage facility the *Sulabh* system is the best system, is not a superficial view of the situation; rather it presents a realistic picture based upon the understanding of the problems involved in disposing of human excreta. In the light of these findings, it may be concluded that the adopters have switched over to the *Sulabh Shauchalaya* system because it has multi-pronged benefits and, at the same time, it facilitates the process of liberation of scavengers. Keeping in view the social and economic conditions of the scavengers as also of the common people, *Sulabh Shauchalaya* appears to be the most adequate system for disposing of night-soil.

The adopters are persons who are experiencing the actual working of the *Sulabh Shauchalaya* system. They are the best persons to tell about the troubles, if any, facing under this system. The information furnished by the adopters clearly suggests that the *Sulabh Shauchalaya* system adopted by them does not show any significant defect. Hence it may be stated that the adopters are fully satisfied with the working of the *Sulabh Shauchalaya* scheme.

Lastly, the attitudes and views of the adopters about the scavenging system, carrying of night-soil by the scavengers, their social status and position in the society, the desirability or undesirability of continuing the scavenging system in a democratic social set-up and other related problems lead to the conclusion that the scavengers are looked down upon in the society because the nature of the work performed by them is dirty and sub-human. Carrying human excreta by human beings is a slur on the society and it must be stopped forth with. The adopters fully agreed to this point that the ideals of democracy, common welfare and social justice cannot be attained so long as the scavenging work continues to persist. If we want to make Indian society a welfare society characterised by equality, equity and distributive justice, scavenging must be abolished. They have also endorsed the view that in case scavenging is abandoned and the scavengers are liberated, it will help in raising their social status and position. In due course the traditional social stigma against them will disappear and, like other sections of the society, they will also be allowed free access to all social, religious and cultural places and will have free and unrestricted social interaction with other sections of the community. For developing a democratic society in the real sense of the term, the liberation of scavengers is unavoidable. These views and attitudes expressed by the adopters throw light on the fact that the scheme of liberation of scavengers initiated by low-cost sanitation, popularly known as the *Sulabh Shauchalaya* system, is the demand of the age and is rendering positive service not only to the downtrodden section of the scavengers, but also to the society and to the whole of the nation.

The data analysed and discussed above show how the project, initiated and carried on by the *Sulabh Shauchalaya Sansthan* (now called *Sulabh International*), has won wide recognition, support and appreciation. The programme of the liberation of scavengers through low-cost sanitation is not only supported by the people, but is also regarded as the most suitable alternative to meet the demands of the climatic, hygienic, economic, social and political conditions prevailing in India today. The programme is favoured not only by the liberated scavengers, who have been relieved of the sub-human work of cleaning night-soil, but also by the non-adopters. The programme has mobilised the opinion of the people in its own favour and the benefits derived from the programme are not confined to the community of scavengers, but also to the adopters as well as to the people of the country in general. Hence, in the concluding remarks it may be summed up as below:

1. The *Sulabh Shauchalaya* scheme being multi-dimensional, stands for the liberation of *Bhangis*, improvement in the hygienic condition of the environment and checks the possibility of infections.

2. The *Sulabh Shauchalaya* scheme is not only beneficial to scavengers, but to society as a whole. The ideals of social justice, common welfare and democracy will remain unfulfilled so long as the scavenging work continues to persist. Hence, for the development of social order characterised by equality, equity and non-exploitation, the abolition of scavenging is inevitable and consequently the liberation of scavengers is a pre-requisite for the development of a healthy society.

3. The *Sulabh Shauchalaya* scheme is now widely known to the people living in urban communities, including *Bhangis* and also the

people of different castes, religions, occupations, income groups and educational attainments.

4. The opinions and views expresed by people from different shades of life in respect of the *Sulabh* scheme are positive. They have not only supported the scheme, but have expressed their desirability to implement it and to extend its area of operation. Those who are not so far covered by the programme are willing to be benefitted by the same and consider the scheme to be essential for eradication of the evil of scavenging and for developing a healthy social order.

5. The troubles arising from the service latrine system are unbearable for the users. The foul smell, the infections caused by night-soil and the unhygienic condition caused by irregular cleaning of night-soil by scavengers are the problems with which users are fed up. In view of the economic hardship they are unable to adopt any other alternative system and hence, they favour the adoption of *Sulabh Shauchalaya* which relieves them of the trouble at the lowest cost.

6. Those who are well acquainted with the working of the sewerage, septic and *Sulabh* systems, subscribe to the view that the septic system does not held in eradicating the scavenging work at all stages. They know that at the time of cleaning septic tanks, the services of scavengers are needed. It is only the sewerage system of the western countries which does not require scavenging. They also know the fact that scavenging at any level is not required in the *Sulabh Shauchalaya* system al o, because the pits where night-soil is deposited are designed and constructed in such a way that human excreta starts decomposing and is transformed into a material like soil which is a good manure.

The cleaning of pits can, therefore, be taken up by any person irrespective of his caste, creed or religion. These people are also aware that the sewerage system is a costly affair and that a poor country like India cannot afford to introduce this system at the national level. On the other hand, the *Sulabh* system is a system of low-cost sanitation, which may be implemented at a much lesser cost. In a country like India the *Sulabh Shauchalaya* system, according to them, is the best and the most adequate system. Hence, the consideration of the economic aspect of the problem leads them to the conclusion that the only suitable and acceptable alternative left to the people of this country in general and Bihar in Particular is the *Sulabh Shauchalaya* scheme.

7. The families of the non-adopters are mostly from lower income groups and are backward from the educational point of view. They are still having the service latrine system and cannot switch over to this low-cost system due to poverty and social as well as educatioal backwardness. The majority of these non-adopters prefer *Sulabh Shauchalaya* because it involves lower cost and removes the possibility of scavenging at all stages. Moreover, the factor of getting economic subsidy in constructing *Sulabh Shauchalaya* is another important consideration for the poor and economically hard-pressed families.

8. The non-adopter families are still having the service latrine system not because they like it, but because they are compelled to tolerate this irritating and trouble-generating system. They are pulling on with this system either because they are poor and cannot afford to meet the cost of conversion or because they are living in rented houses of old type and house-owners do not want to invest any amount over converting the existing system.

9. There has been marked change in the social position and outlook of the liberated scavengers when compared with unliberated scavengers. The liberated scavengers are themselves conscious that they have given up the dirty job of scavenging and are different from the unliberated scavengers.

In addition to it, they have themselves declared that their social interaction with other castes has increased after their liberation. Moreover, the normative restrictions imposed upon the unliberated scavengers in respect of taking food in hotels and restaurants and entry into temples visited by other caste people are also vanishing after liberation. It suggests that the social position has considerably improved after the liberation and the patterns of social interaction and social relations are changing.

10. The unliberated scavengers are also acquainted with the *Sulabh Shauchalaya* scheme and are aware that a large number of scavengers have already been liberated. They have also expressed their eagerness to get rid of the scavenging work, believing as they do that only the *Sulabh Shauchalaya* scheme can liberate them from scavenging.

11. The *Sulabh Shauchalaya* scheme has proved significantly

effective and instrumental not only in liberating the scavengers or in initiating the process of abolishing the scavenging work, but also in mobilising public opinion in favour of the programme. It has created a stir in the whole of Indian society and has drawn the attention of the world outside. The scheme is so positive and constructive that it goes against no one, no ideology and no shade of life. It benefits all and operates with the spirit of delivering good to all in general and the weaker sections of the society in particular. The scheme is revolutionary in spirit, but not coercive or violent in nature, for it corresponds to the ideals of service to humanity and welfare of all. In fact, the *Sulabh Shauchalaya* scheme presents the ideology of *Sarvodaya* in actual action and practice, yielding fruitful positive results. The positive results of the programme of liberation of scavengers through low-cost sanitation are based on positive thinking and positivistic programme of social reconstruction.

Comte, the father of sociology, presented a programme of social development under his philosophy of positivism, but he never enacted the scheme. The scheme of liberation of scavengers has gone one step ahead because along with drawing the scheme the organization of *Sulabh Shauchalaya* has actually implemented it and desired results have been achieved. The author of the scheme himself initiated it and translated the idea into action. The action-aspect of the scheme presented by sociologists has added a new dimension to the discipline which is ahead of the spheres of theoretical sociology, empirical sociology and applied sociology. This new dimension of the discipline may rightly be described as 'Action Sociology', a concept later on developed and popularized by the present author.

TABLE 2
Age Classification

Town	Up to 20	21-30	31-40	41-50	51-60	Total
Patna	1 (2%)	11 (22%)	17 (34%)	17 (34%)	4 (8%)	50
Muzaffarpur	2 (4%)	12 (24%)	21 (42%)	11 (22%)	4 (8%)	50
Arrah	3 (6%)	13 (26%)	15 (30%)	17 (34%)	2 (4%)	50
Total	6 (4%)	36 (24%)	54 (35.3%)	45 (30%)	10 (6.6%)	150

TABLE 3
Educational Classification

Town	1st-2nd class	3rd-4th class	5th-6th class	7th-8th class	9th +	Illiterate	Total
Patna	—	6 (12%)	4 (8%)	4 (8%)	1 (2%)	35 (70%)	50
Muzaffarpur	—	1 (2%)	3 (6%)	—	—	46 (92%)	50
Arrah	1 (2%)	1 (2%)	2 (4%)	2 (4%)	1 (2%)	43 (86%)	50
Total	1 (0.66%)	8 (5.3%)	9 (6%)	6 (4.0%)	2 (1.3%)	124 (82.6%)	150

TABLE 4
Income Classification (Monthly)

Town	Up to Rs. 400	Rs. 401-800	Rs. 801-1200	Rs. 1201-1600	Rs. 1601-2000	Rs. 2000+	Total
Patna	2 (4%)	6 (12%)	22 (44%)	16 (32%)	2 (4%)	2 (4%)	50
Muzaffarpur	4 (8%)	19 (38%)	20 (40%)	4 (8%)	1 (2%)	2 (4%)	50
Arrah	7 (14%)	24 (48%)	15 (30%)	4 (8%)	—	—	50
Total	13 (8.6%)	49 (32.7%)	57 (38%)	24 (16%)	3 (2.0%)	4 (2.8%)	150

TABLE 5
Number of Adults in the Family (Male)

Income (Rs.)	None			1-2			3-4			5-6			Total			Grand total
	P	M	A	P	M	A	P	M	A	P	M	A	P	M	A	
Up to 400	—	3 75%	2 28.5%	2 100%	1 25%	5 71.5%	—	—	—	—	—	—	2	4	7	13
401-800	2 33.3%	—	—	4 66.7%	19 100%	24 100%	—	—	—	—	—	—	6	19	24	49
801-1200	—	—	—	21 95.5%	16 80%	12 80%	1 4.5%	4 20%	3 20%	—	—	—	22	20	15	57
1201-1600	—	—	—	13 81.2%	1 25%	3 75%	3 18.8%	3 75%	1 25%	—	—	—	16	4	4	24
1601-2000	—	—	—	2 100%	1 100%	—	—	—	—	—	—	—	2	1	—	3
2001+	—	—	—	1 50%	—	—	1 50%	1 50%	—	—	1 50%	—	2	2	—	4
Total	2 1.3%	3 2%	2 1.3%	43 28.7%	38 25.3%	44 29.3%	5 3.3%	8 5.3%	4 2.7%	—	1 0.7%	—	50	50	50	150

P—Patna; M—Muzaffarpur; A—Arrah.

confined only to this section of the community, rather it is for the Scheduled Castes in general in which other sub-castes of the Harijans are also included. As compared to the sub-caste of *Bhangis*, the other Harijan sub-castes are more advanced, more conscious and more aware of these facilities and they enjoy the benefits.

It may, therefore, be concluded that so long as scavenging continues, the *Bhangis* will be looked down upon in society and will continue to be backward in all respects. Consequently, the economic condition will not improve and the section of scavengers will not be able to enjoy the privileges and facilities provided to the weaker sections in India. Hence, the ideal of equity and social justice inherent in the Constitution and the Welfare State will remain unfulfilled because this section will remain deprived of the distributive social justice.

It may, therefore, be concluded that for improving the lot of this weaker section and for achieving the ideals of democracy and social justice, the occupation of scavenging should be engaged in other alternative jobs as is being done in Bihar (and now partly in several States of the country) at present. Moreover, along with the rehabilitation of the scavengers, it is also necessary that arrangements should be made for vocational training and guidance to the new generation so that, in future, there may not be any problem of joblessness and economic hardship for the youth. This vocational training and guidance will also be helpful in improving their economic condition which will lead to a better social position. These factors will contribute to the uplift of this community and improvement in their social, educational and economic spheres of life.

The study of unliberated scavengers has brought this fact also to light that the scavenging work is generally done by females and most of the scavengers are women. It is important to point out that the unliberated scavengers covered by this study are those who are employed in municipalities or corporations. Those who are employed as scavengers from this caste or sub-caste are both males and females. But the male scavengers are generally engaged in other works allotted by employers and the female scavengers are generally deputed for scavenging.

The economic condition of the unliberated scavengers is poor.

TABLE 6
Number of Adults in the Family (Female)

Income (Rs.)	None			1-2			3-4			5-6			Total			Grand total
	P	M	A	P	M	A	P	M	A	P	M	A	P	M	A	
Up to 400	—	—	1 14.3%	2 100%	4 100%	6 85.7%	—	—	—	—	—	—	2	4	7	13
401-800	1 16.7%	—	—	5 83.3%	18 94.7%	24 100%	—	1 5.3%	—	—	—	—	6	19	24	49
801-1200	—	—	—	21 95.5%	17 85%	15 100%	1 4.5%	3 15%	—	—	—	—	22	20	15	57
1201-1600	—	—	—	13 81.2%	2 50%	3 75%	3 18.8%	2 50%	1 25%	—	—	—	16	4	4	24
1601-2000	—	—	—	2 100%	1 100%	—	—	—	—	—	—	—	2	1	—	3
2001+	—	—	—	2 50%	—	—	—	1 50%	—	1 50%	1 50%	—	2	2	—	4
Total	1 0.7%	—	1 0.7%	44 29.4%	42 28%	48 32%	4 2.7%	7 4.7%	1 0.7%	1 0.7%	1 0.7%	—	50	50	50	150

P—Patna; M—Muzaffarpur; A—Arrah.

TABLE 7
Number of Children in the Family (Male)

Income (Rs.)	None			1-2			3-4			4-5			Total			Grand total
	P	M	A	P	M	A	P	M	A	P	M	A	P	M	A	
Up to 400	1 50%	2 50%	3 42.8%	1 50%	2 50%	3 42.8%	—	—	1 14.4%	—	—	—	2	4	7	13
401-800	2 33.3%	—	6 25%	3 50%	16 84.2%	11 45.8%	1 16.7%	3 15.8%	7 29.2%	—	—	—	6	19	24	49
801-1200	5 22.7%	2 100%	2 13.3%	13 59%	11 55.0%	9 60%	4 18.3%	7 35%	4 26.7%	—	—	—	22	20	15	57
1201-1600	2 12.6%	2 50%	2 50%	7 43.7%	2 50%	2 50%	7 43.7%	—	—	—	—	—	16	4	4	24
1601-2000	—	—	—	1 50%	1 100%	—	1 50%	—	—	—	—	—	2	1	—	3
2001+	1 50%	—	—	—	1 50%	—	1 50%	—	—	—	1 50%	—	2	2	—	4
Total	11 7.3%	6 4%	13 8.7%	25 16.7%	33 22%	25 16.7%	14 9.3%	10 6.7%	12 8%	—	1 0.7%	—	50	50	50	150

P—Patna; M—Muzaffarpur; A—Arrah.

TABLE 8
Number of Children in the Family (Female)

Income (Rs.)	None			1-2			3-4			5-6			Total			Grand total
	P	M	A	P	M	A	P	M	A	P	M	A	P	M	A	
Upto 400	2 100%	—	1 14.2%	—	4 100%	5 71.4%	—	—	1 14.3%	—	—	—	2	4	7	13
401—800	2 33.3%	—	5 20.8%	4 66.7%	13 68.4%	17 70.8%	—	6 31.6%	—	—	—	2 8.4%	6	19	24	49
801—1200	6 27.3%	6 30%	5 33.3%	12 54.5%	9 45%	8 53.3%	4 18.2%	4 20%	2 13.4%	—	1 5%	—	22	20	15	57
1201—1600	2 12.5%	—	1 25%	10 62.5%	4 100%	2 50%	3 18.7%	—	1 25%	1 6.3%	—	—	16	4	4	24
1601—2000	—	—	—	2 100%	—	—	—	1 100%	—	—	—	—	2	1	—	3
2001+	—	—	—	—	1 50%	—	2 100%	1 50%	—	—	—	—	2	2	—	4
Total	12 8%	6 4%	12 8%	28 18.7%	31 20.7%	32 21.3%	9 6%	12 8%	4 2.7%	1 0.7%	1 0.7%	2 1.4%	50	50	50	150

P—Patna; M—Muzaffarpur; A—Arrah.

TABLE 9
Married Members in the Family (Male)

Income (Rs.)	None			1-2			3-4			5-6			Total			Grand total
	P	M	A	P	M	A	P	M	A	P	M	A	P	M	A	
Up to 400	2 100%	3 75%	1 14.3%	—	1 25%	6 85.7%	—	—	—	—	—	—	2	4	7	13
401—800	1 16.7%	—	2 8.3%	5 83.3%	19 100%	22 91.7%	—	—	—	—	—	—	6	19	24	49
801—1200	—	—	—	20 90.9%	19 95%	14 93.3%	2 9.1%	1 5%	1 6.7%	—	—	—	22	20	15	57
1201—1600	—	—	—	16 100%	1 25%	3 75%	—	3 75%	1 25%	—	—	—	16	4	4	24
1601—2000	—	—	—	1 50%	—	—	1 50%	—	—	—	1 100%	—	2	1	—	3
2001+	—	—	—	2 100%	1 50%	—	—	1 50%	—	—	—	—	2	2	—	4
Total	3 2%	3 2%	3 2%	44 29.3%	41 27.3%	45 30%	3 2%	5 3.3%	2 1.3%	—	1 0.7%	—	50	50	50	150

P—Patna; M—Muzaffarpur; A—Arrah.

TABLE 10
Married Members in the Family (Female)

Income (Rs.)	None			1-2			3-4			5-6			Total			Grand total
	P	M	A	P	M	A	P	M	A	P	M	A	P	M	A	
Up to 400	1 50%	3 75%	2 28.6%	1 50%	1 25%	5 71.4%	—	—	—	—	—	—	2	4	7	13
401—800	—	—	—	5 83.3%	18 94.7%	24 100%	1 16.7%	1 5.3%	—	—	—	—	6	19	24	49
801—1200	—	—	—	20 90.9%	17 85%	14 93.3%	2 9.1%	3 15%	1 6.7%	—	—	—	22	20	15	57
1201—1600	—	—	—	15 93.8%	2 50%	3 75%	1 6.2%	2 50%	1 25%	—	—	—	16	4	4	24
1601—2000	—	—	—	2 100%	—	—	—	—	—	—	1 100%	—	2	1	—	3
2001+	—	—	—	2 100%	1 50%	—	—	1 50%	—	—	—	—	2	2	—	4
Total	1 0.7%	3 2%	2 4%	45 30%	39 26%	46 30.7%	4 2.7%	7 4.7%	2 1.3%	—	1 0.7%	—	50	50	50	150

P—Patna; M—Muzaffarpur; A—Arrah.

TABLE 11
Number of Illiterates in the Family (Male)

Income (Rs.)	None			1-2			3-4			5-6			Total			Grand total
	P	M	A	P	M	A	P	M	A	P	M	A	P	M	A	
Up to 400	2 100%	2 50%	4 57.1%	—	2 50%	3 42.9%	—	—	—	—	—	—	2	4	7	13
401—800	3 50%	10 52.6%	7 29.2%	3 50%	8 42.1%	16 66.7%	—	1 5.3%	1 4.1%	—	—	—	6	19	24	49
801—1200	8 36.4%	6 30%	4 26.7%	12 54.5%	11 55%	10 66.7%	2 9.1%	3 15%	1 6.6%	—	—	—	22	20	15	57
1201—1600	4 25%	1 25%	2 50%	10 62.5%	2 50%	1 25%	2 12.5%	—	1 25%	—	1 25%	—	16	4	4	24
1601—2000	1 50%	—	—	1 50%	1 100%	—	—	—	—	—	—	—	2	1	—	3
2001+	1 50%	—	—	—	2 100%	—	1 50%	—	—	—	—	—	2	2	—	4
Total	19 12.7%	19 12.7%	17 11.3%	26 17.3%	26 17.3%	30 20%	5 3.3%	4 2.6%	3 2%	—	1 0.7%	—	50	50	50	150

P—Patna; M—Muzaffarpur; A—Arrah.

TABLE 12
Number of Illiterates in the Family (Female)

Income (Rs.)	None			1-2			3-4			5-6			Total			Grand total
	P	M	A	P	M	A	P	M	A	P	M	A	P	M	A	
Up to 400	1 50%	—	1 14.3%	1 50%	4 100%	5 71.4%	—	—	1 14.3%	—	—	—	2	4	7	13
401—800	—	—	3 12.6%	5 83.3%	17 89.5%	17 70.8%	1 16.7%	2 10.5%	2 8.3%	—	—	2 8.3%	6	19	24	49
801—1200	—	3 15%	—	17 77.3%	9 45%	12 80%	4 18.2%	7 35%	2 13.3%	1 4.5%	1 5%	1 6.7%	22	20	15	57
1201—1600	2 12.5%	—	—	10 62.5%	2 50%	2 50%	4 25%	2 50%	2 50%	—	—	—	16	4	4	24
1601—2000	—	—	—	1 50%	—	—	1 50%	1 100%	—	—	—	—	2	1	—	3
2001+	—	—	—	1 50%	1 50%	—	—	1 50%	—	1 50%	—	—	2	2	—	4
Total	3 2%	3 2%	4 2.7%	35 23.3%	33 22%	36 24%	10 6.7%	13 8.6%	7 4.6%	2 1.4%	1 0.7%	3 2%	50	50	50	150

P—Patna; M—Muzaffarpur; A—Arrah.

TABLE 13
Level of Education of Male Members (%age)

Town	Illit.	Up to Middle	Under Matric	Matric	Inter	Total
Patna	7 (8.0)	64 (73.6)	9 (10.3)	2 (2.3)	5 (5.8)	87 (100)
Muz.	12 (12.5)	66 (68.8)	11 (11.5)	2 (2.1)	5 (5.2)	96
Arrah	11 (13.9)	52 (65.8)	6 (7.6)	9 (11.4)	1 (1.3)	79
Total	30 (11.5)	182 (69.4)	26 (9.9)	13 (5.0)	11 (4.2)	262

TABLE 14
Level of Education of Female Members (%age)

Town	Illit.	Up to Middle	Under Matric	Matric	Inter	Total
Patna	31 (53.4)	27 (46.5)	—	—	—	58
Muz.	35 (53.0)	28 (42.5)	1 (1.5)	2 (3.0)	—	66
Arrah	36 (65.5)	17 (30.9)	1 (1.8)	1 (1.8)		55
Total	102 (57.0)	72 (40.2)	2 (1.1)	3 (1.7)		179

TABLE 15
Number of Persons who Smoke (Male)

Income (Rs.)	None Grand			1			2			3			4			Total			Grand total
	P	M	A	P	M	A	P	M	A	P	M	A	P	M	A	P	M	A	
Up to 400	—	3 75%	3 42.9%	2 100%	1 25%	4 57.1%	—	—	—	—	—	—	—	—	—	2	4	7	13
401—800	2 33.3%	2 10.5%	1 4.2%	4 66.7%	14 73.7%	19 79.2%	—	3 15.8%	4 16.7%	—	—	—	—	—	—	6	19	24	49
801—1200	3 13.6%	1 5%	—	16 72.7%	11 55%	7 46.7%	3 13.7%	7 35%	8 53.3%	—	1 5%	—	—	—	—	22	20	15	57
1201—1600	1 6.3%	—	—	11 68.8%	1 25%	1 25%	2 12.5%	1 25%	2 50%	2 12.5%	2 50%	—	—	—	—	16	4	4	24
1601—2000	—	—	—	1 50%	—	—	1 50%	1 100%	—	—	—	—	—	—	—	2	1	—	3
2001+	—	—	—	1 50%	1 50%	—	—	1 50%	—	1 50%	—	—	—	—	—	2	1	—	4
Total	6 4%	6 4%	4 2.8%	35 23.3%	28 18.7%	31 20.7%	6 4%	13 8.6%	14 9.3%	3 2%	3 2%	—	—	—	—	50	50	50	150

P—Patna; M—Muzaffarpur; A—Arrah.

TABLE 16
Number of Persons who Smoke (Female)

Income (Rs.)	None			1			2			3			4			Total			Grand total
	P	M	A	P	M	A	P	M	A	P	M	A	P	M	A	P	M	A	
Up to 400	1 50%	4 100%	5 71.4%	1 50%	—	2 28.6%	—	—	—	—	—	—	—	—	—	2	4	7	13
401—800	1 16.7%	1 5.3%	1 4.2%	5 83.3%	17 89.5%	23 95.8%	—	1 5.3%	—	—	—	—	—	—	—	6	19	24	49
801—1200	9 40.9%	—	1 6.7%	13 59.1%	17 85%	13 86.7%	—	2 10%	1 6.7%	—	1 5%	—	—	—	—	22	20	15	57
1201—1600	5 31.3%	—	2 50%	10 62.5%	4 100%	2 50%	1 6.3%	—	—	—	—	—	—	—	—	16	4	4	24
1601—2000	—	1 100%	—	—	—	—	2 100%	—	—	—	—	—	—	—	—	2	1	—	3
2001+	—	—	—	1 50%	2 100%	—	—	—	—	—	—	—	1 50%	—	—	2	2	—	4
Total	16 10.6%	6 4%	9 6%	30 20%	40 26.6%	40 26.6%	3 2%	3 2%	1 0.7%	—	1 0.7%	—	1 0.7%	—	—	50	50	50	150

P—Patna; M—Muzaffarpur; A—Arrah.

TABLE 17
Number of Drinkers in the Family (Male)

Income (Rs.)	None			1			2			3			4			Total			Grand total
	P	M	A	P	M	A	P	M	A	P	M	A	P	M	A	P	M	A	
Up to 400	1 50%	3 75%	3 42.9%	1 50%	1 25%	4 57.2%	—	—	—	—	—	—	—	—	—	2	4	7	13
401—800	3 50%	5 26.3%	1 4.2%	3 50%	14 73.7%	22 91.2%	—	—	1 4.2%	—	—	—	—	—	—	6	19	24	49
801—1200	5 22.7%	5 25%	—	16 72.7%	10 50%	9 60%	1 4.6 %	5 25%	6 40%	—	—	—	—	—	—	22	20	15	57
1201—1600	3 18.8%	—	2 50%	11 68.8%	2 50%	1 25%	2 12.5%	—	1 25%	—	2 50%	—	—	—	—	16	4	4	24
1601—2000	—	—	—	1 50%	1 100%	—	1 50%	—	—	—	—	—	—	—	—	2	1	—	3
2001 +	1 50%	1 50%	—	—	1 50%	—	1	—	—	—	—	—	—	—	—	2	2	—	4
Total	13 8.6%	14 9.3%	6 4%	32 21.3%	29 19.3%	36 24%	5 3.3%	5 3.3%	8 5.3%	—	2 1.3%	—	—	—	—	50	50	50	150

P—Patna; M—Muzaffarpur; A—Arrah.

TABLE 18
Number of Drinkers in the Family (Female)

Income (Rs.)	None			1			2			3			4			Total			Grand total
	P	M	A	P	M	A	P	M	A	P	M	A	P	M	A	P	M	A	
Up to 400	2 100%	4 100%	7 100%	—	—	—	—	—	—	—	—	—	—	—	—	2	4	7	13
401—800	6 100%	19 100%	24 100%	—	—	—	—	—	—	—	—	—	—	—	—	6	19	24	49
801—1200	22 100%	20 100%	15 100%	—	—	—	—	—	—	—	—	—	—	—	—	22	20	15	57
1201—1600	16 100%	2 50%	4 100%	—	2 50%	—	—	—	—	—	—	—	—	—	—	16	4	4	24
1601—2000	2 100%	1 100%	—	—	—	—	—	—	—	—	—	—	—	—	—	2	1	—	3
2001+	2 100%	2 100%	—	—	—	—	—	—	—	—	—	—	—	—	—	2	2	—	4
Total	50 33.3%	48 32%	50 33.3%	—	2 1.4%	—	—	—	—	—	—	—	—	—	—	50	50	50	150

P — Patna; M — Muzaffarpur; A — Arrah.

TABLE 19
Total Monthly Expenditure on Drinking & Smoking (Male)

Income (Rs.)	No expense	Upto Rs. 25	Rs. 26-50	Rs. 51-75	Rs. 76-100	Rs. 101-125	Rs. 126-150	Rs. 151 & above	Total
Up to 400	6 (46.1%)	1 (7.5%)	1 (7.5%)	2 (15.1%)	2 (15.1%)	1 (7.5)	—	—	13
401—800	4 (8.1%)	3 (6.1%)	8 (16.3%)	16 (32.6%)	10 (20.4%)	4 (8.1%)	—	4 (8.1%)	49
801—1200	3 (5.2%)	3 (5.2%)	11 (19.2%)	9 (15.7%)	8 (14.0%)	6 (10.4%)	6 (10.4%)	11 (19.2%)	57
1201—1600	—	—	4 (16.6%)	8 (33.3%)	2 (8.3%)	2 (8.3%)	—	8 (33.3%)	24
1601—2000	—	—	—	—	1 (33.3%)	2 (66.6%)	—	—	3
2001+	—	—	3 (75.0%)	—	—	—	—	1 (25.0%)	4
Total	13 (8.6%)	7 (4.6%)	27 (18.0%)	35 (23.3%)	23 (15.3%)	15 (10.0%)	6 (4.0%)	24 (16.0%)	150

Responses from the three towns of Patna, Muzaffarpur and Arrah have been combined.

TABLE 20
Total Monthly Expenditure on Drinking & Smoking (Female)

Income (Rs.)	No expense	Up to Rs. 5	Rs. 6–10	Rs. 11-15	Rs. 16-20	Rs. 21-25	Rs. 26-30	Rs. 31 & above	Total
Upto 400	10 (76.9%)	—	—	—	1 (7.7%)	1 (7.7%)	1 (7.7%)	—	13
401—800	3 (6.1%)	2 (4.0%)	5 (10.2%)	4 (8.2%)	9 (18.4%)	12 (24.5%)	12 (24.5%)	2 (4.0%)	49
801—1200	10 (17.0%)	—	1 (1.7%)	8 (14.0%)	10 (17.5%)	15 (26.3%)	5 (8.8%)	8 (14.0%)	57
1201—1600	7 (29.2%)	—	—	2 (8.3%)	5 (20.8%)	4 (16.6%)	3 (12.5%)	3 (12.5%)	24
1601—2000	1 (33.3%)	—	—	—	—	—	—	2 (66.6%)	3
2001+	—	—	1 (25.0%)	1 (25.0%)				2 (50.0%)	4
Total	31 (20.7%)	2 (1.3%)	7 (4.7%)	15 (10.0%)	25 (16.7%)	32 (21.3%)	21 (14.0%)	17 (11.3%)	150

Responses from the three towns of Patna, Muzaffarpur and Arrah have been combined.

TABLE 21
Frequency of Film Seeing

Age (yrs.)	Frequetnly			Occasionally			Very infrequently			Never			Total			Grand total
	P	M	A	P	M	A	P	M	A	P	M	A	P	M	A	
Up to 20	—	—	—	1 100%	1 50%	3 100%	—	—	—	—	1 50%	—	1	2	3	6
21—30	1 9.1%	—	1 7.7%	4 36.4%	3 25%	10 76.9%	1 9.1%	—	2 15.4%	5 45.5%	9 75%	—	11	12	13	36
31—40	1 5.9%	—	—	9 52.9%	6 28.6%	9 60%	3 17.6%	8 38.1%	3 20%	4 23.5%	7 33.3%	3 20%	17	21	15	53
41—50	—	—	—	6 35.3%	4 86.4%	3 17.6%	3 17.6%	2 18.2%	9 52.9%	8 47.1%	5 45.5%	5 29.4%	17	11	17	45
51—60					3 75%	—	1 25%	—	1 50%	3 75%	1 25%	1 50%	4	4	2	10
Total	2 1.3%	—	1 0.7%	20 13.3%	17 11.3%	25 16.7%	8 5.3%	10 6.7%	15 10%	20 13.3%	23 15.3%	9 6%	50	50	50	150

Responses from the three towns of Patna, Muzaffarpur & Patna have been taken separately.

TABLE 22
Type of Film Liked

Age (yrs.)	Romantic			Directive			Reformative			All types		
	P	M	A	P	M	A	P	M	A	P	M	A
Up to 20	—	—	—	—	—	—	—	—	—	1 100%	—	3 100%
21—30	—	—	—	—	—	—	—	—	—	6 54.5%	1 8.3%	12 92.3%
31—40	—	—	—	—	—	—	5 29.4%	2 9.2%	—	6 35.3%	6 28.6%	12 80%
41—50	—	—	—	1 5.9%	—	—	1 5.9%	2 18.2%	—	7 41.2%	—	9 52.9%
51—60	—	—	—	—	—	—	1 25%	2 50%	—	—	1 25%	1 50%
Total	—	—	—	1 0.7%	—	—	7 4.7%	6 4.0%	—	20 13.3%	8 5.3%	37 21.7%

TABLE 22 (*Contd.*)

Age (yrs.)	Religious			Bhojpuri			None			Total			Grand total
	P	M	A	P	M	A	P	M	A	P	M	A	
Up to 20	—	1 50%	—	—	—	—	—	1 50%	—	1	2	3	6
21—30	—	1 8.3%	1 7.7%	—	1 8.3%	—	5 45.5%	9 75%	—	11	12	13	36
31—40	2 11.8%	6 28.6%	—	—	—	—	4 23.5%	7 33.3%	3 20%	17	21	15	53
41—50	—	4 36.4%	3 17.6%	—	—	—	8 47.1%	5 45.5%	5 29.4%	17	1	17	45
51—60	—	—	—	—	—	—	3 75%	1 25%	1 50%	4	4	2	10
Total	2 1.3%	12 8.0%	4 2.7%	—	1 0.7%	—	20 13.3%	23 15.3%	9 6%	50	50	50	150

P—Patna; M—Muzaffarpur; A—Arrah

TABLE 23

Are you Aware of the Facilities Given by the State for the Welfare of Scheduled Castes?

Age (yrs.)	Yes	No	Know nothing	Total
Up to 20	5 (83.3%)	1 (16.7%)	—	6
21—30	18 (50.0%)	4 (11.1%)	14 (38.9%)	36
31—40	29 (54.7%)	3 (5.7%)	21 (39.6%)	53
41—50	19 (42.2%)	7 (15.6%)	19 (42.2%)	45
51—60	15 (50.0%)	2 (20.0%)	3 (30.0%)	10
Total	76 (50.7%)	17 (11.3%)	57 (38.0%)	150

TABLE 24
Do you Know the Meaning of the Followings?

Age (yrs.)	Democracy		Equality of right		Adult franchise		Mid-term poll		Lok Sabha Vidhan Sabha		Panchayati Raj		Know nothing	Total
	Yes	No	Yes	No	Yes	No	Yes	No	Yes	No	Yes	No		
Up to 20	2 33.3%	2 33.3%	2 33.3%	2 33.3%	3 50%	1 16.7%	1 16.7%	3 50%	2 33.3%	2 33.3%	—	4 66.6%	2 33.3%	6
21—30	20 55.6%	5 13.9%	15 41.7%	10 27.8%	25 69.4%	—	2 5.6%	23 63.9%	15 41.7%	10 27.8%	6 16.7%	19 52.8%	11 30.6%	36
31—40	24 45.3%	12 22.6%	19 35.8%	17 32.1%	33 62.3%	3 5.7%	2 3.8%	34 64.2%	14 26.4%	22 41.5%	5 9.4%	31 58.8%	17 32.1%	53
41—50	21 46.7%	13 28.9%	17 37.8%	17 37.8%	23 51.1%	11 24.4%	1 2.2%	33 73.3%	8 17.8%	26 57.8%	5 11.1%	29 64.4%	11 24.4%	43
51—60	5 50%	3 30%	2 20%	6 60%	7 70%	1 10%	—	8 80%	2 20%	6 60%	1 10%	7 70%	2 20%	10
Total	72 48%	35 23.3%	55 36.7%	52 34.7%	91 60.7%	16 10.7%	6 4.0%	101 63.3%	41 27.3%	66 44%	17 11.3%	90 60%	43 28.7%	150

Responses of the three towns have been taken together.

TABLE 25
Since When you/your Family Members are in this Occupation?

Income (Rs.)	Up to 5 yrs.	6-10	11-15	16-20	21-25	26-30	31 + yrs.	Total
Up to 400	1 7.7%	3 23.1%	1 7.7%	4 30.8%	4 30.8%	—	—	13
401—800	5 10.2%	14 28.6%	11 22.4%	10 20.4%	5 10.2%	3 6.1%	1 2.0%	49
801—1200	7 12.3%	7 12.3%	8 14.0%	16 28.1%	6 10.5%	5 8.8%	8 14.0%	57
1201—1600	2 8.3%	3 12.5%	3 12.5%	4 16.7%	4 16.7%	6 25.0%	2 8.3%	24
1601—2000	—	—	—	1 33.3%	1 33.3%	1 33.3%	—	3
2001+	1 25%	—	—	—	—	—	3 75%	4
Total	16 10.7%	27 18.0%	23 15.3%	35 23.3%	20 13.3%	15 10.0%	14 9.3%	150

TABLE 26
Why did you Take up this Occupation?

(Income-wise)

Income (Rs.)	Traditional occupation	Easily available	No alternative.	Due to poverty	Total
Up to—400	3 (23.1%)	5 (38.5%)	8 (61-5%)	1 (7.7%)	17
401—800	20 (40.8%)	15 (30.6%)	21 (42.9%)	5 (10.2%)	61
801—1200	24 (42.1%)	23 (40.4%)	26 (45.6%)	10 (17.5%)	83
1201—1600	9 (37.5%)	11 (45.8%)	13 (52.2%)	1 (4.2%)	34
1601—2000	1 (33.3%)	1 (33.3%)	3 (100%)	—	5
2001 +	4 (100%)	1 (25%)	2 (50%)	—	7
Total	61 (40.7%)	56 (37.3%)	73 (48.7%)	17 (11.3%)	207

TABLE 27
Why did you take up this occupation?

(Family Structure-wise)

Family Type					Total
Joint = 56	21 (37.5%)	20 (35.7%)	35 (62.5%)	5 (8.9%)	81
Nuclear = 94	40 (42.6%)	36 (38.3%)	38 (40.4%)	12 (12.8%)	126
Total = 150	61 (40.7%)	56 (37.3%)	73 (48.7%)	17 (11.3%)	207

TABLE 28
What are the difficulties felt by you in the Present Occupation?

Income (Rs.)	Less salary	Hard Duty/ Heavy load of work	Delay in payment of salary	Accessories not provided	Exploi- tation	Others	No difficulty	Total
Up to 400 = 13	3 (23.1%)	4 (30.8%)	5 (38.5%)	7 (53.8%)	2 (15.4%)	—	1 (7.7%)	22
401—800 = 49	11 (22.4%)	9 (18.4%)	21 (42.9%)	34 (69.4%)	11 (22.4%)	3 (6.1%)	3 (6.1%)	92
801—1200 = 57	12 (21.1%)	18 (31.6%)	10 (17.5%)	27 (47.4%)	12 (21.1%)	1 (1.8%)	7 (12.3%)	87
1200—1600 = 24	3 (12.5%)	4 (16.7%)	10 (41.7%)	12 (50%)	10 (41.7%)	1 (4.2%)	4 (16.7%)	44
1601—2000 = 3	—	2 (66.7%)	2 (66.7%)	—	1 (33.3%)	—	—	5
2001 + = 4	—	3 (75.0%)	—	1 (25.0%)	3 (75.0%)	—	1 (25.0%)	8
Total = 150	29 (19.3%)	40 (26.7%)	48 (32.0%)	82 (54.0%)	39 (26.0%)	5 (3.3%)	16 (10.7%)	258

TABLE 29

What are the Difficulties Felt by you in the Present Occupation?

Age (Yrs)	Less salary	Hard Duty/ Heavy load of work	Delay in payment of salary	Accessories not provided	Exploi-tation	Others*	No difficulty	Total
Up to 20 = 6	2 (33.3%)	2 (33.3%)	1 (16.7%)	4 (66.7%)	1 (16.7%)	—	—	10
21—30 = 36	7 (19.4%)	7 (19.4%)	14 (38.9%)	21 (58.3%)	13 (36.1%)	1 (2.8%)	4 (11.1%)	67
31—40 = 53	10 (18.9%)	17 (32.1%)	13 (54.5%)	27 (50.9%)	13 (24.5%)	3 (5.7%)	7 (13.2%)	90
41—50 = 45	9 (20.0%)	12 (26.7%)	18 (40.0%)	27 (60.0%)	8 (17.8%)	1 (2.2%)	4 (8.9%)	79
51—60 = 10	1 (10.0%)	2 (20.0%)	2 (20.0%)	2 (20.0%)	4 (40.0%)	—	1 (10.0%)	12
Total = 150	29 (19.3%)	40 (26.7%)	48 (32.0%)	81 (54.0%)	39 (26.6%)	5 (3.3%)	16 (10.7%)	258

*NOTE: 'Others' include health hazard, no job security and no leave in emergency.

TABLE 30
Reasons for Liking Sulabh Shauchalaya Scheme

(% age)

Age (yrs.)	Economic	Hygienic	Liberates scavengers	Free From fourl smell	Scavenging not needed	Better than service latrine	Beneficial for general public.	Total
Up to 20 = 6	—	4 (66.7)	2 (33.3)	1 (16.7)	2 (33.3)	—	—	9
21—30 = 36	3 (8.3)	21 (58.3)	11 (30.6)	9 (25.0)	8 (22.2)	1 (2.8)	2 (5.6)	55
31—40 = 53	—	27 (50.9)	20 (37.7)	14 (26.4)	15 (28.3)	1 (1.9)	5 (9.4)	82
41—50 = 45	—	17 (37.8)	18 (40.0)	6 (13.3)	9 (20.0)	2 (4.4)	4 (8.9)	56
51—60 = 10	—	7 (70.0)	4 (40.0)	1 (10.0)	2 (20.0)	2 (20.0)	1 (10.0)	17
Total = 150	3 (2.0)	76 (50.7)	55 (36.7)	31 (20.7)	36 (24.0)	6 (4.0)	12 (8.0)	219

TABLE 31
Type and Number of Members in the Family

Town	Joint family						Nuclear family					
	1-3	4–6	7–9	10–12	13–15	Total	1–3	4–6	7–9	10–12	13–15	Total
Ranchi	—	5 35.7%	6 42.9%	1 7.1%	2 14.3%	14	6 16.7%	21 58.3%	9 25.0%	—	—	36
Purnea	1 6.2%	7 43.8%	7 43.8%	1 6.2%	—	16	13 38.2%	16 47.1%	4 11.8%	1 2.9%	—	34
Patna	—	9 29%	15 48.4%	6 19.4%	1 3.2%	31	8 42.1%	7 36.8%	4 21.1%	—	—	19
Total	1 1.7%	21 34.4%	28 45.9%	8 13.1%	3 4.9%	61 40.7%	27 30.3%	44 49.5%	17 19.1%	1 1.1%	—	89 59.3%

TABLE 32
Type of House

Sl. No.	Name of town	Residential pattern: Own	Rental	Govt.	Total
1.	Ranchi	17 (34.0%)	13 (26.0%)	20 (40.0%)	50
2.	Purnea	38 (76.0%)	2 (4.0%)	10 (20.0%)	50
3.	Patna	14 (28.0%)	1 (2.0%)	35 (70.0%)	50
	Total	69 (46.0%)	16 (10.7%)	65 (43.3%)	150

TABLE 33
Type of House

Sl. No.	Name of town	Type of house: Katcha	Pucca	Mixed	Total
1.	Ranchi	31 (62.0%)	15 (30.0%)	4 (8.0%)	50
2.	Purnea	40 (80.0%)	5 (10.0%)	5 (10.0%)	50
3.	Patna	12 (24.0%)	9 (18.0%)	29 (58.0%)	50
	Total	83 (55.3%)	29 (19.3%)	38 (25.3%)	150

TABLE 34
Number of Rooms Available in Each House

Sl. No.	Name of town	No. of rooms available in each house: One room	Two rooms	Three rooms	Total
1.	Ranchi	26 (52%)	18 (36%)	6 (12%)	50
2.	Purnea	48 (96%)	1 (2%)	1 (2%)	50
3.	Patna	47 (94%)	2 (4%)	1 (2%)	50
	Total	121 (80.7%)	21 (14.0%)	8 (5.3%)	150

TABLE 35
Adequacy of Accommodation

Sl. No.	Name of town	Accommodation		Total
		Not Sufficient	Sufficient	
1.	Ranchi	36 (72%)	14 (28%)	50
2.	Purnea	43 (86%)	7 (14%)	50
3.	Patna	45 (90%)	5 (10%)	50
	Total	124 (83.8%)	26 (16.3%)	150

TABLE 36
Electricity

Sl. No.	Name of town	Yes	No	Total
1.	Ranchi	6 (12%)	44 (88%)	50
2.	Purnea	1 (2%)	49 (98%)	50
3.	Patna	44 (88%)	6 (12%)	50
	Total	51 (34%)	99 (66%)	150

TABLE 37
Sources of Drinking Water

Sl. No.	Name of town	Sources of drinking water				Total
		Well	Tap	Hand pump	Tube well	
1.	Ranchi	18 (36%)	32 (64%)	—	—	50
2.	Purnea	1 (2%)	10 (20%)	31 (62%)	8 (16%)	50
3.	Patna	1 (2%)	48 (96%)	1 (2%)	—	50
	Total	20 (13.3%)	90 (60%)	32 (21.3%)	8 (5.3%)	150

TABLE 38
Type of Source of Drinking Water

Sl. No.	Name of town	Private	Public	Total
1.	Ranchi	5 (10%)	45 (90%)	50
2.	Purnea	6 (12%)	44 (88%)	50
3.	Patna	1 (2%)	49 (98%)	50
	Total	12 (8%)	138 (92%)	150

TABLE 39
Place of Defecation

Sl. No.	Name of town	Private toilet	Community latrine	Open space	Total
1.	Ranchi	9 (18%)	34 (68%)	7 (14%)	50
2.	Purnea	3 (6%)	—	47 (94%)	50
3.	Patna	—	36 (72%)	14 (28%)	50
	Total	12 (8%)	70 (46.7%)	68 (45.3%)	150

TABLE 40
Sex Ratio

Sl. No.	Name of town	Male	Female	Total
1.	Ranchi	—	50 (100%)	50
2.	Purnea	12 (24%)	38 (76%)	50
3.	Patna	18 (36%)	32 (64%)	50
	Total	30 (20%)	120 (80%)	150

TABLE 41
Age of Liberated Scavengers

Sl. No.	Name of town	Age Level						Total
		Up to 20	21—30	31—40	41—50	51—60	61 & above	
1.	Ranchi	—	14 28%	14 28%	12 24%	10 20%	—	50
2.	Purnea	1 2%	15 30%	17 34%	15 30%	2 4%	—	50
3.	Patna	—	6 12%	15 30%	18 36%	10 20%	1 2%	50
	Total	1 0.7%	35 23.3%	46 30.7%	45 30%	22 14.7%	1 0.7%	150

TABLE 42
Education

Sl. No.	Name of town	Illiterate	Up to 4th	Up to Middle	Total
1.	Ranchi	47 (94%)	3 (6%)	—	50
2.	Purnea	48 (96%)	2 (4%)	—	50
3.	Patna	43 (86%)	6 (12%)	1 (2.0%)	50
	Total	138 (92%)	11 (7.3%)	1 (0.7%)	150

TABLE 43
Interest in Adult Education

Age (Yrs)	Ranchi			Purnea			Patna		
	Yes	No	Total	Yes	No	Total	Yes	No	Total
Up to 20	—	—	—	1 100%	—	1	—	—	—
21—30	13 92.9%	1 7.1%	14	6 40%	9 60%	15	—	6 100%	6
31—40	10 66.7%	5 33.3%	15	6 33..3%	12 66.7%	18	4 26.7%	11 73.3%	15
41—50	4 33.3%	8 66.7%	12	1 7.1%	13 92.9%	14	3 17.6%	14 82.4%	17
51—60	4 44.4%	5 55.6%	9	—	2 100%	2 9.1%	1 9.1%	10 91.9%	11
61 +	—	—	—	—	—	—	—	1 100%	1
Total	31 62%	19 38%	50	14 28%	36 72%	50	8 16%	42 84%	50

TABLE 44
Monthly Income (Personal)

Income range (In Rs.)	Ranchi	Purnea	Patna	Total
Less than 100	—	—	—	—
100—200	—	2 (4%)	5 (10%)	7 (4.7%)
201—300	—	6 (12%)	6 (12%)	12 (8.0%)
301—400	13 (26%)	39 (78%)	15 (30%)	67 (44.7%)
401—500	37 (74%)	3 (6%)	9 (18%)	49 (32.7%)
501—600	—	—	7 (14%)	7 (4.7%)
601 +	—	—	6 (12%)	6 (4.0%)
Total	50	50	50	150

TABLE 45
Total Monthly Income of the Family

income (Rs.)	Ranchi			Purnea			Patna			Grand total
	J.F.	N.F.	Total	J.F.	N.F.	Total	J.F.	N.F.	Total	
Up to Rs. 400	—	1 (100%)	1	2 (10.5%)	17 (89.5%)	19	1 (14.3%)	6 (85.7%)	7	27
Rs. 401—800	8 (24.2%)	25 (75.8%)	33	4 (23.5%)	13 (76.5%)	17	12 (60.0%)	8 (40.0%)	20	70
Rs. 801—1200	5 (35.7%)	9 (64.3%)	14	7 (58.3%)	5 (41.7%)	12	13 (72.2%)	5 (27.7%)	18	44
Rs. 1201—1600	—	—	—	1 (100%)	—	1	3 (100%)	—	4	4
Rs. 1601 +	1 (50%)	1 (50%)	2	1 (100%)	—	1	2 (100%)	—	2	5
Total	14 (9.3%)	36 (24%)	50	15 (10%)	35 (23.3%)	50	31 (20.7%)	19 (12.7%)	50	150

J.F. — Joint Family; N.F. — Nuclear Family.

TABLE 46
Age at Which Scavenging Started

Name of town	10—15 yrs.	16—20 yrs.	21—25 yrs.	26 yrs. & above	Total
Ranchi	—	47 (94.0%)	3 (6%)	—	50
Purnea	10 (20%)	30 (60.0%)	7 (14%)	3 (6%)	50
Patna	18 (36%)	26 (52.0%)	1 (2%)	5 (10%)	50
Total	28 (18.7%)	103 (68.7%)	11 (7.3%)	8 (5.3%)	150

TABLE 47
Age at Which Liberated

Name of town	Below 20 yrs.	20—25 yrs.	26—30 yrs.	31—35 yrs.	36—40 yrs.	41 yrs. & above	Total
Ranchi	—	7 14%	13 26%	8 16%	3 6%	19 38%	50
Purnea	—	9 18%	11 22%	8 16%	7 14%	15 30%	50
Patna	—	6 12%	6 12%	9 18%	9 18%	20 40%	50
Total	—	22 14.7%	30 20%	25 16.7%	19 12.7%	54 36%	150

TABLE 48
Duration of Scavenging before Liberation

Name of town	Less than 5 yrs.	5—10 yrs.	11—15 yrs.	16—20 yrs.	21 yrs. & above	Total
Ranchi	2 4%	13 26%	12 24%	3 6%	20 40%	50
Purnea	8 16%	7 14%	9 18%	7 14%	19 38%	50
Patna	4 8%	7 14%	10 20%	9 18%	20 40%	50
Total	14 9.3%	27 18%	31 20.7%	19 12.7%	59 39.3%	150

TABLE 49
Are you Satisfied with your Present Occupation?

Sex	Ranchi			Purnea			Patna		
	Yes	No	Total	Yes	No	Total	Yes	No	Total
Male	—	—	—	11 91.7%	1 8.3%	12	12 66.7%	6 33.3%	18
Female	50 100%	—	50	32 84.2%	6 15.8%	38	25 78.1%	7 21.9%	32
Total	50 100%	—	50	43 86%	7 14%	50	37 74%	13 26%	50

TABLE 50
Reasons for Dissatisfaction

Sex	Less salary			More responsibility			Absence of service security			Others			No alternative			Total		
	T1	T2	T3	T1	T2	T3	T1	T2	T3	T1	T2	T3	T1	T2	T3	T1	T2	T3
Male	—	2 66.7%	2 33.3%	—	—	1 16.7%	—	1 33.3%	1 16.7%	—	—	1 16.7%	—	—	1 16.7%	—	3	6
Female	—	3 42.9%	1 14.3%	—	1 14.3%	—	—	3 42.9%	1 14.3%	—	—	3 42.8%	—	—	2 28.6%	—	7	7
Total	—	5 21.7%	3 13.0%	—	1 4.3%	1 4.3%	—	4 17.4%	2 8.7%	—	—	4 17.4%	—	—	3 13.0%	—	10	13 =23

T1 = Ranchi; T2 = Purnea; T3 = Patna. There is multi-response in Purnea.

TABLE 51
Reasons for Dissatisfaction

Family income	Less salary			More responsibility			Absence of service security			Others			No alternative			Total		
	T1	T2	T3	T1	T2	T3	T1	T2	T3	T1	T2	T3	T1	T2	T3	T1	T2	T3
0—400	—	3 60%	—	—	1 20%	—	—	1 20%	1 33.3%	—	—	2 66.7%	—	—	—	—	5	3
401—800	—	1 25%	1 20%	—	—	—	—	3 75%	1 20%	—	—	1 20%	—	—	2 40%	—	4	5
801—1200	—	1 100%	2 50%	—	—	1 25%	—	—	—	—	—	1 25%	—	—	—	—	1	4
1201—1600	—	—	—	—	—	—	—	—	—	—	—	—	—	—	1 100%	—	—	1
1601 +	—	5 21.7%	3 13%	—	1 4.3%	1 4.3%	—	4 17.4%	2 8.7%	—	—	4 17.4%	—	—	3 13%	—	10	13

T1 = Ranchi; T2 = Purnea; T3 = Patna. There is multi-response in Purnea.

TABLE 52
Showing Impact of Liberation

Conditions put to respondents	Ranchi				Purena				Patna			
	Pre-Liberation		Post-Liberation		Pre-Liberation		Post-Liberation		Pre-Liberation		Post-Liberation	
	Yes	No	Yes	No	Yes	No	Yes	No	Yes	No	Yes	No
Visit to temples = 50	50 100%	—	50 100%	—	6 12%	44 88%	21 42%	29 58%	30 60%	20 40%	49 98%	1 2%
Engagement of Brahmins = 50	50 100%	—	50 100%	—	14 28%	36 72%	28 56%	22 44%	30 60%	20 40%	50 100%	—
Invitation by other castes = 50	1 2%	49 98%	50 100%	— —	3 6%	47 94%	8 16%	42 84%	9 18%	41 82%	35 70%	15 30%
Taking water from common source = 50	1 2%	49 98%	50 100%	— —	7 14%	43 86%	43 86%	7 14%	24 48%	26 52%	49 98%	1 2%
Taking food in Hotel = 50	1 2%	49 98%	49 98%	1 2%	7 14%	43 86%	40 80%	10 20%	30 60%	20 40%	49 98%	1 2%
Total	103	147	249	1	37	213	140	110	123	127	232	18

TABLE 53
Do you Send your Children to School?

Level of income (Rs.)	Ranchi				Purnea				Patna			
	Yes	No	NA	Total	Yes	No	NA	Total	Yes	No	NA	Total
Up to 400	—	1 100%	—	1	1 5.3%	15 78.9%	3 15.8%	19	1 14.3%	5 71.4%	1 14.3%	7
401- -800	10 30.3%	23 69.7%	—	33	4 23.5%	12 70.6%	1 5.9%	17	9 45%	8 40%	3 15%	20
801—1200	4 28.6%	10 71.4%	—	14	5 41.7%	5 41.7%	2 16.2%	12	6 33.3%	11 61.1%	1 5.6%	18
1201—1600	—	—	—	—	—	1 100%	—	1	2 66.7%	1 33.3%	—	3
1601 +	1 50%	1 50%	—	2	—	1 100%	—	1	—	2 100%	—	2
Total	15 30%	35 70%	—	50	10 20%	34 68%	6 12%	50	18 36%	27 54%	5 10%	50

TABLE 54
Are there Adequeate Facilities Available for study at Home?

Income Group (Rs.)	Ranchi				Purnea				Patna			
	Yes	No	NA	Total	Yes	No	NA	Total	Yes	No	NA	Total
Up to 400	—	1 100%	—	1	1 5.3%	14 73.7%	4 21.1%	19	1 14.3%	4 57.1%	2 28.6%	7
401—800	5 15.2%	28 84.8%	—	33	5 29.4%	11 64.7%	1 5.8%	17	6 30%	8 40%	6 30%	20
801—1200	4 28.6%	10 71.4%	—	14	—	11 91.7%	1 8.3%	12	8 44.4%	7 38.9%	3 16.3%	18
1201—1600	—	—	—	—	—	1 100%	—	1	1 33.3%	1 33.3%	1 33.3%	3
1601 +	—	2 100%	—	2	—	1 100%	—	1	2 100%	—	—	2
Total	9 18%	41 82%	—	50	6 12%	38 76%	6 12%	50	18 36%	20 40%	12 24%	50

TABLE 55
Do your Children Study at Home?

Name of town	Yes	No	Not applicable	Total
Ranchi	19 (38%)	29 (58%)	2 (4%)	50
Purnea	11 (22%)	28 (56%)	11 (22%)	50
Patna	24 (48%)	13 (26%)	13 (26%)	50
Total	54(36%)	70(46.7%)	26(17.3%)	150

TABLE 56
Number of Persons in Family Needing Employment

Name of town	Male						Female					
	One person	Two persons	Three persons	Four/ more	Total	Nobody	One person	Two persons	Three persons	Four/ more	Total	Nobody
Ranchi	21	6	—	—	27	23	10	1	—	—	11	39
Purnea	9	1	1	—	11	39	18	3	1	—	22	28
Patna	19	5	1	1	26	24	15	12	1	1	29	21
Total	49	12	2	1	64	86	43	16	2	1	62	88

TABLE 57
Preference for Nature of Employment for Males and Females

Name of town	Male								Female					
	Peon	Clerk	Driver mech.	Police	Industry	Any other	Total	NA	Peon	Nurse	Maid servant	Any other	Total	NA
Ranchi	21 60%	5 14.3%	5 14.3%	10 28.6%	26 74.3%	29 82.9%	96	15	8 22.9%	6 17.1%	11 31.4%	13 37.1%	38	15
Purnea	8 26.7%	3 10%	6 20%	2 6.7%	5 16.7%	12 40%	36	20	12 40%	3 10%	21 70%	21 70%	57	20
Patna	19 54.3%	1 2.9.%	14 40%	2 5.7%	23 37.1%	12 34.3%	61	15	21 60%	18 51.4%	29 82.9%	25 71.4%	93	15
Total	48 48%	9 9%	25 25%	14 14%	44 44%	53 53%	193	50 50%	41 41%	27 27%	61 61%	59 59%	188	50

TABLE 58
Did you ever try to get jobs for your Family Members?

Name of town	Yes	No	N.A.	Total
Ranchi	23 (46.0%)	7 (14.0%)	20 (40.0%)	50
Purnea	16 (32.0%)	11 (22.0%)	23 (46.0%)	50
Patna	21 (42.0%)	15 (30.0%)	14 (28.0%)	50
Total	60 (40%)	33 (22%)	57 (38%)	150

TABLE 59
Age Classification

Name of town	Up to 20	21–30	31–40	41–50	51–60	61–70	70 +	Total
Patna	0	7 14%	14 28%	17 34%	3 6%	6 12%	3 6%	50
Muzaffarpur	0	2 4%	10 20%	17 34%	10 20%	6 12%	5 10%	50
Arrah	1 2%	4 8%	12 24%	9 18%	9 18%	11 22%	4 8%	50
Total	1 0.7%	13 8.7%	36 24%	43 28.7%	22 14.7%	23 15.3%	12 8.0%	150 100%

TABLE 60
Sex Distribution

Name of town	Male	Female	Total
Patna	48 (96%)	2 (4%)	50
Muzaffarpur	44 (88%)	6 (12%)	50
Arrah	45 (90%)	5 (10%)	50
Total	137 (91.3%)	13 (8.7%)	150(100%)

TABLE 61
Educational Classification

Name of town	Illiterate	Up to Middle	Up to Matric	Inter-mediate	Graduate	Post-Grad.	Total
Patna	5 10%	13 26%	29 58%	—	2 4%	1 2%	50
Muzaffarpur	6 12%	16 32%	18 36%	6 12%	3 6%	1 2%	50
Arrah	6 12%	19 38%	14 28%	5 10%	6 12%	—	50
Total	17 (11.3%)	48 (32%)	61 (40.7%)	11 (7.3%)	11 (7.3%)	2 (1.3%)	150

TABLE 62
Religious Distribution

Name of town	Hindu	Muslim	Total
Patna	41(82%)	9(18%)	50
Muzaffarpur	38(76%)	12(24%)	50
Arrah	38(76%)	12(24%)	50
Total	117(78%)	33(22%)	150

TABLE 63
Caste-wise Distribution

Name of town	Upper caste	Lower caste	Scheduled caste	Total
Patna	16 (32%)	29 (58%)	5 (10%)	50
Muzaffarpur	21 (42%)	24 (48%)	5 (10%)	50
Arrah	19 (38%)	31 (62%)	—	50
Total	56 (37.3%)	84 (56%)	10 (6.6%)	150

TABLE 64
Occupational Classification

Name of town	Service	Labour	House-wife	Business	Retired	Professional	Cultivator	Total
Patna	17 34%	4 8%	1 2%	24 48%	1 2%	3 6%	—	50
Muzaffarpur.	13 26%	3 6%	5 10%	21 42%	—	2 4%	6 12%	50
Arrah	20 40%	3 6%	5 10%	14 28%	6 12%	2 4%	—	50
Total	50 33.3%	10 6.7%	11 7.4%	59 39.3%	7 4.3%	7 4.3%	6 4%	150

TABLE 65

How did you come to Know about Sulabh Shauchalaya Scheme?

(Education wise)

Educational level	Through friedns/rel.	Through neighbours	Through Sulabh Int.	Through mass media	Through adopters	Public Sulabh Shauch. Compl.	Others (N.A.)	Total
Illiterate = 17	3	8 17.6%	2 47.1%	6 11.8%	4 35.3%	2 23.5%	2 11.8%	25
Middle = 48	4 8.3%	7 14.6%	31 64.6%	13 27.1%	10 20.8%	21 43.8%	3 6.3%	89
Matric = 61	8 13.1%	10 16.4%	41 67.2%	14 22.9%	30 49.2%	19 31.1%	4 6.6%	126
Intermediate = 11	1 9.1%	—	7 63.6%	4 36.4%	5 45.5%	3 27.3%	2 18.2%	22
Graduate = 11	—	—	11 100%	1 9.1%	5 45.5%	2 18.2%	1 9.1%	20
Post-Graduate = 2	—	—	2 100%	1 50%	1 50%	—	—	4
Total	13 8.7%	20 13.3%	100 66.7%	35 23.3%	57 38.0%	49 32.7%	12 8.0%	286

TABLE 66

How did you come to Know about Sulabh Shauchalaya Scheme?

(Caste-wise)

Caste	Through friedns/rel.	Through neighbours	Through Sulabh Int.	Through mass media	Through adopters	Public Sulabh Shauch. Compl.	Others (N.A.)	Total
Upper = 56	8 14.3%	5 8.9%	40 71.4%	13 23.2%	20 35.7%	12 21.4%	8 5.3%	106
Lower = 84	3 3.6%	14 16.7%	55 65.5%	21 25.5%	30 35.7%	34 40.5%	4 4.8%	161
Scheduled = 10	2 20%	1 10%	5 50%	1 10%	7 70%	3 30%	—	19
Total = 150	13 8.7%	20 13.3%	100 66.7%	35 23.3%	57 38.0%	49 32.7%	12 8.0%	286

TABLE 67

What Problems do You Face Due to the Service Latrine in Your House?

Qccupational level	Unhygienic	Foul smell	Irregular scavenging	Foul smell at the time of scavenging	Presence of some family members is essential at the time of scavenging	Foul smell unbearable	Total
	(i)	(ii)	(iii)	(iv)	(v)	(vi)	
Service = 50	50 100%	18 36%	4 8%	25 50%	1 2%	34 68%	132
Business = 59	59 100%	11 18.6%	7 11.8%	34 57.6%	5 8.5%	50 84.7%	166
Labour = 10	10 100%	3 30%	—	7 70%	—	7 70%	27
House-lady = 11	11 100%	3 27.2%	—	6 54.5%	—	7 63.6%	27
Retired = 7	7 100%	5 71.4%	1 14.3%	5 71.5%	—	3 42.8%	21
Professional = 7	7 100%	2 28.6%	1 14.3%	3 42.8%	1 14.3%	5 71.4%	19
Cultivator & others= 6	6 100%	1 16.6%	1 53.3%	2 53.3%	—	6 100%	16
Total = 150	150 100%	43 28.7%	14 9.3%	82 54.6%	7 4.7%	112 74.6%	408

TABLE 68
What Problems do You Face Due to the Service Latrine in Your House?

Occupational	Unhygienic	Foul smell	Irregular scavenging	Foul smell at the time of scavenging	Presence of some family members is essential at the time of scavenging	Foul smell unbearable	Total
	(i)	(ii)	(iii)	(iv)	(v)	(vi)	
Illiterate = 17	17 100%	6 35.3%	2 11.7%	13 76.5%	2 11.7%	11 64.7%	51
Up to Middle = 48	48 100%	15 31.2%	4 8.3%	30 6.3%	1 2.0%	36 75.0%	134
Up to Matric = 61	61 100%	12 19.7%	5 8.2%	27 44.3%	2 3.3%	50 81.9%	157
Intermediate = 11	11 100%	5 45.4%	1 9.1%	6 54.5%	1 9.1%	6 54.5%	30
Graduate = 11	11 100%	55 45.4%	2 18.2%	6 54.5%	1 9.1%	7 63.6%	32
Post-Graduate = 2	2 100%	—	—	—	—	2 100%	4
Total = 150	150 100%	43 28.7%	14 9.3%	82 54.6%	7 4.7%	112 74.6%	408

TABLE 69
Which of the Following Systems did You have in Your House Before Adopting the Sulabh System?

Caste	Service latrine	Septic latrine	Open space	Com-munity latrine	Sandas	Total
Upper Caste	45 75.0%	3 5.0%	3 5.0%	5 8.3%	4 6.7%	60
Lower Caste	70 81.4%	—	12 13.9%	2 2.3%	2 2.3%	86
Scheduled Caste	2 66.7%	—	—	—	1 33.3%	3
Scheduled Tribe	1 100%	—	—	—	—	1
Total	118 78.7%	3 2.0%	15 10.0%	7 4.7%	7 4.7%	150 100%

TABLE 70
How did you Come to Know About the Sulabh Shauchalaya?

Occupational level	Sources of Information							Total
	Relat/ Friends	Adopters	S.I. Agency	Tech. Expert	Munici-pality	Mass convener	Mass media	
Service = 26	6 23.1%	5 19.2%	26 100%	0	1 3.8%	0	2 7.7%	40
Labour = 11	0	3 27.3%	8 72.7%	0	0	0	1 9.1%	12
Business = 64	6 9.4%	21 32.8%	59 92.2%	1 1.6%	6 9.4%	5 7.8%	2 3.1%	100
Retired = 10	—	6 60%	10 100%	—	—	2 20%	—	18
House-lady = 28	1 3.6%	13 46.4%	28 100%	—	—	—	2 7.1%	44
Jobless = 7	—	3 42.9%	7 100%	—	—	—	—	10
Cultivator = 4	—	1 25%	4 100%	—	1 25%	—	—	6
Total	13 8.7%	52 34.7%	142 94.7%	1 0.7%	8 5.3%	7 4.7%	7 4.7%	230 100%

TABLE 71
How Did You Come to Know About the Sulabh Shauchalaya?

Educational level	Sources of Information							
	Relat/ Friends	Adopters	S.I. Agency	Tech. Expert	Munici- pality	Mass conver.	Mass media	Total
Illiterate = 17	2 11.8%	6 35.3%	14 82.4%	—	1 5.9%	1 5.9%	1 5.9%	25
Up to Middle = 61	3 4.9%	20 32.8%	61 100%	—	3 4.9%	—	1 1.6%	88
Up to Matric = 43	6 15.4%	15 53.8%	43 61.5%	1 2.3%	3 6.9%	4 9.3%	2 4.7%	74
Intermed. = 13	2 15.4%	7 53.8%	8 61.5%	—	1 7.7%	2 15.4%	1 7.7%	21
Graduate = 15	—	4 26.7%	15 100%	—	—	—	—	19
Post-Graduate = 1	—	—	1 100%	—	—	—	2	3
Total =150	13 8.7%	52 34.7%	142 94.7%	1 0.7%	8 5.3%	7 4.7%	7 4.7%	230 100%

TABLE 72
Please Mention the Reasons for Abandoning the Previous System Operating in Your House

Caste Level	Unhygienic	Foul Smell	Costly	No provision for sewerage	Scavenging problem	By order of higher authority	Others	Not applicable	Total
Upper = 60	47 (78.3%)	6 (10%)	16 (26.7%)	27 (45%)	18 (30%)	2 (3.3%)	2 (3.3%)	10 (16.7%)	128
Lower = 86	71 (82.6%)	14 (16.3%)	22 (25.6%)	39 (45.3%)	28 (32.6%)	6 (6.9%)	—	14 (16.3%)	194
S/C = 3	2 (66.7%)	1 (33.3%)	2 (66.7%)	1 (33.3%)	1 (33.3%)	1 (33.3%)	—	—	8
S/T = 1	1 (100%)	1 (100%)	—	—	1 (100%)	—	—	—	3
Total = 150	121 (80.7%)	22 (14.7%)	40 (26.7%)	67 (44.7%)	48 (32.0%)	9 (5.0%)	2 (1.3%)	24 (16.0%)	333

TABLE 73
Please Mention the Reasons for Abandoning the Previous System Operating in Your House

Education	Unhy-gienic	Foul smell	Costly	No provi-sion for sewerage	Scaveng-ing problem	By order of higher authority	Others	Not applicable	Total
Illiterate = 17	11 (64.7%)	3 (17.6%)	7 (41.2%)	4 (23.5%)	8 (47.1%)	2 (11.8%)	—	4 (23.5%)	39
Up to Middle = 61	48 (78.7%)	8 (13.1%)	17 (27.9%)	26 (42.6%)	14 (22.9%)	3 (4.9%)	2 (3.3%)	12 (19.7%)	130
Matric = 43	36 (83.7%)	9 (20.0%)	11 (25.6%)	18 (41.9%)	13 (30.2%)	3 (6.9%)	—	5 (11.6%)	95
Intermediate = 13	11 (84.6%)	1 (7.7%)	1 (7.7%)	9 (69.2%)	5 (38.5%)	—	—	9 (15.9%)	29
Gradiate = 15	14 (93.3%)	1 (6.7%)	4 (26.7%)	9 (60.0%)	7 (46.7%)	1 (6.7%)	—	1 (6.7%)	37
P.G. = 1	1 (100%)	—	—	1 (100%)	1 (100%)	—	—	—	3
Total = 150	121 (80.7%)	22 (14.7%)	40 (26.7%)	67 (44.7%)	48 (32.0%)	9 (6.0%)	2 (1.3%)	24 (16.0%)	333

TABLE 74
In What Way Did You Adopt the Sulabh Shauchalaya System?

Educational level	By converting ser. l.	Constructed for the first time	Conversion from sandas to Sulabh	Others	Total
Illiterate	11 (64.7%)	4 (23.5%)	2 (11.8%)	--	17
Up to Middle	46 (75.4%)	11 (18.0%)	3 (4.9%)	1 (1.6%)	61
Matric	35 (81.4%)	5 (11.6%)	2 (4.7%)	1 (2.3%)	43
Intermediate	11 (84.6%)	1 (2.3%)	—	1 (2.3%)	13
Graduate	14 (93.3%)	1 (6.7%)	—	—	15
Post-Graduate	1 (100%)	—	—	—	1
Total	118 (78.7%)	22 (14.7%)	7 (4.7%)	3 (2.0%)	150

TABLE 75
What Inspired You to Adopt the Sulabh Shauchalaya System?

Caste Level	Hygienic	Involves less expenditure	No foul smell	Suited to our climatic condition	The best system in absence of sewerage facility	Advantage of subsidy or economic assist.	It does not require scavenging	It gives a higher grade of manure	Others	Total
Upper Caste = 60	60 100%	2 3.3%	46 76.7%	5 8.3%	33 55.0%	20 33.3%	47 78.3%	14 23.3%	2 3.3%	229
Lower Caste = 86	86 100%	5 5.8%	76 88.4%	3 3.5%	59 68.6%	26 30.2%	67 77.9%	18 20.9%	2 2.3%	342
Scheduled Caste = 3	3 100%	1 33.3%	3 100%	—	—	3 100%	3 100%	1 33.3%	—	14
Scheduled Tribe = 1	1 100%	1 100%	—	—	—	1 100%	—	—	—	3
Total = 150	150 100%	9 6.9%	125 83.3%	8 5.3%	92 61.3%	50 33.3%	117 78.0%	33 22.0%	4 2.7%	588

TABLE 76
Nature of Defects

Sl. No.	Name of town	Defects					Total
		Defect in pits	Floor crack	Leaking in Slabs	Others	No defect	
1.	Patna	1 (2%)	—	—	1 (2%)	48 (96%)	50
2.	Chaibasa	—	2 (4%)	1 (2%)	—	47 (94%)	50
3.	Madhubani	—	—	—	—	50 (100%)	50
	Total	1 (0.7%)	2 (1.4%)	1 (0.7%)	1 (0.7%)	145 (96.5%)	150

Bibliography

Ahmed, Z.: *Evaluation Report on Low-Cost Water-Seal Latrines in Bihar,* Department of Sociology, Patna University, Patna, 1980.

Barve, B.N.: *The Scavengers' Living Conditions Enquiry Committee* Government of Bombay, 1949.

Bhaskaran, T.R.: *Review of work done on Rural Latrines in India,* Indian Council of Medical Research, Special Report Series No. 54, New Delhi, 1966.

Chaturvedi, D.S.: Patit Prabhakar, Quoted from *Nachyo Bahut Gopal,* Rajpal & Sons, Kashmiri Gate, Delhi, 1980.

Chaturvedi, J.C.: *Mathematical Statistics*, Student Friends & Co., Rajamandi, Agra, 1947.

Consortium on Rural Technology Institute of Social Studies Trust.: *Rural Sanitation Technology Options*, Institute of Social Studies Trust, New Delhi, 1981.

Duncan, M.: *Appropriate Technology for Water Supply and Sanitation; Sanitation Alternative for Low-Income Communities—A Brief Introduction,* World Bank, Washington, 1982.

Goode, W.J., Hatt, P.K.: *Methods in Social Research*, McGraw-Hill, Kogakusha Ltd., London 1952.

Gould, H.A.: Lucknow Rickshawala: The Social Organization of an Occupational Category, Quoted from *Urban Sociology in India* by M.S.A. Rao, Orient Longman Ltd., New Delhi, 1974.

Government of Haryana: *Commission to Enquire into the Living Conditions of Safai Mazdoors Employed by Local Bodies and Private Scavengers Working in Haryana State*, 1969-72.

Government of India, UNICEF: *National Seminar on Low-Cost Techniques for Disposal of Human Wastes in Urban Communities*, Patna, 1978.

Government of India, UNDP: *International Seminar on Low-Cost Techniques for Disposal of Human Wastes in Urban Communities*, Calcutta, 1980.

Government of India, Government of Rajasthan, UNDP: *Regional Conference on Low-Cost Pour-Flush Latrines*, Udaipur, 1982.

Government of India, UNDP: *Regional Seminar on Low-Cost Sanitation*, Ministry of Works and Housing, 1982.

Hamlin, Christophere: Sewage: Waste of Resource? A Historical Perspective: *Scavenger, 12* (3), 1982.

Hutton, J.H.: Census of India, 1931; Volume I—India, Part II—Imperial Tables; Manager of Publications, Delhi, 1933.

Hutton, J.H.: *Caste in India—Its Nature, Function and Origin*, Oxford University Press, Delhi, 1981.

Indian Institute of Public Administration: *National Seminar on Integrated Development of Small and Medium Towns*, New Delhi, 1982.

Kalbermatten, J.M.: *Sanitation-Convenience for a Few or Health for Many; the Report on the International Seminar on Low-Cost Techniques for Disposal of Human Wastes in Urban Communities*, Calcutta, 1980; Annexure ii.

Kalbermatten, J.M.: *Appropriate Technology for Water Supply and Sanitation—A Sanitation Field Manual*, Washington, World Bank, 1980.

Lundberg, G.: *Social Research Longmans*, Green & Co., New York, 1949.

Malkani, N.R.: *Report of the Scavenging Conditions Enquiry Committee*, Ministry of Home Affairs, Central Advisory Board for Harijan Welfare, New Delhi, 1960.

Malkani, N.R.: *The Committee on Customary Rights to Scavengers*, 1969.

Menon, A.S.: *Wage Board for Municipal Workers*, Government of Kerala, 1971.

Moser, C.A., Calton, G.: *Survey Methods in Social Investigation*, Heinemann Educational Books Ltd., London, 1980.

Nagar, Amrit Lal: *Nachyo Bahut Gopal*, Rajpal & Sons, Kashmiri Gate, Delhi, 1980.

O'Malley, L.S.S.: *Census of India*, 1911: Volume 5, Bengal, Bihar, Orissa and Sikkim, Bengal Secretariat Book Depot, Calcutta, 1913.

Pandya, B.P.: *Committee on Conditions of Sweepers and Scavengers*, National Commission on Labour, 1969.

Parten, Mildred: *Survey, Polls and Samples*, Harper & Brothers, 1950.

Pathak, B.: *Sulabh Shauchalaya: (Hand-flush Water-seal Latrine): A Simple Idea that Worked,* Amola Prakashan, Patna, 1981.

Pathak, B.: *Sulabh Shauchalaya: A Study of Directed Change*, Amola Press & Publications, Patna, 1982.

Roy, A.K. et al: *Manual on the Design, Construction and Maintenance of Low-Cost Pour Flush Water-seal Latrines in India*, TAG Technical Note No. 10, UNDP International Project, The World Bank, Washington, 1984.

Salappa, I.P.D.: *Committee on Improvement of Living and Working Conditions of Sweepers and Scavengers*, Government of Karnataka, 1976.

UNDP: *Special Studies done by TAG* (India), New Delhi, 1982.

Uno Winblad: *Sanitation Without Water*, WHO Regional Office for Eastern Mediterranean, P.O. Box 1517, Alexandria, Egypt, 1980.

Vachaspati Sri: *Artha Sashtra of Kautilya*, The Chaukhamba Surabharati Prakashan, Varanasi, 1977.

Wagner, E.G., Lanoix, J.N.: *Excreta Disposal for Rural Areas and Small Communities*, World Health Organization, Geneva, 1958.

Young, P.V.: *Scientific Social Survey and Research*, Prentice-Hall, Inc. Engleword Cliffs, N.J. Charles E. Tuttle Company, Tokyo, Japan, 1965.

Index